Roman Theatre

Timothy J. Moore

CAMBRIDGE UNIVERSITY PRESS
Cambridge, New York, Melbourne, Madrid, Cape Town,
Singapore, São Paulo, Delhi, Mexico City

Cambridge University Press
The Edinburgh Building, Cambridge CB2 8RU, UK

www.cambridge.org
Information on this title: www.cambridge.org/9780521138185

© Cambridge University Press 2012

This publication is in copyright. Subject to statutory exception
and to the provisions of relevant collective licensing agreements,
no reproduction of any part may take place without the written
permission of Cambridge University Press.

First published 2012

Printed in India by Replika Press Pvt. Ltd

A catalogue record for this publication is available from the British Library

ISBN 978-0-521-13818-5 Paperback

Cambridge University Press has no responsibility for the persistence or
accuracy of URLs for external or third-party internet websites referred to in
this publication, and does not guarantee that any content on such websites is,
or will remain, accurate or appropriate.

Contents

Preface	v
Historical introduction	vii
1 The origins of Roman theatre	1
The Etruscans	5
2 Roman comedy in performance	7
Getting a play to the stage	7
Performance conditions	9
The setting	15
Actors	19
Movement, gesture and acting styles	21
Costumes	24
Props	27
Masks	28
Music and dance	33
3 Plautus	37
4 Terence	61
5 Tragedy in the Roman Republic	90
6 Mime	97
7 Pantomime	112
Theatres of the Empire	112
8 Seneca	130
9 The legacy of Roman theatre	150
Mime, pantomime and theatre architecture	150
Seneca	151
Plautus and Terence	155
Recommended reading	165
Glossary	170

Acknowledgements

The authors and publishers acknowledge the following sources of copyright material and are grateful for the permissions granted. While every effort has been made, it has not always been possible to identify the sources of all the material used, or to trace all copyright holders. If any omissions are brought to our notice, we will be happy to include the appropriate acknowledgements on reprinting.

Cover, p. 26, akg-images/Erich Lessing; p. 5 The Art Gallery Collection/Alamy; p. 6 from *The History of the Greek and Roman Theatre* (2nd edition) by Margarete Bieber, Princeton University Press, 1961; p. 9 from "Scavi nell'area del Tempio della Vittoria e del Santuario della Magna Mater sul Palatino", Pensabene P., in *Archeologia Laziale* (1988), reproduced in "Plautus on the Palatine", Goldberg, S.M. (1998) in *Journal of Roman Studies*; p. 17 akg-images/Bildarchiv Steffen; pp. 23, 28, 32, 64, 78 from Vat.lat. 3868 reproduced by permission of Biblioteca Apostolica Vaticana, with all rights reserved; p. 31*t* image © Professor Michael Lyons, College of Image Arts and Sciences, Ritsumeikan University, Kyoto, Japan. The images were originally published in "The Noh Mask effect: vertical viewpoint dependence of facial expression perception", Michael Lyons, Ruth Campbell, Andre Plante, Mike Coleman, Miyuki Kamachi & Shigeru Akamatsu, *Proceedings of the Royal Society of London B* 267:2239–2247 (2000); p. 31*b* akg-images/Nimtallah; p. 34 Italy, Campania, The Libation Painter (attributed to), Bell krater (Campanian red-figure ware), Side A: (Two comic actors on stage), Late Classical/Hellenistic period 350–325 BC, fired clay, 36.6 x 33.5 cm diameter, Felton Bequest, 1973 from The National Gallery of Victoria; p. 41 The Art Archive/Musée Archéologique Naples/Collection Dagli Orti; p. 59 The J. Paul Getty Museum, Villa Collection, Malibu, California, Thymiaterion in the form of a comic actor seated on an altar and a theatrical wig, unknown artist, first half of 1st century AD, bronze and silver inlay; p.93 Vanni/Art Resource, NY; p. 109 Roman art: Circus scenes – detail (dancer and musician), Vatican Museo Pio-Clementino © Photo Scala, Florence; p. 112 computer visualisation of the Theatre of Pompey, Rome, created by Martin Blazeby for the King's Visualization Lab, Department of Digital Humanities, King's College London; pp. 113, 119 Fototeca Unione, The American Academy in Rome, Photographic Archive; p. 114 Rolf Richardson/Alamy; p. 117 bpk/Antikensammlung, SMB/Ingrid Geske; p. 130 'Tantalus, after Titian' by Giulio Santo (c. 1565), Blanton Museum of Art, The University of Texas at Austin, The Leo Steinberg Collection, 2002, photo by Rick Hall; p. 135 Herm of Seneca (ca. 4BCE–65 CE), Roman double Herm, 1st half of 3rd century CE, Berlin Antikensammlung, Staatliche Museen zu Berlin, marble (frontal view) h. 28cm, Inv. Sk. 391, photo Johannes Laurentius © 2011 Photo Scala, Florence/BPK, Bildagentur für Kunst, Kultur und Geschichte, Berlin; p. 151 akg-images/Cameraphoto

pp. 161–163 Excerpts from *A Funny Thing Happened on the Way to the Forum*, book by Burt Shevelove and Larry Gelbart, music and lyrics by Stephen Sondheim, based on the plays of Plautus, are copyright © 1963 by Burt Shevelove, Larry Gelbart and Stephen Sondheim, reproduced by permission of the publishers, Nick Hern Books Ltd www.nickhernbooks.co.uk

Artworks and maps throughout by Peter Simmonett

Preface

When we think of ancient theatre today, we tend to think of Greek theatre. Yet the Romans also had a lively and varied set of theatrical traditions, which have had a considerable influence on later drama. This book offers an introduction to these traditions, including the origins of Roman theatre, the extant plays of Plautus, Terence and Seneca, and the many works of comedy, tragedy, **mime** and **pantomime** that no longer survive as written texts. The emphasis throughout is on performance, the role of these theatrical works within Roman society, and Roman theatre's legacy.

As we have no videos, stage directions or recordings of Roman theatre, and for some periods we do not even have eyewitness accounts of performance or contemporary archaeological evidence, it can be very hard to reconstruct just what Roman theatre would have been like in performance. The attempt is well worth the effort, however. An awareness of their performance context brings to life both the surviving plays and the traditions for which no texts survive. In all that follows, therefore, readers will want to try to imagine how the works discussed were performed.

Theatrical performances had a large and enthusiastic following throughout most of Rome's history. That passion for theatre says in itself something about Roman society, and the reader will find that all the works discussed here reflect in important ways Roman daily life, politics, values and prejudices. I encourage readers to think not only about performances, but about how a Roman audience might have responded to those performances, and what Roman theatre tells us about the world in which it was produced.

Readers will find some aspects of Roman theatre bizarre, and sometimes perhaps even repulsive. At the same time, much will be familiar, for Roman theatre is the foundation of many later theatrical traditions. I encourage readers to consider throughout which elements of Roman theatre are strange, and which we still find on stage or screen today.

This book includes numerous translations of excerpts from Roman plays and ancient works about theatre: it is hoped that readers will be inspired to read more of these works in their entirety. English translations of the surviving plays are included in the list of recommended reading on pp. 165–9. Works of Roman art, where theatrical motifs are remarkably frequent, also play an important role in what follows. All the relevant sources, both written and visual, present their own challenges for anyone seeking to use them as evidence: some are much later than the works to which they are relevant, and all reflect the idiosyncrasies of their genres and the biases of their producers. This book thus offers readers a good opportunity to think critically about how to evaluate sources and their reliability.

All translations are my own. **Bold type** marks the first occurrence of a word that appears in the glossary on pp. 170–4.

The help of series editors Eric Dugdale and James Morwood, and of my editor Lucy Mitchell and copy editor Belinda Baker, has been invaluable in the writing of this book. I also received valuable aid from Dan McGowan, Marc Bizer, Franziska Wenzel, Sinclair Bell and Eric Dodson-Robinson. I received financial support as I completed this book from the Department of Classics (my thanks to chair Stephen A. White) and the College of Liberal Arts at the University of Texas at Austin, the Deutscher Akademischer Austausch Dienst and the Ruhr-Universität Bochum (special thanks to Wolfgang Polleichtner). I dedicate this book to the memory of my grandparents, William G. and Wilma H. Moore and Donald J. and Erma C. Armitage.

Historical introduction

The history of theatre in Rome is closely intertwined with Rome's political and social history. According to Roman tradition, Rome was founded in 753 BC and was ruled for its first two and a half centuries by a set of seven kings, the last three of whom were **Etruscans**. The last king, Tarquinius Superbus ('Tarquin the Proud'), was allegedly driven from Rome in 509 BC. In fact, Rome was probably subject to the Etruscans during much of its early history, and the story of the expulsion of the last king reflects the end of Etruscan rule.

With the end of the **Monarchy** Rome became a **Republic**, led by several magistrates, most importantly a pair of **consuls**, who were elected for one-year terms. Although the magistrates were elected by an assembly of the Roman people, most of the power in the Roman Republic lay in the hands of the **Senate**, a group of several hundred ex-magistrates, all members of Rome's highest social class. During the first two centuries of the Roman Republic, Rome conquered a large portion of the Italian peninsula. It was during this time, according to Roman tradition, that theatre started in Rome (see chapter 1).

In the third and second centuries BC Rome extended its domain over much of the Mediterranean world, including the rest of Italy, Sicily, Sardinia, Corsica, Greece, part of North Africa and most of Spain. It was during this period that Plautus, Terence and some other comic playwrights wrote (see chapters 2–4), as well as several writers of tragedy (see chapter 5). This period also saw a thriving tradition of mime (see chapter 6) and perhaps the first stirrings of pantomime (see chapter 7).

The immense influx of wealth that came with the new conquests, along with the strain of trying to rule an empire with a government made for a small state, led to social upheaval in the late second and first centuries BC. This unrest culminated in a series of bloody civil wars, which included Julius Caesar's rise to dictatorship and his assassination. During this period comedy and tragedy continued to be performed, mime became increasingly popular, and there were probably further developments in pantomime.

The civil wars finally ended with the triumph of Julius Caesar's grandnephew Octavian in 31 BC. In 27 BC Octavian took the name Augustus and became the first Roman emperor. It is from this year, therefore, that we date the period known as the **Empire**. During Augustus' reign pantomime reached its maturity and mime thrived. Performances of tragedy and comedy continued but were probably less common than they had been.

Augustus started a dynasty known as the Julio-Claudian dynasty, which lasted until the death of his great-great-grandson Nero in AD 68. It was during this period that Seneca wrote his tragedies (see chapter 8). During this dynasty and in the next centuries, mime, pantomime and tragic singing (see chapter 7) dominated the Roman stage.

In the third century AD Rome experienced 50 years of civil wars, foreign invasions and economic collapse. Diocletian restored stability beginning in 285, instituting a new, much more autocratic style of government. This system of government continued under Constantine, the first Christian emperor, and his successors. It was during this period (in the second half of the fourth century AD) that *Querolus*, the last surviving play from ancient Rome, was written.

In the late fourth and fifth centuries AD, Rome became increasingly subjected to invasions by Germanic peoples, until in the late fifth century the western half of the Roman empire ceased to exist. The eastern half of the empire survived in the form of the Byzantine empire for many more centuries, but because of the antitheatrical bias of the Christian church, state-sponsored theatrical performances soon ended there as well.

Timeline

Dates in theatrical history	Other relevant dates
BC	**BC**
	753: Traditional date of the founding of Rome and the beginning of the Monarchy
	509: Traditional date of the expulsion of the last Roman king and the foundation of the Republic
364: Traditional date of the beginning of theatre in Rome	
	272: Rome has conquered all of Italy south of the Po River
c. 264–c. 184: Plautus	264–241: First Punic War: Rome defeats the Carthaginians and gains control over Sardinia, Corsica and most of Sicily
240: Traditional date of the first translation of a Greek play into Latin, by Livius Andronicus	
239–169: Ennius	
c. 235–c. 204: Theatrical career of Naevius	
c. 220–c. 130: Pacuvius	218–201: Second Punic War: Rome defeats the Carthaginians under Hannibal and gains control over much of Spain
c. 190–159: Terence	200–167: In a series of wars, Rome gains control of Greece

168: death of Caecilius	
170–c. 86: Accius	133: Beginning of a century of social unrest and civil wars
c. 106–c. 43: Laberius	
55: Building of the **Theatre of Pompey**	
46: Alleged competition between Laberius and Publilius Syrus	49–46: Caesar defeats Pompey and his followers in a civil war and becomes dictator
	44: Assassination of Julius Caesar
	27: Augustus becomes the first Roman emperor; beginning of the Empire
22: Alleged date of Pylades' introduction of pantomime to Rome	
AD	**AD**
c. 1–65: Seneca	14: Death of Augustus
	14–37: Reign of Tiberius
	37–41: Reign of Caligula
	41–54: Reign of Claudius
	54–68: Reign of Nero
	79: The eruption of Mount Vesuvius buries Pompeii and Herculaneum
	c. 120: Birth of Lucian
Second century: Probable date of Chariton mime	c. 125: Birth of Apuleius
	235–85: Chaos and economic decline caused by civil wars and invasions by barbarians
	285–305: Diocletian establishes order through more autocratic and bureaucratic government
	312–37: Reign of Constantine, first Christian emperor
	330: Constantine moves the capital of the Roman empire to Constantinople (now Istanbul)
Second half of the fourth century: *Querolus*	
	476: Romulus Augustulus, last Western Roman emperor, deposed
	527–65: Reign of Justinian
	1453: Eastern Roman empire ends as Constantinople falls to Turks

Historical introduction

The eastern Mediterranean.

1 The origins of Roman theatre

Livy (Titus Livius in Latin, *c.* 59 BC–*c.* AD 17) wrote a history of Rome from its beginnings to his own day. Convinced that Rome had reached a state of moral decay by his time, Livy sought both to present examples of Rome's superior morality in the years when she built her empire and to explain how moral decline set in. His description of the events of 364 BC includes an account of the origins of theatre at Rome that reflects both of these aims (*From the Founding of the City* 7.2).

1.1 Both in this year [365 BC] and in the next, when **Gaius Sulpicius Peticus and Gaius Licinius Stolo were consuls**, there was a plague. For that reason nothing worth recording happened, except that for the third time since the city had been founded there was a *lectisternium* to **pacify the gods**.

When neither human remedies nor divine help diminished the power of the plague, it is said that the Romans, their minds overcome by superstition, included even theatrical games among the rites they established in order to appease the gods' anger. Such games were something new for this warlike people, who had previously known only **games in the circus**. The thing itself, however, was a small affair, and of foreign origin, as is generally the case when things first get started. Dancers, summoned from **Etruria**, dancing to tunes provided by

---

Gaius Sulpicius Peticus and Gaius Licinius Stolo were consuls Romans identified dates by the consuls (the two chief magistrates) who served during the year.

lectisternium a religious ritual at which couches – one for each of the major gods – were covered with cloth, and the gods were offered a banquet. The word *lectisternium* means literally 'strewing of the couches'.

pacify the gods Roman religion held that disasters such as plagues occurred because the gods were angry, usually because a religious ritual had not been performed properly. It was believed that special rites, such as the rarely held *lectisternium*, could appease the gods' anger.

games in the circus *circus* here means the *Circus Maximus*, a huge track surrounded by grandstands in the centre of Rome, where chariot-races had been held since Rome's earliest days and where large events such as rock concerts are still held today.

Etruria the homeland of the Etruscans, from whom the name of modern Tuscany is derived (see map on p. x).

a *tibia* player, performed quite refined dances in the Etruscan manner, without singing or imitating any specific action. Then the youth began to mimic them, at the same time hurling insults at each other with rude verses; and their motions were in agreement with their voices. And so the institution was imported, and more frequent performances stirred up greater interest in it.

Professional actors got the name *histriones* because *ister* is the Etruscan name for a dancer. These actors did not exchange primitive rough verses similar to **Fescennine verses**, the way it had been done before; but they acted out *saturae* filled out with tunes, with a **written song** performed to the accompaniment of the *tibia* player, and with corresponding movement.

After some years **Livius Andronicus** first dared to go beyond *saturae* and produce a play with a plot. Like all playwrights of his day, he himself acted in his own plays. It is said that when he had worn out his voice from too many encores, he asked and received permission to have a slave stand in front of the *tibia* player and sing, while

---

tibia   (also known by the plural form *tibiae*) a pair of pipes played simultaneously (see **1.2** and box on p. 3).

Fescennine verses   insults, often obscene, which were directed at the bride and groom at wedding ceremonies and were also delivered on other occasions. Like the teasing of brides and grooms at modern weddings, the Fescennine verses probably started as an apotropaic ritual: that is, it was believed that subjecting fortunate people to insults would ward off evil spirits. The name Fescennine derives from the Etruscan town of Fescennia, from where the verses allegedly first came (see map on p. x).

saturae   no examples of these *saturae* survive, and it is unknown what their exact nature was, though Livy's text suggests songs with a mixture of different tunes. The word *satura* elsewhere means 'stuffed full', as in *satura lanx*, a plate loaded down with food. It is unknown what if any relation there is between these dramatic *saturae* and the later non-dramatic poetic genre of *satira* (satire), in which poets mocked the foibles and vices of their contemporaries.

written song   although this marks the beginning of written drama in Rome, much theatre remained unwritten improvisation throughout Roman history, including the **Atellan plays** mentioned later in this passage and farcical skits known as mimes (see p. 97). Livy almost certainly refers to the text of the songs here, not to musical notes. Although the Romans borrowed from the Greeks a system of musical notation, most music appears to have been learned orally.

Livius Andronicus   Roman tradition held that in 240 BC Livius Andronicus (no relation to Titus Livius) translated Homer's *Odyssey* into Latin, thus producing the first work of Latin literature, and that in the same year he presented the first adaptations of Greek tragedies and comedies on the Roman stage. He is recorded to have been a freed slave from the Greek city of Tarentum in southern Italy (see map on p. x).

> **The *tibia***
>
> The *tibia* was a woodwind instrument made up of two pipes. At the top end of each pipe was a double reed, similar to those used in modern oboes or bassoons. The *tibia* produced a piercing, buzz-like tone. The two pipes could play either in unison or with separate pitches and rhythms, though the Romans did not employ the kind of harmony used in Western music since the Renaissance. The *tibia* was the standard accompanying instrument for all Roman theatrical performances, and it also played an essential role elsewhere in Roman religious life: it was required for most sacrifices, and it accompanied the processions that began festivals. It was virtually identical to the *aulos*, which was used to accompany all genres of Greek theatre. Other sources tell us that unlike in classical Athens, where playwrights created their own melodies, in Rome the player of the *tibia* (called the **tibicen**) composed the melodies to go along with the playwright's words.

he performed the **canticum** with somewhat more energetic motion, because use of the voice did not get in the way. From then the practice began whereby someone else sang while the actor gestured, and only the **deverbia** were left to the actors' own voices.

Later, when this mode of drama was causing plays to develop beyond just laughter and scattered jokes, and acting had little by little changed into a professional skill, the youth left the performance of plays to professional actors, and they themselves began to toss back and forth jokes intermixed with verses, just as they had done in the old days. That was the origin of the pieces later called **exodia** and joined especially to **Atellan plays**. The Atellan plays were received from the **Oscans**. The youth held on to them and did not allow them to be polluted by the professional actors. For this reason the policy has remained that actors in Atellan plays are not

---

canticum, deverbia   a *canticum* (plural *cantica*) was a passage of Roman drama sung to the accompaniment of the *tibia*. A **deverbium** (plural *deverbia*) was delivered without accompaniment.

exodia   short farcical afterpieces appended to other dramas (compare the jigs of Elizabethan and Jacobean theatre). No examples of *exodia* survive.

Atellan plays   short farcical plays with **stock characters**, thought to have come originally from Atella, a town in Campania south of Rome (see map on p. x). Atellan plays were often used as *exodia* after other plays, and they were improvised rather than based on a script. Although in the first century BC some authors began to write down Atellan plays, no examples of the genre survive.

Oscans   an Italic people, ethnically related to the Romans, who inhabited Atella and the area around it.

removed from their tribes, and they can **serve in the army** as if they had no part in theatrical performance.

It seemed to me that just as I describe how various other institutions have grown from modest beginnings, I should also discuss the origins of the theatrical games, so that it will be clear how from reasonable beginnings this institution has now progressed to such a state of madness that **even great wealth can scarcely sustain it**.

> 1 The first written history of Rome was not produced until just about 200 BC. Almost the only written records of what happened in Rome before that date were bare lists of events such as plagues, wars and who held political offices, and records of some upper-class families. There was also an oral tradition of stories handed down over the generations. Given this mixture of possible sources, how reliable do you think Livy's story is likely to be?
>
> 2 What does this passage suggest about the nature of theatrical performance in Rome?
>
> 3 What does Livy himself think about theatre? How might his attitude have affected his account?
>
> 4 What does this passage tell us about Roman attitudes towards actors?
>
> 5 Romans encountered Greeks early in their history, trading with Greeks who had inhabited the southern part of Italy. By the early third century BC Rome had conquered the Greek cities of Italy, and in the first half of the second century BC the Romans gained control of mainland Greece. Exactly how much of Rome's earliest theatre was influenced by Greek theatre is unclear, but by the time of Livius Andronicus that influence was profound: many Roman plays were direct adaptations of Greek ones. Yet Livy makes no reference to Greek influence on Roman theatre. Why do you think he left the Greeks out?
>
> 6 Many have found unbelievable Livy's apparent claim that actors on the Roman stage often only mimed the sung portions of plays while someone else sang. Do you think such a mode of performance is possible?

removed from their tribes   the citizenship of Rome was divided into 35 tribes for the purposes of voting. Most actors in Rome were subject to the loss of most citizen rights, including removal from their tribes (see **2.15**).

serve in the army   most actors in Rome were forbidden to serve in the army.

even great wealth can scarcely sustain it   by Livy's day, in the last years of the Roman Republic, the theatrical games had become the site of intense political rivalry, as politicians tried to win popular support through ever more elaborate theatrical productions. We thus read, for example, of huge temporary theatres adorned with marble, glass and gold even though they were used for only a single festival (see **2.4**) and of theatrical processions with hundreds of animals. It was also during Livy's lifetime that the first permanent stone theatre in the city of Rome was built: the massive and incredibly opulent Theatre of Pompey (55 BC, see **7.1**). When, during the time Livy was writing, Rome changed from a republic to an empire under the rule of one man, the political competition ceased; but extravagant theatrical performances continued, as emperors used them to keep the goodwill of their subjects.

The Etruscans

The Etruscans are a people of unknown origin (their language is not related to any other ancient Italian languages). A number of very powerful Etruscan cities thrived between 800 and 300 BC, after which time they were conquered by Rome. Rome itself was probably under Etruscan rule in the sixth century BC, and the Etruscans left an unmistakable imprint on numerous aspects of Roman society, including architecture, religious practices and language: the Romans themselves were aware of the importance of the Etruscans in their own traditions, and some leading Romans boasted that they had Etruscan ancestors. No Etruscan literature survives, but they left behind an impressive array of artistic creations, most notably elaborate tomb paintings. Many of these paintings include dancers and players of the *tibia* (**1.2**), and one shows a group of spectators at some kind of performance (**1.3**).

This Etruscan **fresco** from the Tomb of the Leopards (early fifth century BC) in Tarquinia, north of Rome (see map on p. x), probably shows a celebration in honour of a person buried in the tomb. At the centre is a *tibia* player. The man on his right holds a bowl used for drinking wine called a *kylix*, the man on his left a lyre.

1.2

In this fresco from another Etruscan tomb in Tarquinia, the figures on a higher level, many wearing typically Etruscan round caps, are watching something (a dance? a theatrical presentation? a race or other athletic contest?) intently from a kind of grandstand. The reason for their raised-arm gestures is not clear. Below them are probably slaves, compelled to watch (or ignore) the event from below the stands where free persons sat. Compare the distinctions between free and slave spectators made much later by the prologue speaker in Plautus' *The Little Carthaginian* (**2.5**).

1.3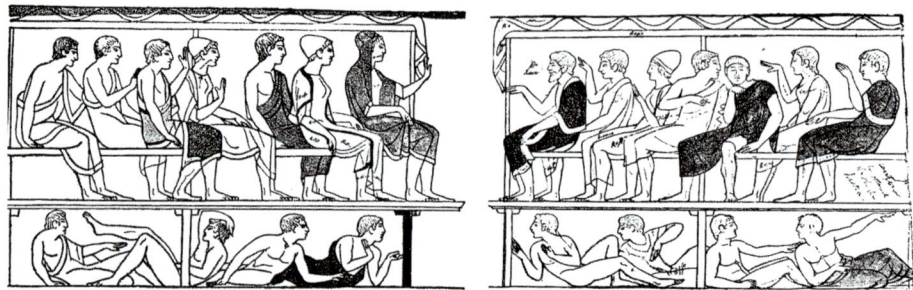

- What do these frescoes suggest about Etruscan life?

6 *The origins of Roman theatre*

2 Roman comedy in performance

The earliest Roman plays to survive, and the largest collection of plays we still have, are 21 comedies by Plautus (Titus Maccius Plautus, *c.* 264–*c.* 184 BC) and six by Terence (Publius Terentius Afer, *c.* 190–159 BC). We can learn much about the performance of these plays from the texts of the plays, works by later Roman authors and Roman art.

Getting a play to the stage

Almost all Roman plays were performed as part of religious festivals called **ludi** (games). As the Romans did not have the concept of the weekend, these festivals were important breaks in the daily schedule of work and business. Some *ludi* were regular annual festivals, such as the **Ludi Romani**, held every September in honour of Jupiter, king of the gods, and the **Ludi Megalenses**, held in April in honour of Cybele (the Great Mother). Leading citizens also held *ludi* at funerals for their relatives and to fulfil vows they had made to the gods. Besides theatrical performances of various types, *ludi* could also feature chariot-races, gladiatorial contests and other forms of entertainment such as boxing and dancing.

Production notices called **didascaliae**, preserved with the manuscripts of several plays, describe some of the personnel involved in theatrical *ludi*. This is the *didascalia* from Terence's *Phormio*.

2.1   Here begins Terence's *Phormio*. It was performed at the *Ludi Romani* under **curule aediles** Lucius Postumius Albinus and Lucius Cornelius Merula. Lucius Ambivius Turpio and Lucius Hatilius Praenestinus brought it to the stage. Flaccus, the slave of Claudius, produced the music on **unequal *tibiae*** through the

---

curule aediles   magistrates responsible for both the *Ludi Romani* and the *Ludi Megalenses*, who also had jurisdiction over trade. Curule **aediles** were usually young aristocrats, who looked to successful games to help in their political careers.

unequal *tibiae*   both pipes of equal *tibiae* were of the same length. In unequal *tibiae* the left pipe was longer than the right.

whole play. The play comes from the **Greek play** *The Petitioner* by **Apollodorus**. It was the fourth play of Terence produced, **in the consulship of Gaius Fannius and Marcus Valerius**.

> 1 What does the material preserved in the *didascalia* suggest about the personnel involved in mounting a theatrical production in Republican Rome?
> 2 How do the activities of these people compare with what happens as a play comes to the stage in our day?
> 3 Why do you think the authors of Roman comedy chose to adapt Greek plays rather than write new plays from scratch?

> **The business side of Roman theatre**
>
> Our knowledge of the economics of Roman theatre is sketchy. Passages like the *didascalia* in **2.1** appear to suggest that actor-producers such as Lucius Ambivius Turpio or Lucius Hatilius Praenestinus bought plays from playwrights, hired or owned actors and *tibia* players, and were paid by the magistrates in charge of games, like the curule aediles mentioned here, to put on the plays. The magistrates got some funds from the Senate and used their own resources as well. A businessman known as the **choragus** provided costumes and perhaps props: he appears to have been hired sometimes by the actor-producer, sometimes by the magistrate (see **2.24**, **2.25**). For a later period we have evidence of several other figures, including the *locator*, a kind of agent whose job was to hire out actors, and, under the emperors, the *procurator*, an important official whose job was to manage the *ludi*.

Greek play most, if not all, Roman comedies were adaptations of comedies written in Athens in the late fourth and early third centuries BC, called 'New Comedies' to distinguish them from the 'Old Comedies' written by Aristophanes and his contemporaries in the fifth and early fourth centuries. The writers of **New Comedy** – the greatest of whom was Menander (c. 344–c. 292 BC) – wrote domestic comedies that often revolved around the tortured but ultimately successful attempts of a young man to win the hand of a young woman despite all obstacles. The Roman playwrights kept these basic plots but made extensive changes, including the removal of the Greek plays' choruses; deletion of some characters and expansion of others' roles; addition of musical solos, verbal humour and farcical scenes; and substitution of dialogues for monologues and vice versa.

Apollodorus a contemporary of Menander.

in the consulship of Gaius Fannius and Marcus Valerius 161 BC.

Performance conditions

As we saw in chapter 1, the city of Rome had no permanent stone theatre until 55 BC. The reason for the long delay was allegedly moral: leading citizens claimed that spending too much time in the theatre would corrupt the populace. In fact, those leaders are more likely to have been reluctant to allow a permanent place for citizens to assemble, fearing sedition. Before Rome had permanent theatres, dramatic performances required just two elements: a place for spectators to stand or sit (***cavea***), and a stage (***scaena***) with a backdrop (***scaenae frons***) and space in front of the backdrop (***proscaenium***).

Often plays were performed in front of temples. Because Roman temples were raised high off the ground, the steps in front of a temple could serve as the *cavea*. Sander Goldberg has demonstrated (2.2) how during the *Ludi Megalenses*, for example, a stage was set up in front of the temple of the Great Mother, on the steps of which 1,300 or more spectators could sit and watch the plays.

2.2

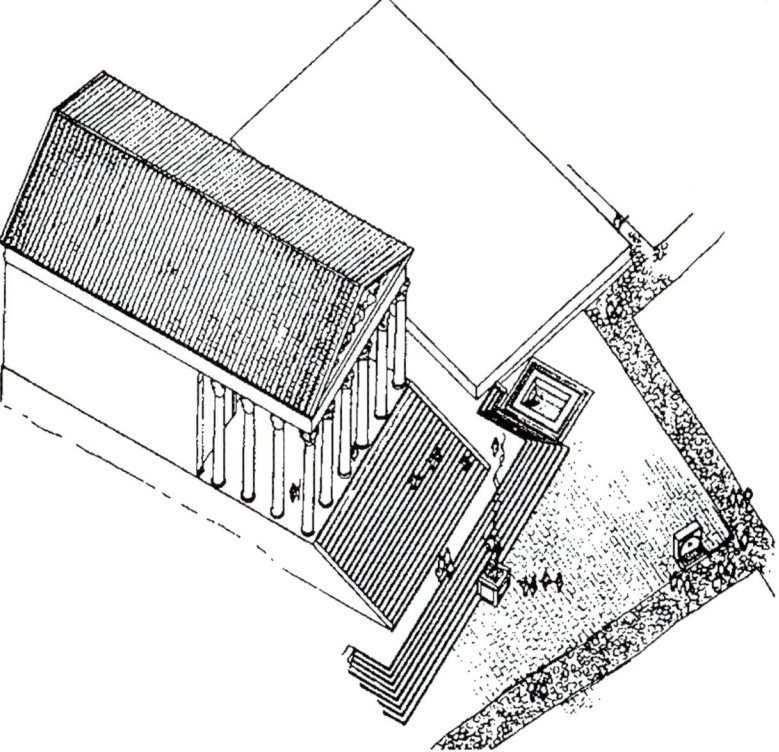

Reconstruction of the temple of the Great Mother on the Palatine Hill in Rome.

Sometimes plays were performed on a *scaena* set up in the **forum** (Rome's central square). The plan in 2.3 shows the Roman forum in Plautus' day. A character in Plautus' *Curculio* gives a tour of the forum in which he mentions each of the places shown here, suggesting that that play may have been performed in the middle of the forum. Because *Curculio* is ostensibly set in the Greek city of Epidaurus, the tour of the forum is an extreme version of what modern scholars such as Niall Slater have called 'metatheatre' in Plautus' plays: comical reminders that the supposedly Greek setting is really part of a theatrical performance in Rome.

2.3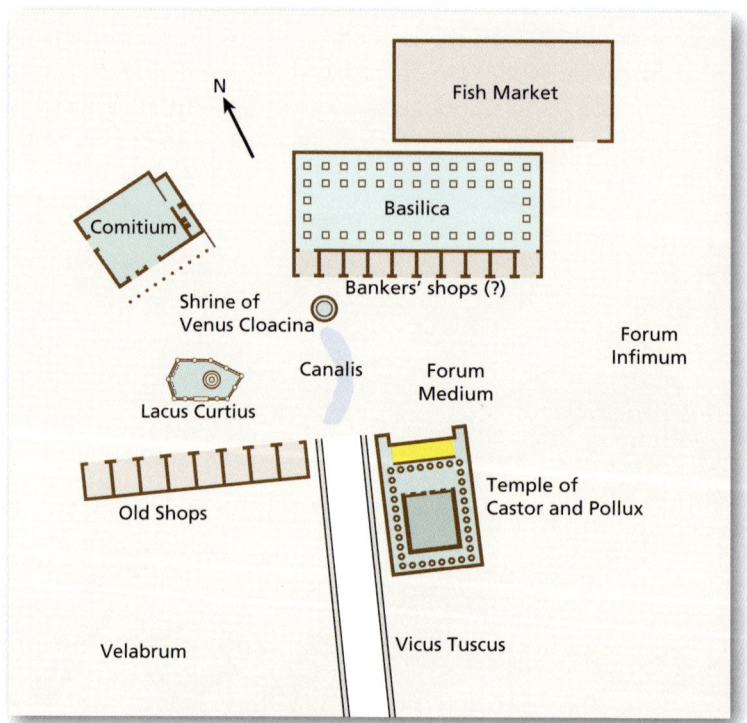

Plautus' forum.

At some point (probably after Plautus' and Terence's time) magistrates in charge of *ludi* began to set up larger temporary theatres that included a full semicircular *cavea* joined to a *scaenae frons* with a stage in front of it. By the first century BC some magistrates, eager to further their political careers through the generosity they showed in sponsoring games, started to create temporary theatres of enormous size and elaborate ornamentation. Pliny the Elder (AD 23–79) describes the most extravagant of these theatres in his encyclopedia (*Natural History* 36.114–15).

2.4 **When he was aedile** Marcus Scaurus made the greatest work of all those that had ever been made by human hands, not only among those that were temporary, but even among those meant for eternity. This was his theatre. It had a three-storey stage with 360 columns … The lowest storey of the stage was marble, the middle glass … and the highest was made of gilded planks. The columns of the lowest storey were … 38 feet high. There were 3,000 bronze statues … in the spaces in between the columns, and the *cavea* held 80,000 spectators … The rest of the furnishings, with gold-embroidered fabric, paintings and other material, were so valuable that when what was left had been carried to his villa in Tusculum for use in everyday pleasures and the villa was burned by angry slaves, the loss was 30,000,000 *sestertii* …

> 1 How would the fact that all performances were held outdoors in the daytime have affected the experience of watching a play in ancient Rome?
> 2 In what ways would each of the three kinds of location available have affected the audience's experience?
> 3 Some scholars have considered Pliny's description of Scaurus' theatre an exaggeration. What do you think?

An anonymous actor delivering the prologue of Plautus' *The Little Carthaginian* (*Poenulus* 1–54) gives a glimpse into what watching a play might have been like.

2.5 I'd like to begin by quoting **Aristarchus' Achilles**. That's right, I'll start with words from that tragedy:

'Be silent and pay attention: your general orders you to listen …'

Your **actor-general**, that is. That's me, and I order all of you to sit on your benches with a good attitude, whether you have arrived hungry or full. Those of you who ate first were a lot smarter. If you didn't eat… well, you can fill up on plays. 'Cause if you had some food prepared, it was really dumb to come in and sit down for our sake without eating it.

'Announcer, get up and make the people listen.'

When he was aedile   58 BC.

sestertii   the *sestertius* was a Roman coin. Its value varied over time, but at any time 30,000,000 *sestertii* would have been an enormous amount of money.

Aristarchus' Achilles   the prologue speaker quotes from a translation by the Roman tragic playwright Ennius (see p. 90) of *Achilles* by the Greek playwright Aristarchus (late fifth century BC).

actor-general   note the irony of the actor's pretensions. As an actor, he belongs to one of Rome's lowest social classes, but he takes on the role of a military leader.

I've been waiting for a long time for you to do your job: work that voice that earns your keep. If you don't shout, you see, you'll starve in silence. OK, now, **sit back down, so you can make double pay**.

'Now everybody: be good and obey my decrees.'

Male prostitutes: no sitting on the *proscaenium*.

Lictors: no noise, either from your mouths or your rods.

Ushers: no walking in front of people's faces or leading anyone to a seat while an actor is on stage. Those lazy folks who overslept should either stand without complaining or learn to get up earlier.

Slaves: no sitting down. We need the seats for free people. Or pay for your freedom. If you can't do that, go home. Otherwise you risk two beatings: one with rods here and one with whips at home, if you haven't done your work when your masters get home.

Wet-nurses: take care of your tiny little babies at home and don't bring them to the play. Otherwise you'll run dry and the babies will die of hunger. And while they starve they'll bleat like goats.

Wives: watch in silence, laugh in silence. Keep your resonant melodious voices from ringing and take your gossip home, so you're not a pain to your husbands here as well as at home.

Officials in charge of the games: no **prize** is to be given to any performer unjustly, and nobody is to lose his chance for a prize because somebody else used bribery: that puts the worse ones ahead of the good ones.

Oh, I almost forgot:

Slave attendants: as long as the games are on, make an attack on the snack stand. Run, now, while you have the chance, while the pastries are hot.

These are the orders of your actor-general: everybody, remember to do your part well.

---

sit back down, so you can make double pay   the prologue speaker jokingly suggests that the announcer is also a male prostitute: the word for 'sit down' in Latin can also mean to be penetrated sexually.

Lictors   Roman magistrates were accompanied by a retinue of lictors, who preceded the magistrate and cleared the way for him. Lictors carried *fasces*, tightly bound bundles of rods with an axe in the middle, as a symbol of the magistrate's authority.

prize   there is no evidence that plays competed for prizes during the Roman games as they did in the Athenian festivals, but this passage and some others reveal that at least sometimes individual actors competed for prizes. We do not know what these prizes were.

Now I want to wander back to the **background** of this play: I want you to know what I know. First I will set out its districts, its borders and its limits: I've been made its surveyor. If you don't mind, I want to give you the name of this comedy: 50 if you do mind, I'll give it anyway, as long as those in charge give me permission. This play is called *The Carthaginian* **in Greek**. Plautus, the **porridge-eating** Roman, calls it *The Uncle* in Latin.

> Ambivius Turpio, the producer and lead actor who brought Terence's plays to the stage, delivers the prologue of Terence's *The Mother-in-Law* (*Hecyra* 29–57).

2.6 I'm bringing back to you *The Mother-in-Law*, which I have never been allowed to perform with an attentive audience: disaster has always squashed it. Your 30 intelligence will put an end to this disaster, if you lend your support to our hard work.

When I first began to put this play on, news of a boxing match, anticipation of rope-walking on top of that, people rushing in to meet their friends, a big commotion and women shouting made me give up on the performance before it 35 even got started. So I did what I had done before in similar situations: I brought it to the stage again. That time the first scenes went well. But then a rumour started that there were going to be gladiators. People rushed in. There was confusion, 40 shouting and fighting for places: I couldn't hold on to my place.

Now it's peaceful and quiet, with no disturbance. I've been given time for performing, and you've been given the chance to bring glory to our dramatic 45 games. Don't let your behaviour restrict the art of playwriting to just a few people: see to it that your influence favours and enhances mine. If I have never been greedy in asking a price for my work, and if I have considered my profit to be to 50

---

background most prologue speakers in Plautus (though not in Terence) give background information on the plot of the plays they introduce.

in Greek Plautus' play is an adaptation of a Greek play called *The Carthaginian*. It is not known who the author of the Greek play was. Plautus' play offers a surprisingly sympathetic portrayal of some Carthaginian characters, even though when the play was first produced Rome had just ended a long and bloody war with the Carthaginians under their general Hannibal (the Second Punic War, 218–201 BC. *The Little Carthaginian* was probably first produced in the 190s BC).

porridge-eating joking about his countrymen's fondness for porridge, Plautus ironically adapts the Greek stereotype of Romans as unsophisticated.

The Uncle if this is the correct reading of the Latin (there is some controversy about that), the name *The Little Carthaginian* must have been given to the play in the years after its first production, by analogy with the name of the Greek original. One of the main characters in the play is the Carthaginian uncle of the young man in love.

please you as much as possible, let me get from you what I ask: let this playwright, who has entrusted his work to my protection and himself to your good faith, not suffer ruin and humiliation, done in by his **enemies**. For my sake take up this 55 cause and be silent, so that others will want to write plays, and so that you will continue to have plenty of opportunity to see new plays that I have purchased for production.

> In a society as rigidly stratified as ancient Rome, spectators of the lower classes probably yielded better seats to their social superiors (note the slaves ordered to stand in **2.5**). Livy reports, however, that there was no official division of seats according to class until 194 BC and that the new division was controversial (*From the Founding of the City* 34.44.5, 34.54.4–7).

2.7 [The **censors**] won enormous goodwill from the senatorial class because they commanded the curule aediles to separate the senators' seats from the people's at the *Ludi Romani*. Before this everyone had watched mixed together …

It was at the *Ludi Romani* … that the Senate first watched separated from the people. This change, like everything new, caused discussion. Some thought that the highest class was finally getting a privilege it should have received long before. Others felt that whatever was added to the dignity of the senators was taken away from the people's honour and that all such distinctions that separate the classes were equally harmful to both civic harmony and liberty. For 558 years the classes had been mixed together in audiences: what had suddenly happened that the senators didn't want to mingle with the people in the *cavea*? Why should a rich man be reluctant to sit next to a poor man? This, they said, was a new and haughty craving, which had been neither desired nor established by the Senate of any other people.

---

enemies Terence's other prologues describe bitter opposition to Terence from other playwrights, especially one named Luscius Lanuvinus. Among the accusations allegedly made against Terence were that he improperly joined two different Greek plays into one Roman one, that he plagiarized from other Roman playwrights, that his plays were anaemic and that he had aristocratic ghost-writers.

censors two censors were elected from among Rome's elder statesmen every five years. They were primarily responsible for public works, taking the census and determining if any members should be removed from the Senate for immorality.

1 What do passages 2.5–7 suggest about the conditions under which Roman comedies were performed?
2 How seriously do you think we should take the prologue speaker of *The Little Carthaginian* when he gives his orders?
3 What kind of relationship do these two prologue speakers have (or try to have) with their audiences?
4 What does the prologue of *The Little Carthaginian* suggest about the participation of different genders and social classes in the Roman theatre audience?
5 How does Ambivius Turpio describe his role as producer in the prologue of *The Mother-in-Law*?
6 How do these prologues compare with the opening scenes of modern plays with which you are familiar?
7 What does it suggest about Roman attitudes towards watching plays that the censors ordered the classes to have separate seats and that the move was controversial?

The setting

All the action of every Roman comedy occurs outdoors in one location: the backdrop (the *scaenae frons*) for each play contained between one and three doors, each belonging to a building facing the street on which the action occurs. Actors could exit from the *proscaenium* through these doors or by departing to the left or right of the stage, where exits were assumed to lead on one side to the forum, on the other to the countryside or harbour. Often, if not always, there was an altar on the stage.

The following plan shows how the stage setting of Plautus' *The Haunted House* may have appeared.

2.8

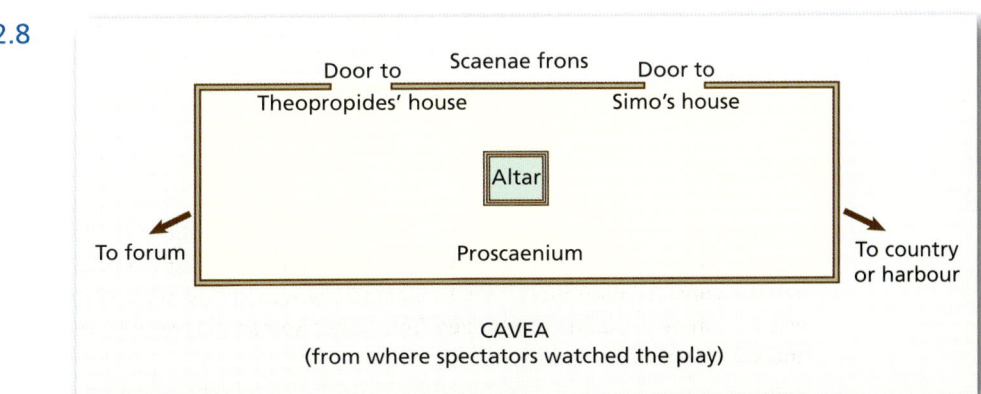

Prologue speakers and other characters often refer to the houses portrayed on stage. The god Mercury, who delivers the prologue of Plautus' *Amphitryo*, describes a backdrop with just one door (97–8).

2.9 This city is **Thebes**. In that house lives Amphitryo.

Terence's *The Brothers* (*Adelphoe*), like most Roman comedies, requires two houses. As they prepare for a wedding, the characters reveal that we are to assume a common garden divided by a wall unseen behind the two houses (903–10).

2.10 DEMEA   But why don't you summon your bride home?
AESCHINUS   I want to, but I'm waiting for a **tibicina** and people to sing the wedding hymn.
DEMEA   Well, do you want to listen to this old man?
AESCHINUS   What?
DEMEA   Forget about all these things, the wedding hymn, crowds, **torches**, *tibicinae*, and order the garden wall to be torn down as fast as possible: bring her over this way: make one household; bring along her mother and all her family to us.

Plautus' *The Pot of Gold* (*Aulularia*) requires three doors: the houses of the miser Euclio and his neighbour Megadorus and a shrine of the goddess *Fides* (Trustworthiness), where Euclio hides his gold during the play (580–6).

2.11 EUCLIO   I tell you, my dear pot, you have many enemies, as does that gold that's been entrusted to you. Now here's what I think is the best thing to do: I'll take you out, pot, to the shrine of *Fides*: there I will hide you well. *Fides*, you know me and I know you: take care that you don't change your name if I entrust this to you. I'll go to you, *Fides*, trusting in your guarantee.

Thebes   a city in Greece. All Roman comedies are set in Greek cities, though the characters often speak and act in ways distinctly Roman. As was noted in **2.3**, the disjuncture between Greek and Roman was often part of the plays' humour.

tibicina   female players of the *tibia* were hired to accompany wedding hymns.

torches   as a part of Roman weddings the bride was led to the groom's home accompanied by singing and torches.

The prologue speaker of Plautus' *The Menaechmus Brothers* (*Menaechmi*) comments on how the same stage can serve for many different settings (72–6). Note again the metatheatre: the prologue reminds the audience that they are watching a play.

2.12 This city is **Epidamnus**, so long as this play is being performed: when another one is performed it will become another town. In the same way the households usually change: now a **pimp** lives here, now a **young man**, now an **old man**, a poor man, a beggar, a **patron**, a **parasite**, a soothsayer.

A number of paintings from the walls of Roman houses show scenes that look like doorways opening onto streets. These may represent stage sets like those used in Roman comedies. The so-called 'Room of the Masks' (2.13) in the House of the Emperor Augustus in Rome (late first century BC) appears to show two doors with little porches, between which are a space for a third door and alcoves decorated with theatrical masks.

2.13

Epidamnus   another Greek city.

pimp, **young man**, **old man**, **patron**, **parasite**   some of the stock characters of Roman comedy.

Roman comedy in performance **17**

This marble relief of unknown date, though it is a copy of an earlier Greek work of art, shows many elements typical of Roman comedy. An angry father, holding a staff, is held back by his friend as he responds to the sight of his son returning home drunk from a party. The son holds a garland (a standard feature of Greek and Roman parties). He is joined by his slave, who props him up, and by a *tibicina*, who may be his girlfriend. Masks on the male characters have been identified as – from left to right – those of the 'leading old man', the 'long-bearded wavy-haired old man', the 'second wavy-haired youth' and the 'wavy-haired leading slave' (see **2.37**). The *tibicina* does not wear a mask: this may have been a typical practice for 'extras'. The free male characters wear long cloaks, but the slave wears a short tunic. Note the very physical nature of the acting, as characters grab onto others on both sides of the stage.

Behind the two fathers is a house door. The elaborate decoration of the door suggests that this performance is in a lavishly equipped theatre. The relief shows the left side of a backdrop with three doors. Because the play being performed calls for only two houses, a curtain, shown on the right side of the relief, covers up the middle door.

2.14

> 1 How does the stage setting for Roman comedy compare with the settings of modern plays with which you are familiar?
> 2 What limitations would the inevitable setting on a single street place on the playwrights? What might be the advantages of such a stage setting?
> 3 Why do you think the Roman comic playwrights set all their plays in the Greek world?
> 4 Do you think the painting in 2.13 is a stage setting? If it is, what does it reveal about such settings? Why might the emperor Augustus have included such a painting in his house?
> 5 Why do you think prologue speakers take such pains to point out who lives in what house and even joke about the setting?

Actors

All speaking actors in Roman comedy, as in almost all Roman theatrical genres, were men (it is possible that women sometimes played characters who did not speak, like the *tibicina* in **2.14**). As we saw in chapter 1, actors were forbidden from serving in the military and were denied other civic rights. They shared this status, which was called **infamia**, with prostitutes, gladiators and criminals. Actors could also be subject to beating by magistrates. They had a reputation for frivolity and loose sexual morals. Such disdain for actors is found in many societies, including Shakespearean England; but it is distinctly different from what one finds in Athens, where acting was a respectable profession.

> To many Romans, it seems, acting was similar to prostitution, an offering of one's body for others' pleasure in return for money. The biographer Cornelius Nepos (*c.* 100–*c.* 24 BC), for example, includes views on actors among the cultural differences between Greece and Rome (*On Famous Men*, Preface 5).

2.15 In just about all of Greece it was a source of great glory to be named as a victor at the Olympian games. And even to go on stage and present oneself for people to watch was not a source of shame for those peoples. But among us Romans all those things are considered either a reason for removal of civic rights, or at the very least lowly and far removed from the respectable.

> Some actors were slaves, others freed slaves. This passage from the prologue of Plautus' *The Donkey Play* (*Asinaria*) appears to refer to slave actors performing under the leadership of head actors, who served as both impresarios and masters (1–3).

2.16 Please pay attention now, spectators, and may this turn out well for me and for you and for this troupe and for our masters and hirers.

> The **epilogue** of Plautus' *The Basket* (*Cistellaria*) suggests that actors could be beaten if their performances were considered inadequate (782–5).

2.17 Spectators, don't expect them to come out here to you: no one will come out; they will all take care of the business inside. When that has been done, they will put aside their costumes; afterwards the one who has messed up will get a beating and the one who has not messed up will get a drink.

> Most ancient Greek plays were subject to a rule whereby they could use only three speaking actors. Roman companies were not subject to that rule, as the following scene from Plautus' *The Donkey Play*, which requires five speaking actors, reveals. Artemona has been told by a parasite (a man who supports himself by getting free meals from others) that her husband, Demaenetus, and her son, Argyrippus, are sharing the prostitute Philaenium. She and the parasite eavesdrop on the party the others are holding across the stage (878–84, 891–6).

2.18
PARASITE	If you happened to catch sight of your husband reclining with a wreath on his head, hugging his girlfriend, do you think you could recognize him?	
ARTEMONA	I sure could.	880
PARASITE	Well, there he is.	
ARTEMONA	Oh no!	
PARASITE	Wait here a minute. Let's listen in and find out what they're up to.	
ARGYRIPPUS	Father, when are you gonna stop hugging her?	
DEMAENETUS	I confess, son …	
ARGYRIPPUS	What do you confess?	
DEMAENETUS	That I'm madly in love with this girl.	
PARASITE	Do you hear what he's saying?	
ARTEMONA	I hear.	
…		
DEMAENETUS	Come on now, give me a kiss from the far side of the couch there.	
ARTEMONA	Oh damn it! Look at how that bastard kisses her, though he's old enough to be dead.	
DEMAENETUS	Wow! Your breath is a lot sweeter than my wife's!	
PHILAENIUM	Tell me, please, is your wife's breath foul?	
DEMAENETUS	I'd rather drink bilge water, if I had to, than kiss her.	895
ARTEMONA	Oh you would, would you?	

> Very few scenes require more than five actors, however, suggesting that with doubling of roles a very small company could perform the plays.

> 1 How does the status of actors in Republican Rome compare with the social position of actors in our society?
> 2 How might the status of the actors have affected how they interacted with the audience from the stage?
> 3 How would the probable doubling of roles have affected the way the audience experienced a Roman comedy?
> 4 What difference, if any, would it have made to a scene like the one from *The Donkey Play* quoted in 2.18 that men played all the speaking parts, including the women's roles?

Movement, gesture and acting styles

Plautus' and Terence's texts do not include explicit stage directions, but they often give a good indication of what movement, including gestures, would occur on stage. In the large parts of the plays that were accompanied by the *tibia*, gestures may have been made in time with the music as a form of dance.

In Plautus' *The Braggart Soldier* (*Miles Gloriosus*), the old man Periplectomenus watches as the clever slave Palaestrio plans a deception (200–9, 213).

2.19 Look at that, will you: look how he stands, worrying and thinking with a stern brow. He strikes his chest with his fingers: I think he's going to summon up his heart. Look! He turns away. Leaning, he holds his left hand on his left thigh. His right does reckoning with its fingers. He strikes his right thigh. Look how hard he strikes it! He must just barely have an idea what to do. He's snapped his fingers. He's working at it. He keeps changing positions. But look! He's nodding his head. He doesn't like what he's come up with. Whatever it is, he won't let it out uncooked but will see that it's well done. Look! He's building something: he's putting a column under his chin ... Wow! I tell you, he's standing beautifully, just like a slave in a comedy.

The Roman orator and philosopher Cicero (Marcus Tullius Cicero, 106–43 BC) describes the gestures of Aesopus and Roscius, the two most famous actors of his day (*On the Orator* 3.102).

2.20 When Roscius performs the verse, 'For the wise man seeks honour as the reward for virtue, not as its plunder', he never uses the gesture he could use. Instead he throws the line away, so that in the next verse, when he says, 'But what do I see? Armed, he sits in the sacred place', he can speed up, gaze, marvel and be astounded. And what about Aesopus when he performs 'What bulwark shall I seek?' in such a gentle, relaxed, unenergetic manner! He presses upon the words 'O my father! O my fatherland! O house of Priam!': he would not be able to arouse such energy here if it had been used up and exhausted by the previous motion. And the actors have not discovered this before the poets themselves, or indeed before those who made the music. By each of them something is held back and then increased, stretched out, inflated, varied, made distinct.

> Valerius Maximus, who recorded examples from history in the first century AD, writes of Roscius' careful attention to gesture (*Memorable Words and Deeds* 8.7.7).

2.21 Nor should we forget Roscius, the most outstanding example of an actor who worked very hard: he never dared to present any gesture before an audience unless he had planned it out at home.

> Roman orators (i.e. public speakers) often took pains to distinguish themselves from lowly actors. Yet in fact orators and actors shared many techniques, including an elaborate system of gestures. The educator Quintilian (Marcus Fabius Quintilianus, born *c.* AD 35) describes the gestures used by Roman orators in his *The Education of the Orator*. He also includes in his discussion some thoughts about the movement of actors (11.3.111–12, 181–2).

2.22 But when vehemence has stirred up the speech, the gesturing will grow along with the speed of the discourse. A swift pronunciation will be appropriate for some places, a deliberate mode of delivery for others. With swift speech we hasten from one point to another, pile arguments on and hurry along. With deliberate speech we press upon a point, drive it home, and fix it in the minds of our hearers. Slower things, moreover, have more emotional impact. That's why Roscius is faster and Aesopus slower, because Roscius performs comedies and Aesopus tragedies. The same practice applies to movement: in plays youths, old men, soldiers and married women walk in a more sombre fashion, but male and female slaves, parasites and fishermen have more lively movements … 112

Moderation should be the most powerful precept, for I want my student to be an orator, not a comic actor. Therefore we will not pursue every refinement in gesture, nor in speaking will we use pauses, changes in tempo and expressiveness in an annoying way. Take the **following verses**: 182

> So what should I do? Surely I should go now, when she summons me of her own accord? Or should I make up my mind not to endure the insults of prostitutes?

An actor on the stage would perform these words with hesitations, variations in his voice and a variety of gestures and nods. Oratory knows better, and it does not want to be too elaborate: for it consists of **action, not imitation**.

---

following verses   Quintilian quotes some verses spoken by a young lover in Terence's *The Eunuch* (*Eunuchus* 46–8).

action, not imitation   that is, orators are expected to accomplish something with their words, whereas actors are imitating the actions of someone else.

Some manuscripts of Terence's plays from the ninth century AD and later include illustrations. The manuscripts, including the illustrations, are copies of earlier manuscripts from sometime between the second and fifth centuries AD. Though they show many signs of their late date, it is possible that at least in some ways they reflect performance traditions going back to the time of Plautus and Terence. The illustrations include a large number of hand gestures, which may retain some traces of the gestures used in the plays when they were first performed.

In the scene from *The Mother-in-Law* (*Hecyra*) shown in 2.23, the old man Laches overhears his wife, Sostrata, telling their son, Pamphilus, that she will leave the city because Pamphilus' wife evidently does not get along with her. Each character uses a gesture that underlines explicitly his or her actions or words. Laches, for example, uses the standard gesture for a character eavesdropping on another character. The characters are identified both by their names and their character types: *mulier* (woman), *adulescens* (young man) and *senex* (old man).

2.23

1. Taken together, what do passages 2.19–22 and illustration 2.23 suggest about how actors may have moved on the Roman stage?
2. Why might Plautus have Periplectomenus deliver a running commentary to accompany the gestures of Palaestrio? Are we to conclude that the gestures were not self-evident, or are there other possible explanations?
3. Periplectomenus says that Palaestrio moves 'like a slave in a comedy'. What does this imply about the gestures of actors playing slaves?
4. What features of stage movement does Cicero point to in the performances of Aesopus and Roscius?
5. What does Quintilian suggest about the style of acting in Rome? What qualities do you think Quintilian would like orators to convey that he seems to believe actors are unlikely to possess?

Costumes

Plautus' and Terence's plays belong to a genre called the ***fabula palliata*** ('play where people wear *pallia*') because most characters wore a cloak called a ***pallium*** (plural *pallia*, see **2.14**). Female characters sometimes wore a similar cloak called a *palla*. Because the Romans associated the *pallium* with Greeks, the costumes identified the characters as Greeks. The *pallium* was worn over a simpler cloak called a tunic (***tunica***); sometimes slave characters wore just the tunic. Almost all characters wore slipper-like footwear known as ***socci***.

> As was noted on p. 8, costumes were provided by the *choragus*. In Plautus' *Curculio* the *choragus* himself (or an actor impersonating him) enters after the title character, a parasite, has left the stage to carry out some deception for his patron, Phaedromus (462–6).

2.24 By **Pollux**, Phaedromus has nicely found himself a nice liar here. I don't know whether I should call him a con man or a swindler. I'm afraid I won't be able to get back the costumes I rented out; but I don't have business with him: I entrusted them to **Phaedromus** himself; still, I'll keep watch.

> In this passage characters in Plautus' *The Persian* (*Persa*) describe how they will get costumes from the *choragus* (157–60).

2.25   TOXILUS   Bring your daughter, costumed nicely **like a foreigner**.
        SATURIO   *De donde* the costumes?
        TOXILUS   Get them from the *choragus*: he has to give them to you. The aediles gave him the contract to provide them.

> The **grammarian** Aelius Donatus (fourth century AD), who wrote a commentary on the plays of Terence, describes variations in costume based on character type. It is not certain whether these distinctions are accurate records of performance practice or guesses by later scholars (*On Comedy* 8.6).

Pollux   one of a pair of divine brothers, Castor and Pollux.

Phaedromus   it appears that the actor playing Phaedromus is the chief actor, to whom the *choragus* rented the costumes.

like a foreigner   Toxilus wants Saturio's daughter to pretend to be a foreigner as part of a plot to deceive a pimp who owns the woman Toxilus is in love with.

De donde   Saturio throws in a word of Greek (hence the Spanish here). Greek words in Plautus' plays sometimes reflect elevated language, but more often they represent the Greek that was mixed in with the slang of Rome's lower classes (many slaves came from the Greek-speaking eastern Mediterranean).

2.26 Comic old men wear white clothing, because that is said to have been the oldest style. Young men wear clothing of various colours. Comic slaves wear a small cloak, either because of their long-standing poverty or so that they can move around more efficiently. Parasites enter with twisted *pallia*. A happy character has white clothing, one in debt has out-of-date garments. A rich man gets purple garments, a poor man scarlet. A soldier gets a purple **chlamys**, a girl a foreign style of dress. A pimp wears a *pallium* of various colours and a prostitute, because of her greed, wears a **yellowish** *pallium*.

> The texts of the plays reveal numerous variations in costume, especially in scenes where characters dress up to carry out deceptions.
>
> In Plautus' *The Three-Penny Day* (*Trinummus*), Charinus observes someone disguised as a traveller (840–1, 851).

2.27 But who is this, who walks onto the square with this novel costume and appearance? ... By Pollux, he's some kind of mushroom: he **covers his whole self with his head**.

> At the end of Plautus' *The Braggart Soldier* (*Miles Gloriosus*) the cook Cario punishes the soldier Pyrgopolynices, who has been caught in attempted adultery and beaten (1423).

2.28 CARIO Don't have any hope for your tunic, your *chlamys* and your sword: you won't get them back.

> In Plautus' *The Prisoners* (*Captivi*), the parasite Ergasilus runs to tell Hegio that his son, captured in war, has returned home. As he does so he takes on the role of the 'running slave', who in many comedies frantically brings news to his master (776–9).

2.29 Now I will run to old Hegio here. I'm bringing him as much good as he hopes for from the gods, and even more. Now I've made up my mind; I'll throw my *pallium* over my shoulder just like comic slaves do, so that he can hear about this from me first.

---

chlamys a kind of cloak worn, like the *pallium*, over the tunic.

yellowish presumably because the yellow looks like gold.

covers his whole self with his head the person observed wears a broad-brimmed hat called a *petasus*, commonly worn by travellers.

This fresco was painted before AD 79 on the wall of a house in Pompeii. A slave, with a padded stomach typical of comic slaves, addresses two figures, probably a young man and his girlfriend. Note the slave's short tunic and the *pallium* slung over his shoulder: this is probably a 'running slave scene' like the one described in **2.29**. The gaze of all three characters towards stage right suggests that the slave is reporting the unwanted arrival of someone – perhaps a pimp who owns the woman, perhaps the young man's father – who opposes the couple being together.

The free characters wear longer *pallia*, and all the characters have *socci* on their feet. The masks in this scene have been identified as – from left to right – those of the 'old slave', the 'second **false maiden**', and the 'admirable young man' (see **2.37**).

2.30

Comic scene from the House of Theatrical Paintings, Pompeii.

1 What do passages 2.24–29 and illustration 2.30 suggest about the nature and use of costume in Roman comedy?
2 What would be the effect of the introduction of the *choragus* as a character in the play?
3 How important do you think costumes were in helping the audience distinguish between character types and individual characters?
4 It is clear from passages both here and in earlier sections of this chapter that actors in Roman comedy were not shy about addressing the audience directly and discussing their own position as actors. How does that compare with practice in the modern theatre?

Props

The *choragus* may also have provided props. In several plays props, like Euclio's pot of gold mentioned in **2.11**, play a central role. The title of Plautus' *The Rope* (*Rudens*) refers to a rope tied to a chest that the slave Gripus has found in the sea. The slave Trachalio knows that the chest contains tokens (i.e. personal effects/objects) that will prove that the play's heroine is freeborn and therefore marriageable (936, 938–9, 944–6, 963–5).

2.31 GRIPUS   Now I'll put this chest away.
     ...
     TRACHALIO   (*enters holding the rope to which the chest is tied*) Hey, wait a minute!
     GRIPUS   Why?
     TRACHALIO   Let me fold up this rope you're dragging.
     GRIPUS   Just let go of it.
     TRACHALIO   But really, I want to help you: a good deed done for the good is not done in vain.
     ...
     GRIPUS   You're boring me to death, whoever you are.
     TRACHALIO   I won't let you get away. Wait.
     GRIPUS   You'd better watch out! Dammit, why are you dragging me back?   945
     TRACHALIO   Listen.
     GRIPUS   I won't listen.
     TRACHALIO   I'll make you listen!
     GRIPUS   All right, say what you want.
     ...
     TRACHALIO   I've known the person who owns that chest for a long time.
     GRIPUS   So?
     TRACHALIO   And I know how it got lost.
     GRIPUS   But I know how it got found, and I know the guy who found it, and I know who owns it now.

Many scenes from the illustrated manuscripts of Terence show props that are mentioned in or implied by the text. This illustration shows the first scene of *The Woman from Andros* (*Andria*), in which the old man Simo addresses his freed slave Sosia, who is followed by slaves bringing provisions for a wedding feast. Note also Simo's and Sosia's gestures, and the costumes: a long *pallium* for Simo and one of the slaves, shorter tunics for the other slave and for the freed slave Sosia. The writing above the illustration is the text of the play, between lines of which the illustrations were drawn.

2.32

> 1 How would you envision the scene in 2.31 being played?
> 2 How would the presence of slaves with props have affected the audience's reaction to the scene being performed in 2.32?

Masks

Some ancient sources appear to suggest that Roman actors did not wear masks until after the time of Plautus and Terence. Most scholars now believe that those sources are mistaken or have been misread, and that actors playing speaking roles in Plautus' and Terence's plays did wear masks, made of wood, linen or leather, which covered the actor's entire face. Some mute characters, like the *tibicina* in **2.14**, may have appeared without masks. The use of masks probably had its origins in the ritual beginnings of theatre, but they brought distinct advantages to performers even after those ritual origins were forgotten. They allowed audience members to identify features of characters at sight: playwrights could use the expectations produced by the masks to give a fuller picture of the characters, or they could surprise the audience by having their characters speak and act differently from what the masks would lead the audience to expect.

> Numerous passages from Roman comedy suggest that variations in masks and other aspects of appearance played an important role in the presentation of characters. In Plautus' *Pseudolus*, the pimp Ballio fears that his enemy, the slave Pseudolus, has tricked the messenger Harpax (1217–21).

2.33 **BALLIO** Hey, tell me, what did he look like, the guy you gave the **sealed letter** to?

HARPAX He was a red-haired guy, with a big belly and fat calves, kind of swarthy, with a big head, sharp eyes, a reddish face and really big feet.

BALLIO Oh no! You've ruined me with those words about his feet. It was Pseudolus himself.

> In Plautus' *The Merchant* (*Mercator*) Charinus asks Eutychus about the appearance of an old man, who will later appear in the play (638–40).

2.34 **CHARINUS** What did they say he looked like, Eutychus?

EUTYCHUS I'll tell you: white-haired, bow-legged, with a big belly and fat cheeks, rather short, with blackish eyes, stretched-out jaws, and kind of spay-footed.

> In Plautus' *The Rope* (*Rudens*), Trachalio looks for his master (the young man Plesidippus) and the pimp Labrax, who has stolen Plesidippus' girlfriend (313–20).

2.35 **TRACHALIO** While you've been standing here, have you seen a strong young man, ruddy with an energetic appearance, come by here, bringing with him three men, each of whom was wearing a *chlamys* and carrying a sword?

FISHERMEN We don't know of anybody with that appearance coming by here.

TRACHALIO How about an old man with a receding hairline, who looks like **Silenus**, standing straight, with a big belly, twisted eyebrows and a scowl, a lying bastard, hateful to gods and men, a scoundrel, full of wickedness, vice and disgrace, bringing with him two rather charming little prostitutes?

> Quintilian suggests that masks distinguished different types of characters and that the positioning of eyebrows was an important part of mask construction (*Education of the Orator* 11.3.74).

2.36 In comedies slaves, pimps, parasites, men from the country, soldiers, prostitutes, female attendants, severe and gentle old men, serious and pleasure-loving youths,

---

sealed letter Pseudolus got the letter from Harpax by pretending he was one of Ballio's slaves, then used the letter to steal one of Ballio's prostitutes.

Silenus a demigod known for his animal-like ways, his corpulence and his drunkenness. He often accompanied Bacchus, the god of wine. The description here reflects the use of padding to make the bellies of some characters appear grotesque.

matrons and girls are all distinguished one from the other. In addition, the father, who has the most important role, has one eyebrow lifted up and the other settled in place, since he is sometimes excited and sometimes calm; and actors often make a point of showing the side of the mask that fits the scenes they are performing.

> The Greek scholar Pollux (second century AD) describes 44 masks, each used by a different character type. Pollux describes the masks of Greek New Comedy, but similar distinctions probably carried over into Roman comedy. Here are some of his descriptions, including those that have been associated with the masks in **2.14** and **2.30** (selections from *Book of Words* 4.144–52).

2.37   The leading old man has a crown of hair around his head. His nose is slightly hooked, his face flat, and his right eyebrow is raised.

The long-bearded wavy-haired old man has a crown of hair around his head. He has a fine beard, and his eyebrows are not raised. He looks sluggish …

The admirable young man is reddish, athletic and tanned, having a few wrinkles on his face and a crown of hair, with his eyebrows raised.

The dark youth is younger, and his eyebrows are not raised. He looks studious rather than athletic …

The first wavy-haired young man, a soldier and a braggart, is dark in both his skin and his hair, and his hair is wavy.

The second wavy-haired young man is the same but gentler looking and with blond hair …

The old slave mask is the only one of the slave masks with grey hair, and it can also indicate a freedman.

The leading slave has a coil of red hair and raised eyebrows, and he knits his brow. He is the same among slaves as the leading old man is among free men …

The wavy-haired leading slave is like the leading slave except for his hair …

The maiden has smoothed-down hair with a parting, straight black eyebrows and a pallid whiteness in her skin.

The first **false maiden** is whiter in her skin, has her hair bound around the front part of her head and resembles a newlywed.

The second false maiden is distinguished from the first only because her hair is not parted.

---

false maiden   a freeborn woman, lost at a young age, usually enslaved and about to enter a career as a prostitute, whose status is revealed before the end of the play.

Theatrical masks of other cultures provide analogies to Quintilian's and Pollux's descriptions. This picture, for example, shows the mask called 'Magojiro', used in traditional Japanese Noh drama. Its name and basic characteristics reveal that this is the mask of a certain type of young woman, one who usually suffers grief during the play. By tilting his head forwards or backwards, the actor can make the mask show different expressions.

2.38

Noh mask.

This mosaic of uncertain date shows a pair of masks and a *tibia*. The masks have been identified as those of the 'maiden' and the 'old slave'. Romans loved to decorate their houses with masks, so works of art such as this one are common. Note the conspicuous features identifying the characters portrayed: the yellow ribbon and long locks of the 'maiden' and the garland, thick eyebrows, wide smile and beard of the 'old slave'.

2.39

The illustrations in the medieval manuscripts of Terence show that the importance of masks was recognized even many centuries after the plays were written. Not only do all the characters shown in the illustrations wear masks, but the text of each play in the manuscripts is preceded by a picture of a little building (an *aedicula*) containing masks for each character who appears in the play. This is the *aedicula* for *The Woman from Andros* (*Andria*).

2.40

> 1 What do the passages and images in 2.33–40 suggest about how masks and other features of physical appearance were used to distinguish characters in Roman comedy?
>
> 2 What do Quintilian's claims about the father's mask in 2.36 suggest about the acting style of Roman actors?
>
> 3 Which aspects of physical appearance seem most important to the characters describing other characters? How does this compare with the physical features you yourself notice in others?
>
> 4 Do the descriptions of characters' faces in the Plautus passages appear to match any of Pollux's masks?
>
> 5 Many masks appear in the images shown in this chapter (2.13, 2.14, 2.23, 2.30, 2.32, 2.39, 2.40). How do these masks compare with the descriptions of masks in Plautus, Quintilian and Pollux? What associations seem to be made in the images between characters, character types and masks?

Music and dance

We noted in chapter 1 the importance to Roman drama of song, dance and the *tibia*. The following passage from the end of Plautus' *Stichus* shows how these three musical elements could work together in Roman comedy. The title character, his fellow slave Sangarinus and their girlfriend, the female slave Stephanium, are having a party (755–75).

2.41   STICHUS   [**tr7**] Come, my honeyed sweetness, dance:
and I will dance along with you.

SANGARINUS   I don't think you'll outdo me in lust: I want her
just as much.

STEPHANIUM   OK, then, I'll dance. But you must give our piper
friend a drink.

STICHUS   We'll drink too.

SANGARINUS   Go on, *tibicen*; drink this down, just like before.
After drinking play a song that's sweet, to stir up all   760
our lust.
Make us tingle from our toes. But first have wine,
and **water too**.
[**ia6**] All right now, drink this down. Before he
liked his drink,
So now he takes it eagerly. Go on now: drink.
And while he drinks it down, my sweet, give me a kiss.

STICHUS   What's this? Is she a common whore, to kiss you here,   765
Right in the street? (*Stephanium slaps Sangarinus or makes a similar gesture of rejection.*) Touché! That's what you
get, you thief!

SANGARINUS   Come on now, puff your cheeks, play something
sweet for us.
We want to hear a song that's new for wine that's old.
(*dancing as the* tibicen *begins to play*)
[**ia8**] **Cinaedi and Ionians** can't dance as well as
I do now.

---

tr7, ia6, ia8, ia7, versreiz   these abbreviations identify the metres sung or spoken by the actors in the Latin text (see the box on metre, pp. 35–6). They stand, respectively, for **trochaic septenarius, iambic senarius,** iambic octonarius, iambic septenarius and *versus reizianus*.

water too   Greeks and Romans usually drank their wine mixed with water.

Cinaedi and Ionians   *cinaedi* were professional performers known for their lewd dancing. They often did a type of dance known as Ionian dance – named after the Ionians, Greeks who lived in what is now Turkey – which involved lifting up their garments in a suggestive fashion.

STICHUS	[ia7] You've beat me there, but try again, I'm sure I can out-twist you.	770
SANGARINUS	Try this way.	
STICHUS	You try this way too.	
SANGARINUS	Babae!	
STICHUS	Tatae!	
SANGARINUS	Papae!	
STICHUS	Stop!	
SANGARINUS	[versreiz] And now a dance with both of us. Call the *cinaedi*. We just can't get enough of this. Like mushrooms and rain.	
STICHUS	[ia7] OK, it's time to go inside. We've earned our wine by dancing. Spectators, have some parties of your own at home. But clap first.	775

Though this illustration is of a performance in Greek southern Italy a hundred years or so before the time of Plautus, it shows actors and a *tibicina* in a relationship similar to that assumed in the passage above. One actor holds a lit torch that may suggest that a night-time party is being staged: scenes of revelling frequently bring to a close Greek comedies as they do the Plautine play above.

2.42

Bell krater (Campanian red-figure ware), 350–325 BC.

Babae! Tatae! Papae! these are exclamations similar to 'Wow!' or 'Yeah!'.

1 What does the dialogue in 2.41 suggest about the position of the *tibicen* relative to the actors, and the way actor and *tibicen* interacted? How do the assumptions of the dialogue compare with how the actors and *tibicina* are shown on the vase in 2.42?
2 What kind of dance seems to be suggested by this passage?
3 Why do you think this scene occurs at the end of the play, rather than at some earlier point?
4 What connections do you notice between the words of the dialogue and the changes of metre in the passage?
5 Besides 2.42, we have also seen images of *tibiae* in 2.14 and 2.39. What might those images tell us about the *tibia* and its role in comedies?

The metres of Roman comedy

Plautus and Terence used a large variety of metres. All of them, like virtually all Greek and Latin verse forms, were based on patterns of long and short syllables. Replacing these patterns with patterns of stress, the foundation of our own metre, we get the following equivalents for Roman comedy's most common metres (´ marks a stress).

iambic senarius:
> All ríght now, drínk this dówn. Befóre he líked his drínk,

trochaic septenarius:
> Cóme, my hóneyed swéetness, dánce: and Í will dánce alóng with yoú.

iambic septenarius:
> You've beát me thére, but trý agaín, I'm súre I cán out-twíst you.

iambic octonarius:
> Cinaédi ánd Ióniáns can't dánce as wéll as Í do nów.

Plautus also used metres based on the following patterns:

anapests: ⏑ ⏑ – equivalent to:
> 'Now be góne, now be góne, with your laúghter and sóngs'

bacchiacs: ⏑ – – equivalent to:
> 'I dón't like this óld sóng, it's toó slów for dáncíng'

cretics: – ⏑ – equivalent to:
> 'Sweétly síng, shów your chárm, dáncing wéll through the níght'.

There are also some rare metres, like the *versus reiziani* in the passage quoted in **2.41**, a mixture of iambic and other elements. Latin poets generally avoided rhyme.

All these metres except the iambic senarius were usually sung to the accompaniment of the *tibia*. That is, all iambic senarii passages were classified as *deverbia* (passages to be spoken), passages in all other metres as *cantica* (passages to be sung). Note that in the above passage the metre changes to iambic senarius while the *tibicen* takes a drink. Because iambic senarii make up only about 37 per cent of Roman comedy, most verses were performed musically.

Plautus and Terence used primarily what are called **stichic** metres, in which the same verse form (for example, trochaic septenarius) is used for many consecutive verses. About 15 per cent of Roman comedy, however, consists of passages like the one in **2.41**, in which metres change frequently. These passages are called **polymetric** passages, and they often occur at the emotional high points of plays.

3 Plautus

Plautus' 21 surviving plays have a wide variety of characters and plots, but most include some variation of the basic storyline that has been standard in European comedy since antiquity: an obstacle to the union of two lovers is overcome. In *The Haunted House* (*Mostellaria*) we can see some of the character types involved in such plots.

> When *The Haunted House* begins, Theopropides is away on a business trip. His slave Tranio has been aiding and abetting his young master, Philolaches, in wild living, which has culminated in Philolaches borrowing a large sum of money in order to purchase and free Philematium, a slave prostitute with whom he has fallen in love. After an opening dialogue between Tranio and his fellow slave Grumio, Philolaches enters and sings the following song (84–156).

3.1 I've thought a lot and pondered a long time, and I put together lots of arguments in my mind, and I've turned this matter over and over in my heart – if I have a 85
heart – and argued with myself a long time: what is a man like, when he's born, and what kind of simile can best describe him? This is what I've come up with: I 90
think a man, when he's born, is like a new house. I'll tell you my reasons for this … And once you've heard me, I'm sure you yourselves will say it's just the way I 95
say it is, and not a jot different. Listen, while I hold forth on the subject at hand: in this matter I want you to be as knowledgeable as I am. 100

As soon as a house has been built, finished and made just right, they praise the builder and commend the house, and everybody takes that house as his model and wants his to be just like it, sparing no expense or labour. But when a 105

***The Haunted House*: Dramatis personae**

Callidamates (Kahl-li-dáh-mah-tees)	a young man
Delphium (Dél-fee-um)	a prostitute
Grumio (Gróo-mee-oh)	a slave
Misargyrides (Miss-ar-jéer-i-dees)	a moneylender
Philematium (Fill-eh-máy-shee-um)	a prostitute
Philolaches (Fill-láh-lah-kees)	a young man
Scapha (Skáh-fah)	an old woman
Simo (Sí-moh)	an old man
Theopropides (Thay-oh-próh-pi-dees)	an old man
Tranio (Tráh-nee-oh)	a slave

worthless and negligent fellow moves in, who's slovenly and sluggish and has a lazy household, a good house is cared for badly, and it goes downhill. And here's what often happens: a storm comes; it breaks the roof covers and tiles. The lazy owner doesn't want to replace them. The rain comes in, it soaks the walls, and they let the rain right in. It rots the beams and destroys the builder's work. The house becomes worthless. And it's not the builder's fault. That's just how most people are: even if something can be fixed for a penny, they procrastinate and don't do it, until the walls come tumbling down, and the whole house has to be built over again.

OK, that's my argument about buildings. Now I want to convince you that men are like houses. First: parents are children's builders. They lay down the foundation for their children, they build them up, and they carefully set them up on firm ground, so they'll be good and upstanding citizens. They don't skimp at all on building materials, and they don't give any thought to the money they spend. They finish the children well: they teach them letters, private and public law, they try with their money and labour to make others want children just like theirs. When the sons join the army they give them some **relative to look after them**. So far, so good. Then the children leave their builders. When their time in the army is up, then you can tell what will become of the building.

Look at me: I was good and well behaved, as long as I was in the power of my builders. But when I moved into my own nature, at once I completely destroyed my builders' work. Idleness came in: that was my storm. When it arrived it brought in hail and rain. It dislodged my self-restraint and whatever excellence I had and blew them right off me. Afterwards I didn't bother to cover myself back up.

Right away love came into my heart like rain. It dripped deep down into my breast and drenched my heart. Now property, good faith, reputation, excellence, honour, they've all abandoned me. I've become really worthless, good for nothing. And, by Pollux, my beams are rotting so badly that I don't think I can patch up my house. I think it'll go completely to ruin and collapse right down to its foundation, and nobody can do anything about it.

I grieve at heart when I think about what I am now and what I was before. In sports I used to be the most energetic of all the young men: I lived for the discus, the spear, the javelin, for running, fighting and riding. I was the model for others in frugality and toughness: all the best youths took lessons from me. Now I'm worthless, and it's truly my own fault I got that way.

---

relative to look after them it was customary for an upper-class Roman youth to serve in the army in the cohort of a relative or friend of his father, who would act as a mentor.

1. How remorseful do you think Philolaches really is?
2. How good is Philolaches at getting his thoughts across? How would his song have been different if he had used fewer words?
3. How persuasive do you find Philolaches' simile?
4. How do you think this song was acted? Would the actor playing Philolaches appear to be addressing himself, as in many modern soliloquies, or would the song be directed at the audience?
5. Why might Plautus have included this lengthy song at the beginning of his play? What might it achieve?

Plautus' life

Ancient sources report that Titus Maccius Plautus was born in the town of Sarsina, in north-central Italy (see map on p. x). He allegedly moved to Rome and made a fortune in the theatre but then lost all his money in a mercantile adventure and was forced to work in a mill, where he wrote some plays. Eventually he got out of debt and lived to old age as a very successful playwright. We have no way of knowing how much of this tradition is accurate, as ancient biographers often made up biographical facts about playwrights from remarks they found in their plays. The tradition that Sarsina was Plautus' home town, for example, may come from the joke Tranio makes in **3.6**; and writers may have claimed that Plautus himself worked in a mill because of the many passages in which characters like Tranio fear they will be sent to a mill, a frequent punishment for disobedient slaves. Even Plautus' name may be made up. *Titus*, though a common enough Roman name, can also be a slang word for penis; *Maccius* is a clownish stock character of Atellan farce; and *Plautus* means 'flat-footed', a word also used of performers in mime. *Titus Maccius Plautus* could thus be a made-up name meaning something like 'Dick the Flat-footed Clown'. The three-part name would be especially funny in Rome, where members of the aristocracy often had three-part names that included reminders of great ancestors (e.g. Quintus Fabius Maximus, of which the third part 'Maximus' (the Greatest) recalled a great Fabius of the past).

In the ensuing scene Philolaches comments aside as he eavesdrops on a conversation between Philematium and her maid Scapha (194–215, 229–30).

3.2 SCAPHA   You're obviously a fool to think he'll always be affectionate and   195
             kind to you. I'm warning you: he'll desert you when you're old
             and he tires of you.
    PHILEMATIUM   I hope not.

SCAPHA	Things you don't hope for happen more often than things you do. All right, then: if what I say can't persuade you, learn from my own experience how true my words are. You see what I am now, and what I was before. I was no less loved then than you are now, and I gave myself to just one man. By god, as soon as this head of mine grew grey with age, **he ran off and abandoned me**. I think that's what will happen to you.
PHILOLACHES	(*aside*) I can hardly keep myself from tearing out that troublemaker's eyes.
PHILEMATIUM	He freed just me, for just himself and with his own money: I think I ought to be faithful to just him.
PHILOLACHES	(*aside*) Good gods! What a charming and modest woman! I'm glad I went bankrupt for her sake.
SCAPHA	You're really an idiot.
PHILEMATIUM	Why?
SCAPHA	Because you're worried about whether he'll keep loving you.
PHILEMATIUM	Why on earth shouldn't I be?
SCAPHA	You're free now. You've got what you wanted: if he doesn't keep loving you, he'll have wasted all that money he spent to buy you.
PHILOLACHES	(*aside*) Damn me if I don't torture and kill her! The seductive witch, she's corrupting the woman.
PHILEMATIUM	I don't think I can ever pay back what he has earned from me, Scapha, so don't try to persuade me to value him less.
…	
PHILOLACHES	(*aside*) By Hercules, if I had to sell my father, I'd much rather sell him than ever let her be in need or have to go begging.

Line numbers: 200, 205, 210, 215, 230

> 1 What do you think the effect would be of this glimpse into the realities of being a prostitute?
> 2 How would Philolaches' asides affect the audience's response to the dialogue between Philematium and Scapha?
> 3 What do Philolaches' final words about his father suggest about the moral world of Plautus' play?
> 4 How are Philematium and Scapha characterized? Are they being portrayed as stereotypes of prostitutes?

he ran off and abandoned me it should be noted that, although prostitution did not have the moral stigma it has in many modern societies, and there are many examples from Greek and Roman history and literature of long-term relationships between prostitutes and their lovers, by law and custom in both Rome and Greece men of Philolaches' class could not marry women of Philematium and Scapha's class. Philolaches' relationship with Philematium could be condoned but never legally ratified, and he would be expected to marry a freeborn woman in the not-too-distant future.

This mosaic of *c.* 100 BC, signed by the artist Discourides, shows a scene from Menander's *The Women at Lunch* (*Synaristosai*), which Plautus adapted as his play *The Basket* (*Cistellaria*). Both plays begin with a dialogue in which three prostitutes discuss their lives.

Note the white masks on all three women: throughout Greek and Roman art, white faces often help to distinguish women (who spent much of their lives indoors) from men. The old woman, as is usual in Greek and Roman comedy, wears a mask that is considerably more grotesque than those of the young women. She also holds a wine cup: old women in Greek and Roman comedy are often stereotyped as drunks. Two of the prostitutes wear yellow garments, just as Donatus suggests prostitutes do (see **2.26**). A young boy without a mask plays a servant: he is probably an unmasked 'extra' similar to the *tibicina* in **2.14**.

> **Women in Roman comedy**
>
> One of the most conspicuous differences between Roman comedy and most modern romantic comedies is the role of women in their love plots. Both today's romantic comedies and most Roman comedies are about overcoming obstacles to love. While modern romantic comedies tend to emphasize the feelings and actions of both the male and the female partner – e.g. a man successfully wins a woman's love or vice versa – the female lovers of Roman comedy usually play a much more passive role. In most Roman comedies the beloved woman is a prostitute like Philematium, and the male lover must somehow acquire money in order to gain exclusive access to her; or she is a marriageable woman, sometimes one who has been raped by the male lover, and the man must overcome obstacles such as parental opposition or misunderstanding so that he can marry her. Almost never is the desire of the female lover a concern of the plot: frequently, in fact, she remains unseen throughout the play. Characters of Roman comedy often express misogynistic sentiments like those of Simo in **3.6**. Nevertheless, Roman comedy offers a number of strong women characters and fascinating glimpses into women's lives. In addition to the women like Philematium who remain steadfastly loyal to their lovers, several strong wives successfully oppose their husbands' philandering and stand up for their sons, and some clever prostitutes seduce and deceive their victims with impressive efficiency.

Philolaches finally tires of eavesdropping, and he and Philematium settle down for a drinking party. They are soon joined by Philolaches' friend Callidamates, who enters – very drunk – with his girlfriend, the prostitute Delphium (313–47).

3.3 CALLIDAMATES (*to a slave who follows him on*) I want somebody to come and fetch me from Philolaches' house when it's time: that's an order. (*The slave exits.*) I was so bored with the party and the 315 conversation where I was that I took off. Now I'll go party at Philolaches': it's sure to be fun there. Do you think maybe I'm a little d-d-d-drunk?

DELPHIUM You're always like this. Look: you've gone the wrong way. It's this 320 way.

CALLIDAMATES How about a little cuddle?

DELPHIUM All right, if that's what you want.

CALLIDAMATES You're so nice! You lead.

DELPHIUM Whoa, steady! Careful you don't fall.

CALLIDAMATES Oh, oh, oh, you're the apple of my eye. Honey, I'm your baby. 325

DELPHIUM Watch out, now, or you'll fall down in the street: hang on until we can settle down on the nice couch waiting for us there.

CALLIDAMATES	Lemme fall.	
DELPHIUM	All right, but if you fall, so do I.	
CALLIDAMATES	Then they can just pick us both up off the street.	330
DELPHIUM	This guy is drunk.	
CALLIDAMATES	What, you say I'm d-d-d-drunk?	
DELPHIUM	Give me your hand: I don't want you to get hurt.	
CALLIDAMATES	There: hold on.	
DELPHIUM	OK, come with me.	
CALLIDAMATES	Where?	
DELPHIUM	You don't know?	
CALLIDAMATES	Sure. I just remembered: we're going home to party.	335
DELPHIUM	No! Over here!	
CALLIDAMATES	Oh yes. Now I remember.	
PHILOLACHES	You don't mind if I go meet them, do you, my love? I'll be right back.	
PHILEMATIUM	That's a long time for me.	
CALLIDAMATES	Who's this?	
PHILOLACHES	He's here!	
CALLIDAMATES	Oh! Philolaches! Greetings, my very best friend in the world!	340
PHILOLACHES	Bless you, Callidamates. Have a seat. Where are you coming from?	
CALLIDAMATES	Where a really drunk guy comes from.	
PHILEMATIUM	Dear Delphium, why don't you sit down here with us? (*to an attending slave*) Give her something to drink.	
CALLIDAMATES	I'm going to sleep now.	
PHILOLACHES	That's nothing new.	345
DELPHIUM	So what should I do now?	
PHILEMATIUM	Just let him lie there, my dear. (*to slave*) But you take the drinking bowl and give a drink to each of us, starting with Delphium.	

> 1 As was noted in chapter 2, the surviving texts of Roman comedy offer no stage directions. What do you surmise about the stage movement here from the dialogue?
> 2 Think about modern caricatures of drunks in plays and films you have seen. What do they have in common with Plautus' Callidamates?

> **The names of Plautus' characters**
>
> The names of almost all characters of Roman comedy, like their settings, are Greek. Plautus seldom uses typical Greek names, however. Instead, he made up Greek-sounding names. Sometimes the names seem to be chosen arbitrarily, or merely for their jingling sounds; but often the names sound like words in Greek that bring extra humour or irony. Here are the names of the characters from *The Haunted House* that appear in this chapter, along with each name's meaning in Greek.
>
> | Name | Sounds like Greek word or phrase for |
> |---|---|
> | Grumio | Riff-raff |
> | Tranio | Galley slave |
> | Philolaches | Luck-lover |
> | Philematium | Little kissy |
> | Scapha | Ship's hull (perhaps because she can hold as much wine as a ship can, an allusion to the stereotypical drunkenness of old women in Roman comedy) |
> | Callidamates | Lady killer |
> | Delphium | Little dolphin |
> | Theopropides | Son of a prophet |
> | Misargyrides | Money hater |
> | Simo | Monkey nose |

No sooner has the party started than Tranio enters with disastrous news from the harbour, where he had gone to buy food. At first he addresses the audience, unseen by Philolaches and the others (348–403).

3.4   TRANIO   Jupiter almighty, with all his might and main, wants me and my young master dead. Our hope has perished, there's no refuge for 350 confidence. Even **Safety** herself couldn't save us now. I saw such a great mountain of trouble and grief at the harbour just now. My master's come home from abroad: Tranio is finished. Hey! Is there anybody here who'd like to make some money, who could 355 stand to be **crucified** in my place today? Where are all the guys beaten with blows and worn down by iron, or the ones who run up under the enemy's towers for three pennies, where you can

---

Safety Romans personified many abstract qualities as goddesses, including *Salus*, Safety.

crucified Roman citizens could not legally be crucified, but crucifixion was a common penalty for slaves who committed serious crimes.

	get your body pierced with five or ten spears at a time? I'll give a **talent** to the first guy who scampers up onto the cross – on one condition, that he get tied up twice by the feet, twice by the arms. Once that's done, he can come to me to claim the money on the spot. But as for me … Wait? What am I doing? I've got to run home as fast as I can.	360
PHILOLACHES	Hurray, the food's here! Look, Tranio's back from the harbour.	
TRANIO	Philolaches …	
PHILOLACHES	What is it?	365
TRANIO	Both you and me …	
PHILOLACHES	What about you and me?	
TRANIO	We're finished!	
PHILOLACHES	What is it?	
TRANIO	Your father's home!	
PHILOLACHES	What?	
TRANIO	We're ruined. Your father has come home.	
PHILOLACHES	Tell me, please, where is he?	
TRANIO	He's here!	
PHILOLACHES	Who says so? Who saw him?	
TRANIO	I saw him myself.	
PHILOLACHES	Oh no! What am I doing?	
TRANIO	Silly, why do you ask what you're doing? You're relaxing on the couch.	
PHILOLACHES	You say you saw him yourself?	
TRANIO	I did.	
PHILOLACHES	Are you sure?	
TRANIO	Absolutely.	
PHILOLACHES	I'm dead, if you're telling the truth.	370
TRANIO	What would I get out of lying?	
PHILOLACHES	What should I do now?	
TRANIO	Order all this stuff taken away. Who's that sleeping there?	
PHILOLACHES	It's Callidamates.	
TRANIO	Wake him up, Delphium.	
DELPHIUM	Callidamates, Callidamates, wake up!	
CALLIDAMATES	I am awake. Gimme a drink.	
DELPHIUM	Wake up! Philolaches' father has come back from abroad!	
CALLIDAMATES	Good for his father.	
PHILOLACHES	It's good for him, all right, but I'm finished!	375
CALLIDAMATES	You're **Finnish**? How can you be Finnish?	

talent a very large sum of money, equivalent to over 25 kilograms (55 pounds) of silver.

Finnish in the Latin, Philolaches exclaims, *disperii*! ('I'm ruined!') and Callidamates responds, *bis perii*? ('You've died twice?'). Can you think of another way to express the pun in English?

PHILOLACHES	Please, get up! My father's come home!	
CALLIDAMATES	Your father's come home? Tell him to go away again. What's he doing coming back here?	
PHILOLACHES	What should I do? My father's going to get here and find me drunk and the house full of partiers and women. This is really bad. Try digging a well when you're thirsty: that's what it's like for me trying to figure out what to do when my father gets home.	380
TRANIO	Look! He's gone back to sleep. Get him up.	
PHILOLACHES	Are you sleeping again? I tell you, my father's gonna be here any minute.	
CALLIDAMATES	Your father, you say? Gimme my shoes: I'm gonna fetch my weapons. By god, I'll kill your father!	
PHILOLACHES	You're wasting time.	385
DELPHIUM	Quiet, please.	
TRANIO	Grab this guy and carry him inside right away.	
CALLIDAMATES	By Pollux, I'm gonna use you all for a piss jar, if you don't get me one quick.	
PHILOLACHES	I'm finished.	
TRANIO	Buck up. I'll find a nice way to cure you of your fear.	
PHILOLACHES	I'm done for.	
TRANIO	Ssh! I'll think of some way to fix this for you. What if, when your father gets here, I don't just keep him out of the house, but I get him to run far, far away? You all just hurry up and get inside, and take all this stuff with you.	390
PHILOLACHES	Where do I go?	
TRANIO	Wherever you want: with this girl or this one.	
DELPHIUM	Maybe we should get out of here.	
TRANIO	No need, Delphium: just go inside and keep drinking like before.	
PHILOLACHES	Oh dear, that all sounds nice, but what's it leading to? I'm scared stiff!	395
TRANIO	Just calm down and do what I say.	
PHILOLACHES	OK.	
TRANIO	First of all, Philematium, you go on inside. You too, Delphium.	
DELPHIUM	We're both happy to oblige you.	
TRANIO	I wish! Now, you, Philolaches: pay attention and do what I say. First of all, make sure the house is all shut up. Don't let anybody inside so much as make a squeak.	400
PHILOLACHES	Done.	
TRANIO	There's not a soul in the house.	
PHILOLACHES	Got it.	
TRANIO	And nobody's to answer when the old man knocks on the door.	

1 What is Tranio's relationship with the audience in this scene?
2 Where does the humour lie?
3 What features does this scene share with scenes you know from modern comic plays, films and television programmes? What features are different?
4 How does Tranio's reaction to the news of Theopropides' return compare with Philolaches'? What do their reactions reveal about their respective characters?

Plautus' language

Plautus' Latin is remarkable for its colourful exuberance, much of which is lost in translation. Part of that exuberance comes from Plautus' metrical variety, which has been discussed in the previous chapter. In addition, Plautus made great use of such techniques as **alliteration** (use of the same consonant to start words in close proximity to one another), **assonance** (repetition of vowel sounds), piling on of extra words, and word play. In the following verses – the opening of **3.4** in Latin – repeated sounds are marked in bold print. Read the passage aloud. Even if you mispronounce some of the words, you will get a feel for the kinds of effects Plautus' language can produce (348–53):

> I**u**ppiter **s**upremus **s**ummis o**pi**bus atque industriis
> me **p**eriisse et **Phi**lolachetem cupit erilem filium.
> occidit spes **n**ostra, **n**usquam stabulum est confidentiae,
> nec **Sal**us nobis **sal**uti iam esse, si cupiat, potest:
> ita **m**ali, **m**aeroris **m**ontem **m**aximum ad portum **m**odo
> conspicatus sum: erus advenit **per**egre, **per**iit Tranio.

With everyone else safely inside, Tranio waits for Theopropides to return (426–531).

3.5

TRANIO   All right, let him come. I'll put on **games** for the old man while he's here to enjoy them like he'll never get when he's dead. I'll move over here away from the door and watch from a distance; then I'll pile a pack of lies on the old man when he gets here.   430

THEOPROPIDES   **Neptune**, I am terribly grateful that you sent me home from your realm alive, though just barely. If you ever catch me even setting foot on a ship again, I give you permission to do to me

---

games   Tranio puns on the word *ludi*, which can mean games like those described in chapter 2, including funeral games, but also tricks or mockery.

Neptune   it was customary to give thanks to Neptune, god of the sea, upon returning from a sea voyage.

	then what you tried to do this time. No Neptune for me from this day on: I've put myself in your hands for the last time.	435
TRANIO	By Pollux, Neptune, you really messed up, wasting a good opportunity like that.	
THEOPROPIDES	Finally home, after more than two years. I'm sure my family will be happy to see me.	440
TRANIO	By god, they'd be happier to see a messenger with news that you were dead.	
THEOPROPIDES	But what's this? It's the middle of the day, and the door's closed. I'll knock. Hey! Is anybody inside? Open the door, will you!	445
TRANIO	Who's this guy coming right up to our door?	
THEOPROPIDES	Oh! It's my slave, Tranio.	
TRANIO	Oh, Theopropides, my master, greetings! I'm so glad you've come home safe and sound! How have you been?	
THEOPROPIDES	Just fine, as you can see.	
TRANIO	Excellent!	
THEOPROPIDES	What's with you all? Are you crazy?	450
TRANIO	Why?	
THEOPROPIDES	You're out here gallivanting about, and there's nobody home to answer the door. I just about broke down **both these doors** banging on them.	
TRANIO	What? You touched the house?	
THEOPROPIDES	Why shouldn't I touch it? And I didn't just touch it: I banged on the door so hard I almost broke it.	455
TRANIO	You touched it?	
THEOPROPIDES	Yes, and I banged on it.	
TRANIO	Oh no!	
THEOPROPIDES	What is it?	
TRANIO	It's terrible!	
THEOPROPIDES	What's the matter?	
TRANIO	I can't even say what a shocking crime you've committed.	
THEOPROPIDES	What?	460
TRANIO	Get away, please, get away from the house! Quick, come over here, towards me. You say you touched the door?	
THEOPROPIDES	How could I knock on it without touching it?	
TRANIO	You've killed …	
THEOPROPIDES	Killed who?	
TRANIO	Your whole family!	
THEOPROPIDES	That's a bad omen, damn you!	

both these doors Roman doors often had two leaves, which met each other in the middle and each opened outwards.

TRANIO	I'm afraid you may not be able to make atonement enough for yourself and for them.	465
THEOPROPIDES	Why? What is all this?	
TRANIO	Oh dear. Order **both those guys** to go away.	
THEOPROPIDES	Go away.	
TRANIO	And make sure you don't touch the house. But **touch the ground**.	
THEOPROPIDES	Please, tell me. What is this all about?	
TRANIO	It's been seven months since anybody has set foot in this house, ever since we moved out.	470
THEOPROPIDES	What?	
TRANIO	Look around. Is there anybody who could overhear us?	
THEOPROPIDES	All clear.	
TRANIO	Look around again.	
THEOPROPIDES	Nobody. Tell me.	
TRANIO	It was a terrible crime.	475
THEOPROPIDES	What? I don't understand.	
TRANIO	A crime from a long time ago, old and ancient.	
THEOPROPIDES	Ancient?	
TRANIO	But we only recently found out about it.	
THEOPROPIDES	What crime? Who did it? Tell me.	
TRANIO	A host grabbed hold of his guest and killed him. As far as I know, it was the guy who sold you this house.	480
THEOPROPIDES	What?	
TRANIO	And the same guy took his guest's gold and buried his guest right here in the house.	
THEOPROPIDES	What makes you think such a crime was committed?	
TRANIO	I'll tell you: listen. It so happened your son had dined out. When he came home from dinner we all went to bed and fell asleep. I happened to forget to put out a lamp. All of a sudden he let out the most piercing scream!	485
THEOPROPIDES	Who? My son?	
TRANIO	Quiet! Just listen. He said the dead guy came to him in his sleep.	490
THEOPROPIDES	In his sleep?	
TRANIO	Yes. Just listen. He said the dead man said this to him …	
THEOPROPIDES	In his sleep?	
TRANIO	I don't imagine he would speak to him when he was awake when he was murdered sixty years ago. Theopropides, sometimes you are really dumb.	495
THEOPROPIDES	OK, I'll shut up.	

both those guys the slaves carrying Theopropides' luggage.
touch the ground touching the ground was a gesture used to ward off evil spirits.

| TRANIO | So this is what he told him in his sleep: 'I am a stranger from across the sea: my name is **Allende el Mar**. This is where I dwell, my allotted habitation. **Orcus** would not allow me into the underworld, because I died before my time. I trusted, and I was deceived. My host killed me, and he buried me without proper rites in this house, the monster: he did it for my gold. Now you, get out of here! This house is cursed. This dwelling is hateful to the gods.' I could hardly tell you in a year all the scary things that keep happening here. | 500

505 |
| --- | --- | --- |
| THEOPROPIDES | Sshh! | |
| TRANIO | Good god, what is it? | |
| THEOPROPIDES | I heard the door creak. | |
| TRANIO | (*to the house*) He's the one who knocked, not me! | |
| THEOPROPIDES | I've hardly got a drop of blood left! The dead are coming to drag me down to Hades alive! | |
| TRANIO | (*aside*) Dammit! They're gonna ruin my story! I'm afraid he'll catch me in the act. | 510 |
| THEOPROPIDES | What are you mumbling to yourself about? | |
| TRANIO | Get away from the door! I beg you by Hercules, run away! | |
| THEOPROPIDES | Where to? Why don't you run away too? | |
| TRANIO | I'm not afraid: I've made my peace with the dead. | |
| A VOICE FROM INSIDE THE HOUSE | Hey, Tranio! | 515 |
| TRANIO | Don't yell at me! I didn't do anything. I wasn't the one who banged on those doors … | |
| THEOPROPIDES | What's the matter, Tranio? Who are you talking to? | |
| TRANIO | Oh, was it you who called me? By the gods, I thought the dead man was complaining because you banged on the doors. But why are you still standing here and ignoring what I say? | 520 |
| THEOPROPIDES | What should I do? | |
| TRANIO | Don't look back! Flee! **Cover your head**! | |
| THEOPROPIDES | Why don't *you* flee? | |
| TRANIO | I've made my peace with the dead. | |
| THEOPROPIDES | I know. But what about just now? Why were you so frightened? | 525 |
| TRANIO | Don't worry about me: I can take care of myself. But as for you: pick up where you left off, run away as fast as you can, and call on Hercules to help you. | |
| THEOPROPIDES | Hercules, I call on you! | |
| TRANIO | And I call on you too, Hercules … to give you a heap of trouble, old man. Immortal gods, be my witnesses: look how much mischief I've accomplished today! | 530 |

Allende el Mar Plautus uses the Greek *Diapontius* ('Mr Across the Sea').

Orcus the god of the underworld.

Cover your head Romans covered their heads to protect themselves from evil spirits.

1 The entire play from the entry of Philolaches at the beginning of 3.1 through to the end of 3.4 is written in metres that were sung to accompaniment. This section, however, is written in unaccompanied iambic senarii (see p. 36). Why do you think Plautus made that change here?
2 What does this scene reveal about Tranio? And about Theopropides?
3 What kind of movement and gestures would have been used in this scene?

The Saturnalian in Roman comedy

Each year in late December the Romans held a festival called the **Saturnalia**, a key feature of which was extreme social inversion: masters waited on their slaves at table. Although plays were not performed as part of the Saturnalia, Roman comedies, especially Plautus' plays, include many elements that Erich Segal and others have described as Saturnalian. Slaves deceive their masters and get away with it, even though in real life a tricky slave like Tranio could face severe punishment, including execution. The power of the *paterfamilias* – the male head of the household – was nearly absolute in Rome: a father could even execute his children if they were guilty of capital offences. Yet Roman comedy abounds in youths like Philolaches who disobey their fathers. Rome was an emphatically patriarchal society, in which women were generally subservient to their male relatives. In Roman comedy, though, wives win in battles with their husbands, and prostitutes gain control over wealthy male citizens. Romans of Plautus' day liked to think of themselves as a morally superior people, especially in terms of their frugality and their good faith; yet dissipation and deception are central features of many Plautine plays. Scholars have differed in their assessments of how these Saturnalian elements would have affected the Roman audience. Some have seen the social inversion as a kind of escape valve, arguing that the inversion, limited to the time of the play, would actually reinforce the hierarchy and moral rules it overturned. Others, like Amy Richlin, have argued that Roman comedy's presentation of a world that flouted society's hierarchies and morality was subversive.

Tranio's tricks meet an unexpected obstacle when Misargyrides, the moneylender who loaned Philolaches the money for Philematium, enters and Theopropides overhears him demanding interest from Tranio. Always a quick thinker, Tranio persuades Theopropides that Philolaches borrowed the money to buy the house of his next-door neighbour, Simo. Simo enters with a song directed at the audience (690–782).

3.6	SIMO	I haven't had it nicer at home, or a meal I liked more, in a year. My wife gave me a very fine lunch. Now she wants me to go to bed. No way! I thought it was no coincidence that lunch was better than it usually is: the old woman wanted to get me into bed! Sleep after lunch is not good. Forget it! I snuck out of the house in secret. I know my wife's waiting for me at home, all excited.	690 695
	TRANIO	(*aside*) This old man's got trouble waiting for him this evening: he won't eat or sleep well.	700
	SIMO	You know, when I think about it, anybody who's got an old wife with a big **dowry** never gets any sleep. They all hate to go to bed, just like me. I've decided I'd rather go out to the **forum** than home to bed. By god, I don't know what your wives are like, but I know mine's got me in a predicament, and later it will get even worse.	705 710
	TRANIO	(*aside*) You'll be sorry you took off, old man, and you won't be able to blame the gods for it. You have every good reason to blame yourself. OK: time for me to talk to him. I've figured out how I can lead this old man on and send my troubles packing with a trick. I'll go up to him. The gods bless you, Simo.	715
	SIMO	Hello, Tranio.	
	TRANIO	How are you?	
	SIMO	Not bad. What are you up to?	
	TRANIO	(*shaking his hand*) I'm holding onto the best of men.	
	SIMO	What a nice thing to say!	720
	TRANIO	You most certainly deserve it.	
	SIMO	And by Hercules, I'm holding onto a slave who's no good at all … So what's up now? What's in the works?	
	TRANIO	What do you mean?	
	SIMO	I mean the usual goings-on inside there.	
	TRANIO	What?	
	SIMO	You know what I'm talking about. That's how it should be. Enjoy yourselves. Remember how short life is.	725
	TRANIO	Oh! I see: you mean what we've been up to.	
	SIMO	You're living your lives elegantly, as you should, with good wine and food, and the choicest fish.	730

dowry dowries were a standard feature of Roman marriages. In most marriages the dowry went back to the woman's family in the case of divorce, so dowries were thought to give women power over their husbands, and in several plays Plautus' characters joke about the power of wives with large dowries.

forum often in Roman comedy the forum, the location of law-courts and political meetings, is associated with business in opposition to pleasure. It is therefore an especially powerful statement that Simo would rather be there than with his wife.

TRANIO	No, that's the way our lives used to be: now we've lost all those things.
SIMO	How?
TRANIO	We're all completely ruined, Simo.
SIMO	Bah! Everything's gone swimmingly for you up to this point. 735
TRANIO	That's true, I don't deny it. We really did live well, just the way we wanted. But now, Simo, the favourable wind has abandoned our ship.
SIMO	What do you mean?
TRANIO	It's terrible!
SIMO	But your ship has come safely to shore!
TRANIO	Oh!
SIMO	What is it?
TRANIO	Poor me, I'm a dead man.
SIMO	Why? 740
TRANIO	Because another ship has come to smash our ship's timbers.
SIMO	Tranio, what are you talking about?
TRANIO	My master has come home from abroad.
SIMO	Oops! That means big trouble for you: first the chain-gang, then the cross.
TRANIO	Please, Simo, I beg you **by your knees**, don't tell the master on me. 745
SIMO	Don't worry: he won't learn anything from me.
TRANIO	Hail, my **patron**.
SIMO	I don't care to have **clients** like you.
TRANIO	Now, about what my old master sent me to you for.
SIMO	But first tell me this: has your old master learned anything about that business?
TRANIO	Not a thing. 750
SIMO	So he hasn't scolded his son?
TRANIO	He's as calm as a sunny day. Now he has ordered me to entreat you most earnestly to let him look over this house of yours.
SIMO	It's not for sale.
TRANIO	I know that, but the old man wants to build women's quarters, baths, a 755 walkway and a **portico** over in his house.
SIMO	What for?

---

by your knees it was customary in the ancient world for suppliants to grab the knees of the persons they were supplicating, a gesture that indicated they were throwing themselves on their mercy.

patron, clients a central feature of Roman society was the system of patrons and clients. A wealthy patron would help his (poorer) clients in financial and legal matters. In return the clients would support their patron in his political career and offer other services.

portico a covered walkway.

TRANIO	He'd like to get his son married as soon as possible, so he wants to build new women's quarters. And he says that some architect or other has praised to the stars the way your house is built. He wants to use your house as a model, if it's OK with you. He especially wants to pattern his house on yours, because he heard that you have good shade in the summer all day long, even on sunny days.	760

765 |
SIMO	What do you mean? Even when there's shade everywhere else, we're always in the sun here from morning to evening. The sunlight's like a **creditor** standing continually at the door. I never have a **patch** of shade anywhere, unless there's some in the well.	
TRANIO	Have you got a **Jane**, then, if you don't have a **Pat**?	770
SIMO	Don't be a pest. It's just as I say it is.	
TRANIO	Well, he still wants to look it over.	
SIMO	Let him look if he wants. If he finds anything he likes, he can copy my house when he builds.	
TRANIO	Shall I go and call him?	
SIMO	Go ahead, call him.	
TRANIO	(*aside*) They say **Alexander the Great** and **Agathocles** are the two men who accomplished the greatest deeds. And what about me, the third? I accomplish immortal deeds all by myself! I've got this old man carrying a load, and this other one too. I've started a new custom that's not bad: mule drivers have mules to carry their burdens, but I've got two men to do it. They can hold a lot: whatever you load them up with, they carry it.	775

780 |

> 1 How do you think men in the audience might have responded to Simo's words about wives with dowries? What about women in the audience?
>
> 2 How does Tranio's interaction with Simo compare with his dialogue with Theopropides?
>
> 3 The metre changes from sung verse to unaccompanied iambic senarii when Tranio says, 'Now, about what my old master sent me to you for.' Why do you think the music stops there?

creditor Simo refers to the practice of *flagitatio*, in which a creditor or someone who had been wronged would publicly rebuke a debtor or transgressor in front of the debtor or transgressor's door.

patch, Jane, Pat this desperate pun replaces one – slightly less lame – in the Latin. Simo complains that his house has no *umbra* (shade). Tranio, pretending to hear *Umbra* (a woman from Umbria, a region north-east of Rome, see map on p. x), asks if Simo has a *Sarsinatis* (a woman from Sarsina).

Alexander the Great Alexander III of Macedon (356–323 BC), who conquered the Persian empire.

Agathocles tyrant of Syracuse (*c.* 361–*c.* 289 BC), who fought a number of successful campaigns against other Greek cities and Carthaginians.

Stock characters

Both genres from which Plautus drew his inspiration – Greek New Comedy and Italian popular farce such as the Atellan plays – used what are known as stock characters. A stock character, reappearing from play to play in different guises, has a set of predictable characteristics, which features of masks and costumes reinforce. The table below shows the stock character types to which some of the characters in our selections from *The Haunted House* come closest, and the typical characteristics of each character type:

Character	Type	Typical characteristics
Philolaches	Young man in love	Hopelessly in love, loquacious, inept
Philematium	Slave prostitute	Kind-hearted, loyal to lover, subservient, innocent
Scapha	Old prostitute or madam	Cynical, grasping, bibulous
Callidamates	Helpful friend	Helpful, more sensible than the young man in love
Theopropides	Harsh old man	Severe, prone to anger, gullible
Simo	Easy-going old man	Believes 'boys will be boys'
Tranio	Clever slave	Clever, tricky, cheeky, loyal to his young master but disobedient to his old master

Very few characters completely conform to the stereotypical characteristics of stock characters, and much of the fun of watching a Roman comedy comes from simultaneously recognizing the familiar features of stock characters and observing how characters transcend the expectations produced by their character types. Thus, for example, Simo, tolerant of Tranio's and Philolaches' peccadilloes in the above passage, will turn on Tranio and align himself with Theopropides later in the play. Most interesting in this respect is Philematium. Free prostitutes of Roman comedy are often grasping and tricky, milking their lovers for all they are worth. Slave prostitutes, however, are usually much more sympathetic, and they are often revealed to be freeborn before the end of the play. Philematium, once a slave but now free, and not destined to be proven freeborn, does not fit exactly into either mould, so the audience will not be sure what to make of her professions of love and loyalty towards Philolaches.

Tranio leads both Theopropides and Simo on a tour of Simo's house. In a masterpiece of comic deception, he simultaneously persuades Simo that Theopropides is looking to buy Simo's house and Theopropides that Philolaches has already bought the house, but that Simo feels so remorseful about the sale that Theopropides should not mention it. Tranio's ruse comes crashing down, however, when two slaves who have come to fetch Callidamates tell Theopropides all that has been going on while he has been gone. Theopropides borrows slaves from Simo and prepares to bind and punish Tranio, but Tranio overhears the plan and seeks refuge at the onstage altar, from where he cannot be removed without sacrilege. Theopropides is livid (1108–81).

3.7

THEOPROPIDES You tricked me!
TRANIO How?
THEOPROPIDES You really **wiped my nose in it**!
TRANIO Let me see, please, there's no snot flowing out of it, is there?
THEOPROPIDES Dammit! You wiped my brain right out of my head. I've found out all your crimes right down to the roots. No: not just down to the roots, but even below the roots. 1110
TRANIO There's no way you're ever gonna get me off this altar.
THEOPROPIDES Well then, I'll have you surrounded with burning brushwood, you jailbird.
TRANIO Don't do that: I generally taste better boiled than roasted. 1115
THEOPROPIDES I'll make an example of you today.
TRANIO You like me so much you want to use me as an example?
THEOPROPIDES Tell me: what kind of son did I leave behind when I went away?
TRANIO One with feet, hands, fingers, ears, eyes, lips.
THEOPROPIDES I meant something else.
TRANIO So I'm telling you something else. But look, there's your son's buddy coming over here. If you want to accuse me, do it in front of him. 1120
CALLIDAMATES After I slept and sobered up, Philolaches told me his father had come home from abroad, and when he got here his slave somehow made fun of him, and he's afraid to face him. Now out of all his friends I've been chosen to plead for him, to make peace with his father. Good: there he is. Theopropides, greetings. I'm very glad you've arrived home safely. Please, **come to our house for dinner today**. 1125

---

wiped my nose in it the Latin here is *emunxti*, which means literally 'you wiped the mucus from my nose' and metaphorically 'you tricked me'.

come to our house for dinner today it was customary to invite returning travellers to dinner.

THEOPROPIDES	Bless you, Callidamates, but no thanks on the dinner.	1130
CALLIDAMATES	Why won't you come?	
TRANIO	Say you'll go. I'll go for you, if you don't feel like it.	
THEOPROPIDES	Damn you, are you still making fun of me?	
TRANIO	Because I say I'll go to dinner for you?	
THEOPROPIDES	You won't go. I'll see you carried off to be crucified, as you deserve.	
CALLIDAMATES	Come on now, forget that and say you'll come to dinner.	
TRANIO	Why don't you answer?	
CALLIDAMATES	You there, what are you doing on that altar?	1135
TRANIO	Some idiot came along and scared me to death. Now make your accusation; here's an arbitrator for the both of us: go on, make your case.	
THEOPROPIDES	I say you corrupted my son.	
TRANIO	Listen now. I confess that he partied and freed his girlfriend while you were away, and he borrowed money at interest, and the money is now all spent. What did he do that's not done in all the best families?	1140
THEOPROPIDES	By Hercules, I'd better watch out for you: you're a really clever **lawyer**.	
CALLIDAMATES	Just let me **judge**. (*to Tranio*) Get up. I'll sit there.	
THEOPROPIDES	Excellent. You be judge for this **case**.	
TRANIO	This looks like a trick to me. Give me some reassurance, so I know you're looking out for me.	1145
THEOPROPIDES	I don't care so much about all the rest: what infuriates me most is all the ways he tricked me.	
TRANIO	Well, you deserved it, and I'm glad I did it: somebody your age, with all that grey hair, ought to have some sense.	
THEOPROPIDES	What do I do now?	
TRANIO	Well, if you're friends with **Diphilus or Philemon**, tell them how your slave made a fool of you: you'll give them some great deception plots for their comedies.	1150
CALLIDAMATES	Be quiet now: listen and let me talk for a minute.	
THEOPROPIDES	OK.	
CALLIDAMATES	You know I'm your son's very best friend. He came to me because he was afraid to face you, because he did what he knows you know he did. Now, I beg you, forgive his youthful foolishness. He's your own son. You know things like this	1155

lawyer, **judge**, **case**   the characters use the language of a Roman law-court. Metaphors like these, drawn from the worlds of law and business, are very common in Roman comedy and shed much light on Roman practices and attitudes in these areas.

Diphilus or Philemon   two writers of Greek New Comedy, contemporaries of Menander.

	happen at his age. Whatever he did, I did it with him: we're both guilty. The interest, the principal, all the money he used to buy his girlfriend, we'll pay it all back. We'll pull the money together at our own expense, not yours.
THEOPROPIDES	No advocate could be more persuasive than you are: now I'm not mad at him any more, and I'm not angry about anything. As a matter of fact, even while I'm here he can have girlfriends, drink, and do what he wants. As long as he's sorry he spent money, that's enough punishment for me.
CALLIDAMATES	He's really sorry.
TRANIO	OK, he's forgiven. What about me?
THEOPROPIDES	*You* are going to be strung up and beaten silly.
TRANIO	But what if I'm sorry?
THEOPROPIDES	By god, I'll kill you if it's the last thing I do.
CALLIDAMATES	Forgive everything. Please, let Tranio off for my sake.
THEOPROPIDES	I'd rather do anything than let this guy live after what he did.
CALLIDAMATES	Please, let him off.
THEOPROPIDES	Let him off? But look at how unrepentant that bastard is!
CALLIDAMATES	Tranio, you'll be quiet if you're smart.
THEOPROPIDES	No, *you* be quiet and stop pleading for him: I'll shut *him* up with a thrashing.
TRANIO	There's really no need for that.
CALLIDAMATES	Come on, give in.
THEOPROPIDES	I don't want to hear it.
CALLIDAMATES	Please.
THEOPROPIDES	I said I don't want to hear it.
CALLIDAMATES	You'll hear it anyway. Please, forgive this one misdeed for my sake.
TRANIO	Why not give in? You know full well I'll be bad again tomorrow; then you can punish me twice over: once for what I did today, and once for what I'll do then.
CALLIDAMATES	Let me persuade you.
THEOPROPIDES	All right, go. Go scot-free. And you can thank him. Spectators: that's the end of our play – now it's time for you to applaud.

1. How has Callidamates changed since his earlier scene?
2. What do you think Tranio's reference to Diphilus and Philemon contributes to the play?
3. What persuades Theopropides to forgive his son? What does that say about Theopropides?
4. Why do you think Theopropides is finally persuaded to forgive Tranio?
5. What do you think of the play's ending? In what ways is it similar to or different from endings of modern comedies with which you are familiar?

Scenes of slaves taking refuge on altars were a common feature of Roman comedy: they show up on numerous works of art, including this incense-burner from the first century AD.

3.8

Plautus' other plays

The Haunted House presents many features typical of Plautus, but each of his 21 surviving plays is unique. Many of the plays, like *The Haunted House*, revolve around deception. Others, known as 'recognition plays', end with the revelation that a woman loved by a young man, thought to be a slave, is in fact freeborn and therefore marriageable. Some plays combine deception with recognition; others provide still greater variety. Below is a list of Plautus' other plays. To give a sense of both the wide variety of Plautus' plots and also of some common elements, basic plot-summaries of some of the plays are included.

Latin title	English title	Basic plot
Amphitruo	Amphitryo	Plautus' only play with a mythological subject: Jupiter, disguised as Amphitryo, sleeps with Amphitryo's wife Alcumena. After much comic confusion, Alcumena gives birth to Jupiter's son Hercules.
Asinaria	The Donkey Play	The old man Daemenetus, aided by the trickery of two clever slaves, helps his son to get access to his prostitute girlfriend, but he wants to sleep with her himself. He is caught by his wife and chastised.
Aulularia	The Pot of Gold	

Bacchides	*The Bacchis Sisters*	Two prostitutes seduce two young men, Mnesilochus and Pistoclerus. Mnesilochus' clever slave tricks Mnesilochus' father three times to get money so that Mnesilochus can buy out one of the prostitutes' contracts and purchase refreshments for their party. When the young men's fathers find out, they attack the prostitutes' home but are seduced themselves.
Captivi	*The Prisoners*	A slave, Tyndarus, and his master, Philocrates, are captured in war and sold to Hegio. They exchange identities so that Philocrates can go home, sent to bring back Hegio's own son, also captured in war. Tyndarus is caught and punished but is rescued when Philocrates returns, bringing not only Hegio's son, but also another slave, who reveals that Tyndarus is Hegio's son.
Casina	*Casina*	
Cistellaria	*The Basket*	
Curculio	*Curculio*	The parasite Curculio uses deception to steal his patron's slave prostitute girlfriend from a pimp and the soldier the pimp has sold her to. The prostitute turns out to be the soldier's sister.
Epidicus	*Epidicus*	
Menaechmi	*The Menaechmus Brothers*	Two identical twins, separated when they were very young, end up in the same town. After much humorous confusion, they discover each other.
Mercator	*The Merchant*	
Miles Gloriosus	*The Braggart Soldier*	
Persa	*The Persian*	
Poenulus	*The Little Carthaginian*	
Pseudolus	*Pseudolus*	
Rudens	*The Rope*	Daemones rescues the slave prostitute Palaestra from the clutches of a greedy pimp, then learns that Palaestra is in fact his own long-lost daughter.
Stichus	*Stichus*	Two sisters, against their father's wishes, refuse to leave their husbands, who have been away for three years on business. The husbands return and all celebrate, except for a parasite, whom the returning husbands reject.
Trinummus	*The Three-Penny Day*	
Truculentus	*The Truculent Slave*	
Vidularia	*The Trunk*	

4 Terence

A generation after Plautus, the freed slave Terence continued the tradition of the *fabula palliata*. While maintaining many of the practices of Plautus and his other predecessors, Terence also took the genre in new directions.

> After a prologue in which the playwright defends himself against his literary enemies, Terence's *The Self-Tormentor* (*Heauton Timoroumenos*) begins with a dialogue between two fathers, Menedemus and Chremes, in the countryside near Athens (53–150).

4.1   **CHREMES**   We've only known each other a little while: just since you bought this land here next to mine. And, of course, we haven't had much interaction at all. Still, you're a good man and my neighbour: I think that makes you practically my friend. So I'm going to be bold enough to give you some personal advice: it seems to me that you are behaving in a way not at all suitable for your age or your wealth. By all the gods and men, what are you after? What are you trying to do? I would guess you're sixty, or even older. Nobody in this region has better or more valuable land. You have a lot of slaves, but you act as if you didn't have a single one, you work so hard doing their jobs. No matter how early I come out in the morning or how late I return home in the evening, I always see you out in the fields, digging or ploughing or carrying some load. You never let up or take a rest. I'm sure you can't be enjoying all this. I suppose you'll say, 'Too little work gets done around here.' Well, if you spent the same energy you spend doing the work yourself on getting your slaves to do it for you, you'd get more accomplished.

The Self-Tormentor: Dramatis personae

Antiphila (An-tí-fill-a)	a young woman
Bacchis (Báh-kiss)	a prostitute
Chremes (Kréh-mees)	an old man
Clinia (Klí-nee-ah)	a young man
Clitipho (Cléye-ti-foh)	a young man
Dromo (Dróh-moh)	a slave
Menedemus (Meh-neh-dée-mus)	an old man
Sostrata (Sóh-strah-tah)	an old woman
Syrus (Seár-us)	a slave

MENEDEMUS	Chremes, do you have so much free time from your own affairs that you can busy yourself with things that are none of your business?	75
CHREMES	**I am a human being: as far as I'm concerned nothing that pertains to human beings is 'none of my business'.** Take what I say as advice, or as just a question. If what you're doing is right, I want to do it too. If not, I want to discourage you from doing it.	
MENEDEMUS	I have to do this. You do what you have to do.	80
CHREMES	Does anybody have to torture himself?	
MENEDEMUS	I do.	
CHREMES	If you've got troubles, I wish you didn't. But what's this punishment all about? What on earth did you do to deserve it?	
MENEDEMUS	Oh!	
CHREMES	Don't cry. Just tell me, whatever it is. Let it out. Don't be afraid. Trust me. I can help, whether it's comfort, advice or help you need.	85
MENEDEMUS	You really want to know?	
CHREMES	Yes: I've already told you why.	
MENEDEMUS	OK, I'll tell you.	
CHREMES	In the meantime, put down that hoe and stop working.	
MENEDEMUS	No.	
CHREMES	Why on earth not?	
MENEDEMUS	Just let me keep working.	90
CHREMES	No, I won't, I say.	
MENEDEMUS	You're not being fair.	
CHREMES	Whoa! It's heavy!	
MENEDEMUS	It's what I deserve.	
CHREMES	Now tell me.	
MENEDEMUS	I have one son, a young man. Oh, why do I say I have one? I had one, Chremes. Now I don't know whether I have one or not.	95
CHREMES	What do you mean?	
MENEDEMUS	You'll see. There's a poor old woman from **Corinth** here. My son fell so madly in love with her young daughter that he treated her almost like a wife. He did all this in secret. When I found out about it, I started to treat him brutally, not the way you	100

I am a human being: as far as I'm concerned nothing that pertains to human beings is 'none of my business' within a century of Terence's death, Chremes' words, in their Latin form ('homo sum: humani nil a me alienum puto') would become a famous proverb espousing concern for one's fellow human beings.

Corinth a city not far from Athens (see map on p. x). The Corinthian woman's daughter would be not only poor, but also a foreigner, and Athenians were required by law to marry Athenians if their children were to be citizens.

	should treat a lovesick young man, but the way fathers usually do. I accused him every day: 'Hey, do you think you can keep doing these things while your father is alive, keeping a mistress practically as if she's your wife? If that's what you think, Clinia, you're wrong, and you don't know me. As far as I'm concerned, you're my son only as long as you behave the way you should. If you don't, I'll figure out what to do with you. Too much free time: that's what causes things like this. When I was your age I didn't have time for love: I was poor, so I went off to **Asia**, and there I earned money and glory as a mercenary.' Finally it came to the point that the young man was worn down by hearing the same things over and over again. He thought that because I was older and loved him I knew more than he did and could look out for him better than he could himself. He went to Asia to be a mercenary for the **king**, Chremes.
CHREMES	What?
MENEDEMUS	He went away in secret and has been gone now for three months.
CHREMES	You're both at fault. But I must say, by taking that step he showed he is a brave man with a sense of honour.
MENEDEMUS	When I found out from those he had confided in, I came home miserably unhappy, confused and not knowing what to do. I sat down: my slaves ran to me. They took off my shoes. I watched other slaves hurrying about, laying out the linens, getting dinner ready. Each one was working hard to relieve my misery. When I saw that, I began to think, 'Look at this! So much work to fulfil just my needs. Should so many slaves help me get dressed? Should I alone have such household expenses? But my only son, who deserves to enjoy these things just as much – and even more – than I do, since he's of an age to enjoy them, I've thrown him out with my unjust actions. If I continued like this, I think I would deserve any punishment you can think of. As long as he leads that life of poverty, an exile because of what I did, I'm going to punish myself for his sake, working, scrimping, earning more money, serving him.' That's what I've done from that point on. I haven't left one nice dish or piece of clothing in the house: I gathered them all up

Asia also called Asia Minor, part of western Turkey (see map on p. x). Asia was known for its wealth and would therefore be a good place for a mercenary to make money.

king in Terence's day most of the lands around the eastern Mediterranean were ruled by several kings, descendants of Alexander's generals, who had divided up his empire after Alexander died in 323 BC. These kings often hired mercenaries for their wars against each other and other powers.

and got rid of them. I sold all my slaves except for those who could
easily earn their keep doing farm work. I put the house up for sale   145
and sold it for about fifteen talents. I bought this farm. Here I put
myself to work. I decided that I do just a little less injustice to my
son as long as I'm miserable, Chremes. It's not right for me to
enjoy any pleasure here until he returns safely and can share the   150
pleasure with me.

Here is a moment from the scene between Menedemus and Chremes in one of the illustrated manuscripts discussed on p. 23. The characters are labelled 'Chremes Senex' ('Chremes the Old Man') and 'Menedemus II' ('Menedemus the Second Old Man').

4.2

1 What does the text suggest about actors' movements in this scene? In what respect has the manuscript illustration succeeded or failed in capturing the action of the scene?
2 Other ancient playwrights often provided much of the background necessary for their plots in the prologue. How does Terence provide the background for this play? What do you think of his method?
3 Some have considered Chremes here a model of *humanitas*, a generous concern for humankind that was much admired in Rome. Others see his words in this scene as those of a busybody. What do you think?
4 What do you think of Menedemus' reactions to his son's love affair and then to his self-imposed exile? Were those reactions justified? Why or why not?

Terence's life

Information handed down about the life of Terence (Publius Terentius Afer) is probably more reliable than the tradition surrounding Plautus' life. The scholar Suetonius (born *c.* AD 70) wrote a biography of Terence, in which he reports that Terence was born in Carthage, in modern-day Tunisia in North Africa (see map on p. x). He was later a slave at Rome – whether he was born a slave or became a slave is not certain – but was freed by his master, the Roman senator Terentius Lucanus. He went on to become a successful playwright. For one of his six plays, *The Eunuch* (*Eunuchus*), Terence received the highest fee that had ever been paid for a comedy at Rome. He also had struggles, however. As we have seen (**2.6**) his *The Mother-in-Law* (*Hecyra*) failed twice before it could be performed in its entirety, and Terence complains repeatedly in his prologues about hostile critics. One of the charges levelled against Terence was that he received help in writing his plays from aristocratic friends. Terence never denies the charge. He died, a young man, while on a trip to Greece in 159 BC.

Terence's biography is interesting for a number of reasons. Carthage was settled by Phoenicians, from modern-day Lebanon, but Terence's last name, *Afer*, suggests that he was a native of Africa. He was probably ethnically related to modern-day North Africans, but it is not impossible that he is the world's first extant black author. His status as a freed slave both reveals the social mobility available to a few talented and lucky people in Rome and brings extra poignancy to the many slave characters in his plays. His conflicts with hostile critics reflect lively controversies in Rome in the second century BC about how Greek literature should be adapted for a Roman audience. The allegations of aristocratic 'ghost writers', whether true or not, suggest that Terence was associated with a group of leading Romans with literary interests.

Chremes consoles Menedemus and invites him to celebrate the festival of Dionysus with him, but Menedemus refuses. Soon after Menedemus leaves the stage, Chremes sees his son Clitipho entering from his house, addressing Menedemus' son Clinia, who has returned to Athens in secret and is now inside Chremes' house (175–212).

4.3   CLITIPHO   There's nothing to worry about, Clinia: they're working fast, and I   175
know she'll be here with you today as soon as she gets your message.
So just stop torturing yourself with ungrounded fears.
         CHREMES   Who's my son talking to?

CLITIPHO	Oh! It's my father, **just the person I've been looking for**. I'll go to him. Father, you've come at just the right time.	
CHREMES	What is it?	180
CLITIPHO	You know Menedemus, our neighbour here?	
CHREMES	Very well.	
CLITIPHO	Did you know he has a son?	
CHREMES	I heard he's in Asia.	
CLITIPHO	He's not, father. He's at our house.	
CHREMES	What?	
CLITIPHO	As soon as he got off the ship I brought him here for dinner. We've been very good friends since we were boys, you see.	
CHREMES	What wonderful news! Oh, I wish I'd been more insistent when I invited Menedemus to join us. Then I could be the first to surprise him with this joyful news in my own home! But there's still time.	185
CLITIPHO	Wait! Don't do that, father.	
CHREMES	Why not?	
CLITIPHO	Because he's still not sure what he should do. He just got back. He's apprehensive about everything: his father's anger and his girl's feelings towards him. He's desperately in love with her. All this trouble is because of her.	190
CHREMES	I know.	
CLITIPHO	Now he's sent his slave to her in the city, and I sent our slave Syrus along.	
CHREMES	What does Clinia say?	
CLITIPHO	He says he's terribly unhappy.	
CHREMES	Unhappy? Who could be less unhappy? Out of all the things people value – parents, a secure fatherland, friends, family, relatives, wealth – what's he not got? But these things are only as good as the attitude of the person who has them. They're good for the man who knows how to use them, but bad for the one who doesn't.	195
CLITIPHO	No, father, the problem is his old man. He was always so demanding, and now I'm terribly afraid that in his anger he'll do something awful to him.	
CHREMES	*Him*? (*aside*) But wait, I'll hold back: it might be good for him to stay frightened.	
CLITIPHO	What are you mumbling to yourself about?	200
CHREMES	I'll tell you. Whatever his father was like, Clinia should have stayed. Perhaps his father was a little less fair than he would wish: he should have put up with it. Who should he put up with if not his own father?	

---

just the person I've been looking for coincidence plays a very important role in Roman comedy. Over and over again, characters appear at 'just the right time' for the needs of the plot. Terence may be making a subtle joke about that convention here.

	Should a father live according to the son's ways, or the son according to his father's? And I don't buy that business about his father being too harsh. The wrongs of fathers are generally the same type, if the father is at all a tolerant person: they don't want their sons to go whoring, they don't want them to party too much, and they offer too little spending money. All these things they do to encourage their sons' virtue. Fathers have to act like Clinia's did when their sons are all turned around by desire. It's smart to learn from others' experiences what can be useful for yourself.	205 210
CLITIPHO	Right.	
CHREMES	I'm going inside to see how the preparations for dinner are going. It's late: make sure you don't wander too far.	

> 1 What does this dialogue suggest about the relationship between Clitipho and Chremes?
> 2 What do you think of the words of wisdom Chremes shares with Clitipho here?
> 3 Do you think Chremes makes the right decision in not telling Clitipho what he knows about Menedemus? Why or why not?
> 4 Can you anticipate what will happen next? How much does one scene in a Roman comedy prepare the way for what follows?

When his father has left, Clitipho reveals to the audience that he, too, is in love, with a prostitute named Bacchis. Clinia enters, worried that his beloved, Antiphila, has been corrupted while he has been away. His fears appear to be confirmed when Clinia's slave Dromo and Clitipho's slave Syrus return, followed at a distance by a grand procession of two women and many female attendants. Syrus reveals, however, that he and Dromo found Antiphila leading a life of innocent poverty. Clinia is relieved and asks more (303–80).

4.4	CLINIA	But what did she say when you said my name?	
	SYRUS	When we said that you had come back and wanted her to come to you, she immediately dropped the **cloth she was weaving**, and her whole face filled with tears: she loves you, it's obvious.	305
	CLINIA	I swear, I'm so happy I don't know what to do. I was so frightened.	
	CLITIPHO	I knew all along your fears were groundless, Clinia. But tell me, Syrus, who's that other woman with Antiphila?	310
	SYRUS	We're bringing your Bacchis along, too.	

cloth she was weaving Dromo and Syrus found Antiphila and two female attendants weaving. Weaving the family clothing was for the ancient Romans the exemplary activity of an ideal woman: on tombstones the words 'she worked with wool' are often sufficient to indicate that the deceased was a virtuous wife.

Terence's language and metre

Terence occasionally employs the kind of stylistic exuberance used by Plautus, but usually his language is much less obtrusive and closer to everyday speech. For example, he uses actual Greek names instead of long made-up names. His characters use a very great number of colloquial expressions, and they often leave out words (a practice known as ellipsis), the way most speakers do in casual conversation. Terence's metre is also considerably tamer than Plautus'. He avoids almost entirely the more exotic metres such as bacchiacs, cretics and anapests used by Plautus, and a greater percentage of his verses are in unaccompanied iambic senarii (see pp. 35–6).

Terence was praised in antiquity for the refined purity of his Latin: the famous general and dictator Julius Caesar (100–44 BC), also a man of letters, called Terence a 'lover of pure language'. Centuries later the Dutch scholar Erasmus (c. 1466–1536) looked to Terence as a model for his own Latin, and those who write in Latin still find Terence a good source for many expressions. Below is the opening of the dialogue in **4.3** between Clitipho and Chremes. Note the relative lack of features such as alliteration, assonance and word play so common in Plautus, and the short, matter-of-fact questions and answers when father and son begin to talk to each other. Read it aloud and you will hear the difference from the Plautus passage quoted in the box on p. 47, even if you mispronounce some words (175–82).

CLITIPHO	nil adhuc est quod vereare, Clinia: haudquaquam etiam cessant	175
	et illam simul cum nuntio tibi hic adfuturam hodie scio.	
	proin tu sollicitudinem istam falsam quae te excruciat mittas.	
CHREMES	quicum loquitur filius?	
CLITIPHO	pater adest quem volui: adibo. pater, opportune advenis.	
CHREMES	quid id est?	180
CLITIPHO	hunc Menedemum nostin nostrum vicinum?	
CHREMES	probe.	
CLITIPHO	huic filium scis esse?	
CHREMES	audivi esse in Asia.	
CLITIPHO	non est, pater:	
	apud nos est.	

CLITIPHO	What? Bacchis? You scoundrel! Where are you taking her?
SYRUS	Where am I taking her? Why, to our house of course.
CLITIPHO	To my father's?
SYRUS	Yup.
CLITIPHO	Why, you brazen, impudent bastard!
SYRUS	Hey! No great deed was ever achieved without some risk.

CLITIPHO Wait a minute, you son-of-a-bitch. Are you trying to win glory for 315
yourself at the cost of my life? If you screw up just one little bit, I'm
done for. (*to Clinia*) What would you do with this guy?
SYRUS But really …
CLITIPHO What 'really'?
SYRUS If you let me, I'll tell you.
CLINIA Let him talk.
CLITIPHO OK.
SYRUS Well, it's kind of like when …
CLITIPHO Dammit, what kind of rigmarole is this?
CLINIA He's right, Syrus. Forget all that and get to the point.
SYRUS But really, I have to say this: you're being unfair in all sorts of ways, 320
and I can't stand it.
CLINIA We need to hear him out, Clitipho, so be quiet.
SYRUS You want a lover. You want to possess her. You want to get money
to give her. But you don't want to take any risks. Well, that's really
smart – that is, if you plan on never getting what you want. Either you 325
get the risk along with the pleasure, or you give up the pleasure along
with the risk: decide which you prefer. But the plan I've come up with
is the right one, and it's safe, I'm sure of it. It gives you the chance
to have your lover with you at your father's house with nothing to
fear. Not only that, but using the same plan I'll get that money you
promised her, the money you've been asking for until I'm practically 330
deaf. What else do you want?
CLITIPHO If only this works out.
SYRUS If only? You'll soon see it work out.
CLITIPHO OK, OK. Tell us this plan of yours. What is it?
SYRUS We'll pretend your mistress is his mistress.
CLITIPHO Great. And what will he do with his own girl? Or will we say she's his
mistress too, in case having just one isn't disgraceful enough?
SYRUS No, his girl will be brought to your mother. 335
CLITIPHO Why?
SYRUS I don't have time to spell it all out, but there's a good reason.
CLITIPHO Nonsense! I don't see any good reason why I should take on all this
stress.
SYRUS Hold on. If you're afraid of this plan, I've got another one, which
you'd both agree is without risk.
CLITIPHO Yes, please, find me a plan like that.
CLINIA Yes, please.
SYRUS OK, I go meet them and tell them to go home. 340
CLITIPHO What?
SYRUS That way I'll take away all your fear, so you can sleep like a baby.
CLITIPHO What do I do now?

Terence **69**

CLINIA	You? After the chance you've been given …
CLITIPHO	Syrus! Just tell me the truth.
SYRUS	What do you want? You'll wish you'd listened to me, but it will be too late.
CLINIA	Enjoy it while you can. You never know …
CLITIPHO	Syrus!
SYRUS	Say what you want. I'm taking them back anyway.
CLINIA	… whether you'll ever have that chance again.
CLITIPHO	That's true, by Hercules. Syrus, Syrus, wait! Hey, Syrus!
SYRUS	He's warmed up. What do you want?
CLITIPHO	Come back! Come back!
SYRUS	OK, I'm back. What is it? Now I suppose you'll say you don't like this plan.
CLITIPHO	No, Syrus: I hand over my love and my reputation to you. You're the judge: see that you don't do anything I'll blame you for later.
SYRUS	It's silly to give me such a warning, Clitipho. As if this business affects me any less than you. If by chance anything goes wrong, you just get scolded: I get beaten. So don't worry: no way am I handling this carelessly. But beg your friend here to pretend Bacchis is his mistress.
CLINIA	Of course I'll do that. We've reached the point where there's no way around that.
CLITIPHO	Clinia, I'm really grateful. You're a true friend.
CLINIA	But make sure she doesn't mess things up.
SYRUS	She's been well trained.
CLITIPHO	But I'm amazed you could persuade her to come so easily: she usually spurns all her lovers.
SYRUS	I came to her at just the right time. That's always the most important thing. You see, when I got there I found a soldier, pleading wretchedly for one night with her. She was handling the fellow skilfully, getting him all stirred up and at the same time treating him in a way that would please you. But listen, you, make sure you don't do anything rash! You know how eagle-eyed your father is. I know you, and how out of control you can be. No double entendres or sideways glances; and no groaning, clearing your throat, coughing or smiling at her.
CLITIPHO	You'll be proud of me.
SYRUS	Make sure of it.
CLITIPHO	You'll be amazed.
SYRUS	But look how fast the women have caught up with us!
CLITIPHO	Where are they? Why are you holding me back?
SYRUS	Now remember, she's not yours.
CLITIPHO	I know she's not, at my father's house. But in the meantime …
SYRUS	No, not in the meantime either.
CLITIPHO	Oh, please.
SYRUS	No.

CLITIPHO	Just a little.
SYRUS	No.
CLITIPHO	Let me just say hello.
SYRUS	If you're smart you'll skedaddle.
CLITIPHO	OK. I'm off. What about him? 380
SYRUS	He stays.
CLITIPHO	Lucky fellow!
SYRUS	Get going.

> 1 Why do you think weaving was a sign of an ideal wife for ancient Romans?
> 2 What is the relationship between Syrus and Clitipho like? How do you think their relationship compares with relationships between Roman masters and slaves outside of the theatre?
> 3 How does Syrus get Clitipho to change his mind and go along with his plan?

> **The double plot**
> Terence inherited from some of his Greek models plots in which two sets of characters have parallel and contrasting experiences. In most of his plays Terence either expanded the role of one of the two character sets, or he added a second set of characters to the play. He thus encouraged his audience to compare the actions of different characters in similar situations. Five of his plays have two sets of lovers. In four of these, as in *The Self-Tormentor*, one young man is in love with a marriageable woman but the other loves a prostitute; spectators can thus compare different kinds of love affairs. In Terence's final play, *The Brothers* (*Adelphoe*), the 'double plot' has special significance, as the play presents the actions of two brothers, one raised leniently, one with strict discipline. Terence's 'double plots' have had a profound effect on later comedy, where contrasting sets of characters, especially pairs of lovers, remain a common feature.

Antiphila and Bacchis with all her attendants enter after Clitipho leaves the stage. Bacchis tells Antiphila she envies her, for she can afford to be good, but Bacchis herself, a prostitute dependent on many lovers, must grasp what she can before she gets old (compare Scapha in **3.2**). Antiphila and Clinia have a joyous reunion, and all enter Chremes' house. In the next scene a night has passed. Chremes believes that Clinia and Bacchis, who have stayed at his house for the night, are lovers, and he passes that story on to Menedemus (427–97).

4.5 **CHREMES** **Good morning**, Menedemus. I bring you news you want to hear more than anything else in the world.
MENEDEMUS You haven't heard anything of my son, have you, Chremes?
CHREMES He's alive and well. 430
MENEDEMUS Where? Tell me!
CHREMES He's at my house.
MENEDEMUS My son?
CHREMES Yep.
MENEDEMUS He's come home?
CHREMES Sure has.
MENEDEMUS My Clinia has come home?
CHREMES That's what I said.
MENEDEMUS Then let's go! Take me to him, please!
CHREMES He doesn't want you to know that he's come home, and he's avoiding you. He's afraid your former severity will be even greater 435 now because of what he's done.
MENEDEMUS Didn't you tell him how I feel now?
CHREMES No.
MENEDEMUS Why not, Chremes?
CHREMES Because you're not looking out for yourself or him, if you show him that you're so easy-going and that there's no fight left in you.
MENEDEMUS I can't bear it. I've been a harsh father long enough.
CHREMES Ah, you go too far in both directions, Menedemus: you're either 440 too generous or too stingy. This error will lead you into the same dead end that one did. Before, rather than allow your son to be with a woman who was then content with little and grateful for 445 anything, you frightened him so much he skipped town. Then the woman, forced against her will, began to seek her living as a common whore. Now, when he can't hold onto her without great expense, you want to give him whatever he needs. Let me tell you 450 how well she's been trained for your destruction. First of all, she brought with her more than ten attendants, all loaded down with fine clothing and gold. If a **satrap** were her lover, he couldn't keep up with her expenses. You certainly can't.
MENEDEMUS Is she in your house?
CHREMES Is she ever! I gave one dinner to her and her companions. If I had 455 to give another like it, I'd be finished. Not to mention everything else, she consumed barrels of my wine just by tasting it and spitting

---

Good morning the change to the next morning is striking: the action of almost every other Roman comedy occurs within one day.

satrap a governor of a province of the Persian empire. Persians in general and satraps in particular were known for their wealth and love of luxury.

	it out! She'd say, 'This one's so-so', and, 'Father, this one's bitter. Please get me something smoother.' I opened up every jar of wine I have, the big ones and the small ones. All my slaves were kept busy. And this was just in one night! What do you think will happen to you when she starts eating you out of house and home non-stop? By the gods, I really pity your estate, Menedemus.	460
MENEDEMUS	Let her do whatever she wants: eat, devour, destroy. I've decided to put up with it, so long as I have him with me.	465
CHREMES	If that's what you're determined to do, I think it's really important that you act so he doesn't know you're knowingly giving him all this.	
MENEDEMUS	What should I do?	
CHREMES	Do anything rather than what you're planning to do. Allow yourself to be tricked by your slave, so you can give the money through anybody but yourself. I sense those slaves are at it already: they're scheming between themselves in secret. Syrus whispers with that slave of yours, and they bring their plans to the boys. It's better for you to lose a talent that way than a **mina** in the way you propose. It's not about the money now, but about how we can give it to the young man with the least risk. For if he ever catches an inkling of your attitude – that you'd give up your very life and all your money rather than lose your son – forget it! What a window you will have opened up for his depravity! You wouldn't be able to live in peace. Too much freedom makes us all worse. Whenever he thinks of anything, he'll want it. He'll ask you for it without a thought as to whether it's bad or good. You won't be able to stand to have both your property and him go to ruin, so you'll refuse to give it. He'll go back immediately to what he knows has the greatest power over you: he'll threaten to run away again.	470 475 480 485
MENEDEMUS	I think you're exactly right.	490
CHREMES	By Hercules, I didn't sleep a wink last night, lying awake figuring out how I could restore your son to you.	
MENEDEMUS	Give me your right hand. I want you to do something for me, Chremes.	
CHREMES	I'm ready.	
MENEDEMUS	Do you know what it is?	
CHREMES	Tell me.	495
MENEDEMUS	You sensed that they were beginning to plan a deception against me. Make them do it soon. I want to give him what he wants, and I want to see him in person.	
CHREMES	I'll do my best.	

mina one-sixtieth of a talent, or just under a pound of silver.

1. What do you think of Chremes' arguments to Menedemus about showing Clinia how he feels? Would you have responded as Menedemus does?
2. Once again, readers of the play have differed in their evaluations of Chremes here. Do you think he is being a helpful friend or is meddling?

> **Terence and stock characters**
>
> We have noted how Plautus liked to 'tweak' the stock characters of his tradition, sometimes giving them unexpected characteristics or mixing features of different types in one character. Terence responded much more audaciously to the convention of stock characters. Most of his characters fail in some way to meet the expectations their stock type would produce, and many are blatantly different from what the audience probably expected. Note, for example, Menedemus and Chremes, neither of whom fits comfortably into the category of either 'harsh old man' or 'gentle old man'. Terence's slaves are seldom as clever as they think they are, and their ruses fail in several plays. A common feature of Terence's characters is that they are more complex and sympathetic than characters of comedy often are. Clitipho's lover Bacchis, for example, is in many ways the grasping free prostitute typical of the comic tradition, but she also shows her more human side in her respect for Antiphila's innocence.

As Menedemus has requested, Chremes encourages his slave Syrus to help Menedemus' slave Dromo deceive Menedemus. Clitipho, unable to control himself around Bacchis, almost ruins Syrus' plans when Chremes catches him fondling her (remember they are pretending that Bacchis is Clinia's girlfriend); but Syrus, feigning indignation at Clitipho's behaviour, keeps Chremes in the dark. Syrus then begins a plan to get ten minae, which he has promised Bacchis Clitipho will pay her (595–672).

4.6

CHREMES   And what about you? Have you done anything about what we were just talking about? Have you found some plan you like? 595
SYRUS   You mean about the deception? I've just come up with one.
CHREMES   Good job. Tell me, what is it?
SYRUS   I'll tell you as it unfolds.
CHREMES   What is it, Syrus?
SYRUS   This prostitute of Clinia's is really bad.
CHREMES   So it seems.
SYRUS   Just listen to what she's up to, if you really want to know how bad 600
          she is. There was a certain old woman from Corinth here. Bacchis had loaned her **a thousand drachmas**.

---

a thousand drachmas   a mina is 100 drachmas, so this is ten minae.

CHREMES	So?
SYRUS	The old woman died. She left behind a young daughter, who was handed over to Bacchis as a surety on the loan.
CHREMES	I see.
SYRUS	She brought the girl here with her. She's **the one who's with your wife now**.
CHREMES	So?
SYRUS	Now Bacchis wants the thousand drachmas, so she's demanding that Clinia pay her and take the girl.
CHREMES	She's demanding, no less?
SYRUS	That's certainly what it looked like to me.
CHREMES	So what are you planning to do now?
SYRUS	I'll go to Menedemus. I'll say the girl is a rich and noble captive from **Caria**, and that there's **a lot of money in it if he buys her**.
CHREMES	That won't work.
SYRUS	Why?
CHREMES	Menedemus will just say, 'I'm not buying.' What do you do then?
SYRUS	That's just the answer I want.
CHREMES	Why?
SYRUS	I don't need him to buy her.
CHREMES	You don't?
SYRUS	Nope.
CHREMES	How can that be?
SYRUS	You'll see.
CHREMES	Hang on a minute. What's all that noise coming from our door?
SOSTRATA	(*entering talking to her* **nurse**) Unless my mind is really playing tricks on me, this truly is the ring I think it is, the one my daughter was **exposed** with.
CHREMES	Syrus, what do you think this is all about?
SOSTRATA	Well? Do you think it's the same ring?
NURSE	I said so right away, when you showed it to me.
SOSTRATA	But have you thought it over carefully enough, dear nurse?
NURSE	I have.
SOSTRATA	Go inside now and tell me if she's finished with her bath. Meanwhile I'll wait here for my husband.

---

the one who's with your wife now Syrus refers to Antiphila, whom Chremes does not know is Clinia's girlfriend.

Caria a region in the south-western part of what is now Turkey (see map on p. x).

a lot of money in it if he buys her Antiphila's relatives, Syrus suggests, would pay a high ransom for her.

nurse a slave who takes care of her mistress's infant children.

exposed left to die. See the box on infanticide, p. 78.

SYRUS	She's looking for you. See what she wants. She seems sad somehow: something's up, and it worries me.	620
CHREMES	What could it be? But you know her: she'll probably make a great effort to say a great bit of nonsense.	
SOSTRATA	Oh, my husband!	
CHREMES	Oh, my wife!	
SOSTRATA	I've been looking for you.	
CHREMES	What do you want?	
SOSTRATA	First, I beg you: don't believe that I dared to do anything against your command.	
CHREMES	You want me to believe that, even though it's incredible? OK, I believe it.	
SYRUS	(*aside*) Looks like she's done something wrong.	625
SOSTRATA	Do you remember when I was pregnant, and you insisted that if I gave birth to a girl, you didn't want me to keep it?	
CHREMES	I know what you did: you kept it.	
SYRUS	(*aside*) That's it. Now I've got a new mistress, and the master has new expenses.	
SOSTRATA	No. Not at all. But there was an old woman from Corinth here, who was of upstanding character. I gave it to her to expose.	630
CHREMES	O Jupiter! To think that you could be so stupid!	
SOSTRATA	Goodness, what did I do?	
CHREMES	You have to ask?	
SOSTRATA	If I did wrong, Chremes, I did it in ignorance.	
CHREMES	Oh I know that's true, even if you deny it. You do and say everything in ignorance, never thinking what you're doing. What you did was wrong in so many ways. First, if you really wanted to obey my command, the baby should have been killed. You shouldn't have just said you killed it when in fact you gave it hope of life. Well, I'll let that pass: I grant it was your pity and your maternal instinct. But think a minute: how well did you think through what you did? When you handed our daughter over to that old woman, she would inevitably either make her living as a prostitute or be sold openly. I suppose you thought anything was better than the child's death. What's to be done with people who have no idea what's just or good or right? Good, bad, beneficial, harmful, it's all the same: they only see what they want to see.	635 640
SOSTRATA	Dear Chremes, I confess I did wrong, and you're right. But now I beg you, my husband, since your mind is forgiving by nature, let my foolishness find refuge in your justice.	645
CHREMES	Of course I'll forgive you. Though I'm too easy-going, Sostrata, and it really teaches you a bad lesson. But why have you brought this up now?	

SOSTRATA	We foolish women are all terribly superstitious, so when I handed her over to be exposed, I took a ring off my finger and ordered that it be exposed along with the infant. That way if she died, she would not be completely without anything from us.	650
CHREMES	Good. You protected both yourself and her.	
SOSTRATA	Here is that ring.	
CHREMES	Where did you get it?	
SOSTRATA	The young woman Bacchis brought along with her …	
SYRUS	(*aside*) What?	
CHREMES	(*aside*) What is she saying?	655
SOSTRATA	When she went to bathe, she gave it to me to keep for her. At first I didn't notice. But after I looked at it, right away I recognized it, and I ran out to you.	
CHREMES	What do you think happened, and what have you found out about the girl?	
SOSTRATA	I don't know, but you could ask her where she got the ring, if that can be determined.	
SYRUS	(*aside*) I'm done for! I see more hope here than I want to. If this is all true, she's ours.	660
CHREMES	Is the woman you gave her to still alive?	
SOSTRATA	I don't know.	
CHREMES	What did she say back then, when you gave her the baby?	
SOSTRATA	She said she did what I asked her to.	
CHREMES	Tell me what the woman's name was, so we can investigate.	
SOSTRATA	Philtera.	
SYRUS	(*aside*) **That's the one**. I'll be damned if she's not saved, and I'm ruined.	
CHREMES	Sostrata, follow me in here.	
SOSTRATA	Oh, this has turned out so much better than I expected! I was so afraid you'd be as harsh now as you were then about keeping her, Chremes!	665
CHREMES	Often a man can't act as he would like, if he doesn't have the means. The way things are now, I would like a daughter. Once I wanted nothing less.	

Chremes and Sostrata exit.

SYRUS	Unless my mind is really playing tricks on me, I'm in big trouble. This business has forced my **troops** into a narrow ravine: we're trapped if I don't find some way to keep the old man from finding out that that woman is his son's lover. And it's goodbye to my hopes of getting money or tricking him. I'll have won a great victory if I can just make a retreat with my flanks covered.	670

That's the one   Syrus recognizes the name of Antiphila's alleged mother.

troops   slaves who carry out deception in Roman comedy often use military language, parodying the leaders of Roman society, who were most proud of their accomplishments in the military.

Here is the entrance of Sostrata and the nurse in one of the illustrated manuscripts of Terence. Note the names and types of the characters over the figures (from left to right): Sostrata Mulier ('Sostrata, a woman'), Nutrix Anus ('the nurse, an old woman'), Chremes Senex ('Chremes, an old man') and Syrus Servus ('Syrus, a slave').

4.7

> 1. Because the discovery that Antiphila is Chremes' daughter makes Syrus give up his plan to get money by telling Menedemus that he should buy Antiphila from Bacchis, we never know exactly what that plan was. What do you think Syrus might have been planning to do?
> 2. What does Chremes' behaviour towards Sostrata indicate about his character?
> 3. Does the manuscript illustration seem to you to have captured well the likely staging of this scene? Why or why not? What do the postures of the characters suggest?
> 4. What effect would the comments of the eavesdropping Syrus have on how an audience might respond to this scene of recognition?
> 5. As you can see, after Sostrata leaves, Syrus echoes the words with which she entered. He also repeats her metre. What do you think is the significance of this repetition?

Infanticide

When a child was born in the Greek or Roman world, its father decided whether or not he wished to claim and raise it. If he chose not to raise the child, it would be exposed, either to die or to be picked up by someone else. In real life, exposed infants were sometimes picked up and made slaves (note Chremes' concerns for the infant here). Female infants were exposed more often than male babies because a daughter was expensive: the father would have to provide a dowry for her so that she could get married. In drama, both tragedy and comedy, exposed infants often grow up and are later discovered by their real parents (compare the exposure and rediscovery of Oedipus). Often some token that was left with the baby when it was exposed, like Antiphila's ring here, leads to the recognition.

It would now be easy for Clinia to tell his father that he is in love with Antiphila: as Chremes' and Sostrata's daughter, she is marriageable. Syrus persuades Clinia to keep up the pretence that Bacchis, not Antiphila, is his lover, however, so that he can continue his plans to get money for Clitipho to give to Bacchis. Bacchis and her entourage move from Chremes' house to Menedemus'. The young men and Syrus tell Menedemus the truth – that Bacchis is Clitipho's mistress and Clinia wants to marry Antiphila – but they let Chremes think that Bacchis is Clinia's mistress and that Clinia's desire to marry Antiphila is concocted to deceive Menedemus. Syrus then persuades Chremes to pay Bacchis what is allegedly owed to her for Antiphila (remember his lie that Antiphila was surety on a loan Bacchis made to Antiphila's foster mother): in fact, this is the money Syrus promised Bacchis she would get from Clitipho. Syrus and Clitipho himself bring Bacchis the money (842–948).

4.8

MENEDEMUS (*talking back to Clinia, who is inside the house*) I think I've been made the most fortunate of all men, since I see that you have come to your senses, my son.
CHREMES How wrong he is!
MENEDEMUS Chremes! You're just the man I was looking for. Save my son and my family. You have the power.   845
CHREMES What do you want me to do?
MENEDEMUS You have discovered a daughter today.
CHREMES What of it?
MENEDEMUS Clinia wants to marry her.
CHREMES What kind of man are you?
MENEDEMUS What do you mean?
CHREMES Have you already forgotten what we said about how they would trick you to get money?   850
MENEDEMUS No.
CHREMES Well, that's just what's happening now.
MENEDEMUS What do you mean? The woman at my house is Clitipho's lover.
CHREMES That's what they say. And you swallow it hook, line and sinker. And they say Clinia wants to marry Antiphila. That way, when I give my permission, you'll give him money so he can buy gold and   855 fine clothing and the other things necessary for the wedding.
MENEDEMUS That's it. You're right. He'll hand that all over to his lover.
CHREMES Obviously.
MENEDEMUS Oh! Then I was so happy for nothing, dammit. Still, I'd prefer anything to losing him again. What should I say your answer is, Chremes, so he doesn't know that I know what's going on and am   860 unhappy about it?

CHREMES	So he doesn't know you're unhappy? Menedemus, you'll really spoil him.	
MENEDEMUS	So be it. I'm going to finish what I've started, and I need your help.	
CHREMES	All right. Say we've met and discussed the wedding.	
MENEDEMUS	I will. What else?	
CHREMES	Say I'll do everything, that I'm pleased with my son-in-law, and finally, if you want, even say that I agreed to the engagement.	865
MENEDEMUS	Good, that's what I wanted to hear.	
CHREMES	So he'll demand money from you that much sooner, and you'll pay it out as fast as possible, just the way you want.	
MENEDEMUS	Yes. That's what I want.	
CHREMES	As I see it, you'll have had enough of this before very long. But whatever happens, you'll be careful how much you pay out if you're smart.	870
MENEDEMUS	I will.	
CHREMES	All right, go inside. See what he wants. I'll be at home if you want me for anything.	
MENEDEMUS	I will, since I'm going to keep you informed of whatever I do.	

Both men exit into their respective homes. Menedemus returns almost immediately.

MENEDEMUS	I know I'm no genius. But Chremes, so full of help and advice, is even dumber. I deserve to be called any of those names they call stupid people: dolt, blockhead, jackass, dimwit. But these names are nothing for him: his stupidity outdoes them all.	875
CHREMES	(*back to his wife in the house*) Wife! Enough with the prayers of gratitude. Do you think the gods are as thickheaded as you are, and don't understand anything unless they hear the same thing a hundred times? (*aside*) I wonder why my son's been over there with Syrus so long?	880
MENEDEMUS	Who's that you say is staying so long, Chremes?	
CHREMES	Oh, Menedemus! Are you back? Tell me, did you tell Clinia what I said?	
MENEDEMUS	Everything.	
CHREMES	What did he say?	885
MENEDEMUS	He started to act really happy, like someone who wants to get married.	
CHREMES	Ha ha ha!	
MENEDEMUS	Why are you laughing?	
CHREMES	I was just struck by the cleverness of my slave Syrus.	
MENEDEMUS	Oh?	
CHREMES	The scoundrel. He can even make people's faces do what he wants.	

MENEDEMUS You mean my son, because he pretended he was happy?
CHREMES Exactly.
MENEDEMUS I thought of the same thing.
CHREMES The old fox!
MENEDEMUS If you knew more, you'd be even more impressed with Syrus' cleverness.
CHREMES What do you mean?
MENEDEMUS Just listen.
CHREMES Hold on. First I want to know what you've shelled out. When you announced the engagement to your son, I'm sure Dromo immediately told you how the betrothed needed clothing, gold and female attendants, and that you should give money for that.
MENEDEMUS Nope.
CHREMES What? He didn't?
MENEDEMUS Sure didn't.
CHREMES And your son didn't either?
MENEDEMUS Not a bit, Chremes. The only thing he did was insist that the wedding happen today.
CHREMES That's amazing. What about my Syrus? Didn't he ask for anything?
MENEDEMUS Nothing.
CHREMES I don't understand it.
MENEDEMUS That really surprises me, since you understand everything else so well. But Syrus also did a great job making your son's face do what he wanted, so I couldn't in the slightest think that Bacchis was Clinia's lover.
CHREMES What did he do?
MENEDEMUS I leave out the kissing and hugging. That's nothing.
CHREMES How could he do more than that?
MENEDEMUS Ha ha!
CHREMES What is it?
MENEDEMUS Just listen. I've got a little room at the very back of my house. A bed was laid out there with covers.
CHREMES So?
MENEDEMUS In the wink of an eye, Clitipho went back there.
CHREMES Alone?
MENEDEMUS Alone.
CHREMES Oh dear.
MENEDEMUS Bacchis followed him right away.
CHREMES Alone?
MENEDEMUS Alone.
CHREMES Oh no!

MENEDEMUS   When they went inside, they closed the door.
CHREMES   Oh no! Did Clinia see this?
MENEDEMUS   How could he not? He was right there with me.
CHREMES   So then Bacchis is my son's lover! Menedemus, I'm ruined!
MENEDEMUS   Why?
CHREMES   My household will hardly survive ten days.
MENEDEMUS   What do you mean? Are you concerned because he's helping out his friend? 910
CHREMES   No! Because he's helping out his girlfriend!
MENEDEMUS   If that's what he's doing.
CHREMES   Do you have any doubt? Do you think anyone is so friendly or easy-going that he would let his lover, right in front of his eyes …
MENEDEMUS   Well, why not? They wanted to deceive me.
CHREMES   You're making fun of me, and I deserve it. I'm angry at myself now. They gave so many signs that should have clued me in, if I weren't such an idiot. What things I saw! Oh dammit! But so help me, they won't get away with this. I'll … 915
MENEDEMUS   Hold on there! Look at yourself! Am I not a good enough example for you? 920
CHREMES   Menedemus, I'm beside myself. I'm so angry!
MENEDEMUS   What a thing for you to say! Aren't you ashamed to be so good at giving others advice but unable to help yourself?
CHREMES   What should I do?
MENEDEMUS   Do what you said I didn't do. Let him know you're his father. Make him feel he can tell you everything and can ask you for things, so he doesn't look elsewhere and abandon you. 925
CHREMES   No. I'd rather he go away anywhere on earth rather than stay here and bankrupt his father through shameful behaviour. If I continue to provide for his expenses, Menedemus, I really will have to **dig with a hoe**! 930
MENEDEMUS   This will all end up making you terribly unhappy, if you're not careful! You'll be severe now, and later you'll forgive him, but it will be too late.
CHREMES   Ah, you don't know how I'm suffering.
MENEDEMUS   Do as you wish. But what about my request, that your daughter marry my son? Are you still happy with that? 935

dig with a hoe   Chremes refers back to Menedemus' voluntary use of the hoe in the first scene and suggests that after Bacchis depletes him of all his money he will be forced to do manual labour.

CHREMES	Yes, I'm happy with the son-in-law and the family connection.
MENEDEMUS	How much dowry shall I tell my son you're offering? Why are you silent?
CHREMES	Dowry?
MENEDEMUS	Yes.
CHREMES	Ah!
MENEDEMUS	Chremes, don't worry about how much. The dowry's not important to us.
CHREMES	I've decided that two talents is appropriate, given my resources. But you have to tell him, if you want to save me, my estate and my son, that I've **offered all my property as a dowry**.
MENEDEMUS	What?
CHREMES	Pretend you're surprised at this, and ask him why I would do that.
MENEDEMUS	But I am surprised, and I don't know why you would do that.
CHREMES	Why? So I can drag him back from luxury and dissipation. So he'll be desperate.
MENEDEMUS	What's this all about?
CHREMES	Never mind. Just let me do this my own way.
MENEDEMUS	OK. Is that really what you want?
CHREMES	Yes.
MENEDEMUS	Then so be it.
CHREMES	And now let Clinia prepare to summon his bride.

940

945

---

1. When this scene begins, Menedemus and Chremes speak unaccompanied iambic senarii (see p. 36). Music starts when Menedemus enters with the knowledge that Bacchis is Clitipho's lover, stops again when Chremes realizes the truth, then begins a final time when Chremes says that Clitipho is to be told that his whole estate will go to Antiphila as a dowry. Why do you think Terence chose these places to start and stop the music?
2. Both Menedemus and Chremes agree that Chremes has been exceptionally stupid. What do you think? Should he have been able to see through the deception?
3. What do you think of Chremes' plan to make Clitipho believe he has been disinherited? Is this a good way for him to respond to the dangers of Bacchis?

---

offered all my property as a dowry by giving all his property as a dowry to Antiphila, Chremes would disinherit Clitipho.

Terence

Terence's other plays

Each of Terence's six plays has at its core one or more relationships between fathers and sons.

In *The Woman from Andros* (*Andria*), the young man Pamphilus has been having an affair with Glycerium. Because she is from Andros (see map on p. x) and not Athenian, Pamphilus cannot marry her. Pamphilus' father Simo finds out about the affair but does not tell his son he knows. Instead, he arranges a marriage for Pamphilus to test Pamphilus' loyalty to him. Pamphilus' slave Davos persuades Pamphilus to pretend to go along with the wedding plans, believing he can devise a way of getting Pamphilus out of the agreement. Davos' plans fail, and the marriage almost happens, much to the chagrin of Pamphilus and his friend Charinus, who is in love with the woman Pamphilus is to marry. All is resolved when it is revealed that in fact Glycerium is Athenian, the long-lost daughter of the man whose other daughter Pamphilus was to marry.

When *The Eunuch* (*Eunuchus*) begins, Phaedria is competing with a soldier, Thraso, for the attentions of the prostitute Thais. Thais loves Phaedria but is using Thraso to gain possession of Pamphila, a kidnapped girl whom she wants to return to her Athenian family. Phaedria's brother Chaerea sees Pamphila and falls in love with her. Disguised as the eunuch Phaedria has bought as a gift for Thais, Chaerea enters Thais' house and rapes Pamphila. When she finds out about the rape, Thais agrees that Chaerea can marry Pamphila. In a surprise ending, Thraso's parasite persuades Phaedria to share Thais with Thraso.

When *Phormio* begins, Antipho has fallen in love with and married the poor orphan Phanium. Antipho's father, Demipho, is away, and the parasite Phormio has pretended that he is a relative of Phanium and has taken Antipho to court, bringing the charge that Antipho is Phanium's closest male relative: Athenian law required that an orphan's closest male relative marry her or find her a husband. Meanwhile, Antipho's cousin Phaedria has fallen in love with a slave prostitute. Demipho returns, furious at the marriage, but Phormio counters him effectively and at the same time acquires money from Demipho so that Phaedria can buy the woman he loves. Demipho's brother (Phaedria's father) Chremes also returns to Athens, and it is discovered that Phanium is actually his illegitimate daughter: Chremes has been looking for her, to marry her to Antipho. Phormio finds out Phanium's parentage and tells Chremes' wife Nausistrata, who makes Chremes let Phaedria keep his prostitute and becomes Phormio's patroness.

The Mother-in-Law (*Hecyra*) is Sostrata, whose daughter-in-law Philumena has been living with her while her husband Pamphilus is away on business, but has left her without giving a reason. Sostrata's husband Laches assumes that the two women have feuded and blames Sostrata. Pamphilus returns and discovers that in fact Philumena has given birth, although it has only been a few months since he consummated the marriage. Unwilling to stay with the mother of someone else's child, he tells his father he will leave Philumena because of her quarrel with his mother. Meanwhile, Philumena's father, Phidippus, learns of the birth. He and Laches assume that Philumena's mother, Myrrina, has kept the birth a secret in anger at Pamphilus, because when he married Philumena he was in love with the prostitute Bacchis (he has since grown to love his wife). Laches calls upon Bacchis to reassure Myrrina and Philumena that she is no longer intimate with Pamphilus. When she does so she discovers that a ring Pamphilus gave her in fact belongs to Philumena: shortly before the marriage, Pamphilus had raped Philumena and taken the ring. It was dark, and neither assailant nor victim knew the other's identity. Pamphilus and Philumena are reunited, and Laches and Phidippus are left in the dark about what actually happened.

In *The Brothers* (*Adelphoe*), the stern old man Demea has two sons, now grown to adulthood. One of the sons, Ctesipho, he has raised himself, but the other, Aeschinus, he handed over to his brother Micio, a bachelor and a very lenient father. Aeschinus has stolen a prostitute from a pimp. In fact, the prostitute is for Ctesipho, but the family of the poor woman Pamphila, who is giving birth to Aeschinus' child, thinks Aeschinus has abandoned them, and they remonstrate with Demea and with Micio, whom Aeschinus has not told about the pregnancy. Micio agrees that the remorseful Aeschinus can marry Pamphila. Meanwhile, Micio's slave Syrus sends Demea on two 'wild goose chases' as he looks first for Ctesipho (who is hiding with his prostitute in Micio's house) and then for Micio (whom he wants to tell about Aeschinus' wrongdoing). Finally, Demea learns the truth and is humiliated: Micio seems to have won the day. Demea, however, decides to beat Micio at his own game: pretending to be looking out for Aeschinus, he browbeats Micio into marrying Pamphila's widowed mother, giving away land to Pamphila's relative, and freeing Syrus.

When Clitipho learns that he has been disinherited, he concludes that he must not really be the child of Chremes and Sostrata. He tells this to his mother, who accosts Chremes (1003–67).

4.9 SOSTRATA Unless you watch out, my good man, you'll do real harm to our son. I just can't figure out how anything so stupid could come into your mind. 1005

CHREMES Will you stop acting like a woman? You've opposed everything I've ever wanted. You're so sure of yourself, stupid, but if I asked you now what I'm doing wrong or why you're against it, you wouldn't be able to tell me.

SOSTRATA Wouldn't I?

CHREMES All right, you would. Let's just not start this all over again. 1010

SOSTRATA You're not being fair: I have a right to speak my mind.

CHREMES All right, speak your mind. I'll still do just as I planned.

SOSTRATA You will?

CHREMES I will.

SOSTRATA Don't you see how much harm you're causing with all this? He thinks he's a **foundling**.

CHREMES A foundling?

SOSTRATA Yes. 1015

CHREMES And what do you say? Is he?

SOSTRATA What? Please, wish that on our enemies! Am I to say that my son is not mine, when he is?

CHREMES What? Are you afraid you won't be able to prove he's your son when you want to?

SOSTRATA Because our daughter has been found?

CHREMES No. You can easily prove he's your son because you two are so alike. All his faults are the same as yours, and nobody but you would give birth to a son like that. But here he comes. Look how solemn he is! One look at his face and you can see he's upset. 1020

CLITIPHO Mother, if there was ever a time when you were glad that I was called your son, please, think back on that time and have pity on me now that I'm destitute: show me who my parents are. That's all I want now. 1025

SOSTRATA Please, my son, don't even let the idea cross your mind that you are someone else's.

CLITIPHO But I am.

---

foundling   that is, Clitipho thinks he is someone else's child whom Chremes and Sostrata have pretended is theirs.

Terence

SOSTRATA	(*to Chremes*) So is this what you were after? (*to Clitipho*) I swear you're his son and mine, by your own life, which I hope will outlast both his and mine. And if you love me, don't ever let me hear you say that again.	1030
CHREMES	And if you fear me, don't ever let me see those vices in you again.	
CLITIPHO	What vices?	
CHREMES	Well, if you want to know, I'll tell you: you're a disgrace, a liar, a profligate, a glutton and a spendthrift. Believe that, and believe that you're our son.	
CLITIPHO	That's not the kind of thing a father says.	1035
CHREMES	Clitipho, not even if you were born from my own head, as they say **Minerva was from Jupiter's**, would I stand by and let you ruin my reputation and standing with your bad behaviour.	
SOSTRATA	The gods forbid!	
CHREMES	I don't know about the gods, but I know *I* will do everything I can to prevent it. You're looking for what you already have: parents. You're not looking for what you don't have: a way to obey your father and protect what his hard work has earned. A way not to use tricks to bring right here under my eyes a … I'm ashamed to say that base word in front of your mother. But you weren't at all ashamed to do it.	1040
CLITIPHO	Oh, I'm so completely disgusted with myself! I'm so ashamed! I don't even know how to start trying to regain your favour.	
MENEDEMUS	(*entering from his house*) Chremes is really torturing the young man: he's too severe and too cruel, so I'm coming out to make peace between them. Good: here they both are.	1045
CHREMES	Oh, Menedemus. Why haven't you ordered my daughter to be summoned, and why don't you confirm the dowry I have named?	
SOSTRATA	Dear husband, I beg you, don't do that.	
CLITIPHO	Father, forgive me, I beg you.	
MENEDEMUS	Show him mercy, Chremes: let me persuade you.	1050
CHREMES	I'm knowingly to hand over my estate as a gift to Bacchis? I won't do it.	
MENEDEMUS	But we won't let that happen.	
CLITIPHO	If you want me to live, father, forgive me.	
SOSTRATA	Do it, dear Chremes.	
MENEDEMUS	Do it, please. Don't be so stubborn, Chremes.	
CHREMES	All right. I see I won't be allowed to carry this through as I intended.	

Minerva was from Jupiter's   Jupiter impregnated and then swallowed Minerva's mother, Metis. The blacksmith god Vulcan struck Jupiter's head with an ax, and Minerva sprang forth.

MENEDEMUS	Now you're doing what's right.	
CHREMES	I'll do it under one condition: he must do what I think is right.	1055
CLITIPHO	Father, I'll do anything: give the command.	
CHREMES	You must marry.	
CLITIPHO	Father!	
CHREMES	No excuses.	
SOSTRATA	I'll take responsibility for this: he'll do it.	
CHREMES	I don't hear him saying anything.	
CLITIPHO	Oh no!	
SOSTRATA	Are you hesitating, Clitipho?	
CHREMES	Hold on. Let him decide which choice he wants.	
SOSTRATA	He'll do everything you ask.	
MENEDEMUS	When you begin things like marriage, they're hard, because they're unfamiliar. When you get used to them, though, they're easy.	
CLITIPHO	I'll do it, father.	
SOSTRATA	My son, I will give you that nice daughter of our neighbour Phanocrates: you could easily love her.	1060
CLITIPHO	That redhead, with grey eyes, freckles and a crooked nose? I can't do it, father.	
CHREMES	So fastidious! You'd think he'd actually thought about it!	
SOSTRATA	I'll give you another.	
CLITIPHO	No. Since I have to get married, I have one in mind that I want.	1065
CHREMES	Now you're talking, son.	
CLITIPHO	The daughter of **Archonides** here.	
SOSTRATA	Excellent.	
CLITIPHO	Father, one thing remains.	
CHREMES	What?	
CLITIPHO	I want you to forgive Syrus, who did all this for my sake.	
CHREMES	So be it.	
EPILOGUE SINGER	And you, spectators, farewell! Give us your applause!	

> 1 How does the interaction between Sostrata and Chremes here compare with the way they interacted in their earlier scene?
> 2 What is your assessment of Chremes here? Is he justified in his treatment of Sostrata and Clitipho?
> 3 What do you think of Clitipho's willingness to marry?
> 4 Why do you think Chremes forgives Syrus so easily?

Archonides   one of Chremes' neighbours.

Epilogue Singer   it is not known whether one of the actors, the entire troupe or a special performer delivered the final verse (i.e. the epilogue) of this and Terence's other plays.

5   Think back over the play and try to identify the different kinds of humour that you have encountered: gallows humour, for example, as when Syrus jokes about getting beaten, or humorous insults like Menedemus' 'dolt, blockhead, jackass, dimwit'. See how many other types of humour you can come up with.

6   What types of modern comedy (be it television, film or theatrical comedy) are closest in spirit or subject-matter to the Roman comedy that you have sampled?

7   Imagine that you were directing a production of a play by Plautus or Terence. What might you do to bring it to life for a modern audience?

Other writers of comedy

Plautus and Terence are the only writers of *fabulae palliatae* whose plays have survived, but there were many others. Livius Andronicus, the first Latin playwright (see **1.1**), wrote both comedies and tragedies, as did the poets Naevius and Ennius (see chapter 5). Caecilius, who flourished between Plautus and Terence, was considered by some ancient critics to be the greatest of the comic playwrights. We have a **fragment** of one of his plays in which a husband complains, in a style reminiscent of Plautus, about a wife with a big dowry. In the second century BC another comic genre called the ***fabula togata*** developed. These plays were set in Italy: hence the characters wore the Roman *toga* rather than the Greek *pallium*. After the second century BC, however, very few new *fabulae palliatae* or *fabulae togatae* appear to have been written, and by the first century AD they seem to have been seldom performed, replaced by mime and pantomime performances.

Much later, in the second half of the fourth century AD, an author from Gaul (modern France) wrote a play called *Querolus* (*The Complainer*), also called *The Pot of Gold* (*Aulularia*). This play, written in prose for performance at private dinner parties, is the only Roman comedy to survive in its entirety besides the plays of Plautus and Terence. It shares its title and some character names with Plautus' *The Pot of Gold* but has a completely different plot, in which a parasite tries to trick a young man (the always complaining Querolus) out of a pot of gold left him by his father. The parasite is caught and Querolus gets the gold.

5 Tragedy in the Roman Republic

Roman audiences of Plautus and Terence's day enjoyed tragic as well as comic drama. Several playwrights adapted Athenian tragedies, including those of the great fifth-century playwrights Aeschylus, Sophocles and Euripides, for the Roman stage. None of these plays have survived in their entirety, but we possess many fragments, passages of the tragedies quoted by later Latin authors whose works have survived.

Quintus Ennius (239–169 BC) was probably the greatest Latin poet before the first century BC. Unfortunately, none of his works have survived except in passages quoted by later authors. Originally from southern Italy, he was brought to Rome by the Roman statesman Marcus Porcius Cato in 204 BC. He became friendly with many of Rome's leading citizens, teaching their sons and, on occasion, writing poems in their honour. He wrote comedies, tragedies, philosophical and topical poems and, most notably, the *Annales*, an epic history of Rome in verse from its beginnings up to his own day.

> Here is the opening of Ennius' Latin adaptation of Euripides' *Medea* (253–61 Warmington).

5.1 NURSE I wish the fir planks had never fallen to the earth, cut by axes in the **Pelian** grove, and that therefore no prelude had been made for beginning the ship, which is now called by the name *Argo* because chosen **Argive** men, carried in it, sought the **golden ram's fleece from the Colchians** through trickery, at the command of King Pelias. For if that had not happened my mistress Medea would never have gone away from home, straying off course with her heart sick, wounded by savage love.

Pelian on Mount Pelion, in northern Greece (see map on p. x).

Argive here Argive means Greek.

golden ram's fleece from the Colchians Jason was ordered by his uncle, King Pelias, to acquire the Golden Fleece from Colchis, on the south-eastern shore of the Black Sea. He had the ship *Argo* built, with which he and a large group of Greek heroes sailed to Colchis. Once there, Jason acquired the fleece with the help of Medea, the daughter of the king. She left home with Jason and married him. Now, however, Jason has abandoned Medea for a Greek wife. In the course of the play Medea will take revenge by killing Jason's new bride and her father as well as her own children by Jason.

> **Translation and adaptation**
>
> Like their contemporaries Plautus and Terence, the Roman tragic playwrights adapted their plays from Greek dramas. Sometimes they kept quite close to their originals. Elsewhere they made radical changes. Here is a translation of the opening lines of Euripides' *Medea*, also spoken by Medea's nurse (1–8).
>
> > *I wish the ship Argo had never flown through the dark rocks of the Symplegades to the land of the Colchians, and that the pine had never fallen, cut in the vales of Mount Pelion, and furnished oars for the hands of the best men, who went after the Golden Fleece for Pelias. For then my mistress, Medea, would not have sailed away to the towers of the Iolchian land, struck in her heart with love for Jason.*
>
> - Compare this passage to **5.1**. What kinds of changes has Ennius made?

Ennius' *Iphigenia*, probably an adaptation of Euripides' *Iphigenia at Aulis*, described how the Greek general Agamemnon sacrificed his daughter, Iphigenia, in order to get the gods to change the direction of the winds so that his fleet could sail to Troy. Here a chorus of soldiers complains because the hostile winds have stranded them at Aulis (see map on p. x), where the Greek forces had gathered, and they have nothing to do (241–8 Warmington).

5.2 CHORUS   The one who doesn't know how to handle leisure, when he has leisure, has more **work when he's at leisure** than he has when he's working. For when a task has been set out for someone to do, he does it with no work, he's eager to do it, and in doing it he delights his mind and his soul. But when he's in leisurely leisure his soul is troubled and doesn't know what it wants. That's just the bind we are in. Look, we're neither at peace nor at war now. We go over here, then over there. When we've gone over there, we want to go somewhere else. Our minds wander in uncertainty. We're only half alive.

Ennius' nephew, Marcus Pacuvius (*c.* 220–*c.* 130 BC), was also a successful writer of tragedies. In his play *Teucer* (probably based on a lost play of Sophocles with the same name), a character reports how the Greek fleet, returning from Troy, was beset by a storm (353–62 Warmington).

5.3   Happy at setting out, we watch the frolicking fish, and we never get tired of gazing at them. Meanwhile, at just about sunset, the sea begins to rise up roughly, the shadows are doubled, the blackness of night and of storm clouds blinds us.

---

work when he's at leisure   Ennius is playing here with the Latin words *otium* ('leisure') and *negotium* ('not leisure' or 'work').

Flames flash amid the clouds, the sky trembles with thunder. Hail, mixed with abundant rain, falls suddenly, headlong. Winds break forth from all directions, fierce whirlwinds arise, the sea boils with the tempest …

Swiftly, in the turbulent storm, the waves call up the ship back and forth, headlong, and hurl it up and cast it down in and out of their laps.

> 1 How would you describe Pacuvius' use of language in this scene?
> 2 It is hard to reconstruct the plays as a whole from the few snippets that survive. Based on this passage, though, how do you think this narrative might unfold? If you had to speculate what will happen next, what might you guess about the circumstances in which the narrator tells his story here?

The last of the great tragedians of the Roman Republic was Lucius Accius (170–c. 86 BC). In his *Myrmidons*, perhaps modelled on the *Myrmidons* of Aeschylus, Achilles defends his refusal to fight after the commander-in-chief Agamemnon has insulted him. The play thus offers a moment from Homer's *Iliad*. Surprisingly, Achilles sounds more like a philosopher than a warrior here as he lectures his fellow soldier Antilochus about verbal distinctions. The fragment reflects the interest of both Greek and Roman tragedy in the difficulty of determining what actions are right or wrong (452–7 Warmington).

5.4 ACHILLES You, **Antilochus**, claim that this is obstinacy, but I say it is determination, a quality I want to possess. I am very willing to be called determined, but I don't care at all to be called obstinate. Determination is a quality of the brave; fools have obstinacy. You attribute to me what is blameworthy and refuse to give me credit for what is praiseworthy.

This terracotta relief from the first century BC probably shows a performance of Accius' *Astyanax*. Troy has fallen to the Greeks, and Ulysses (right) demands Astyanax, the son of Hector, from his mother Andromache (centre), so that he can throw him off the walls of the city (the scene also occurs in Euripides' *The Trojan Women*). The smaller figures on the left are less important characters, perhaps the chorus. Note the expressive gestures, tragic masks and elaborate *scaenae frons*: the horse and rider at the top are part of its decoration. All the actors wear platform shoes called *cothurni*, which were standard for tragic performances. Children appear as non-speaking characters in several Greek and Roman tragedies. Astyanax here wears a kind of pointed cap (the 'Phrygian hat') that was often associated with people who lived near Troy.

Antilochus a leading Greek warrior at Troy, son of the old warrior Nestor.

5.5

> 1. What do you notice about the way the characters of Roman tragedy express themselves? Do they use succinct expressions, or extra words? Do they speak literally or metaphorically? Is the train of thought easy or difficult to follow? What effect do you think the characters' mode of expression would have on audiences?
> 2. Accius' Achilles (5.4) and the chorus of Ennius' *Iphigenia* (5.2) both deliver generalizations about human life. Such generalizations were a common feature of Roman tragedy. What purpose might they have served?
> 3. What does the relief in 5.5 suggest about how Roman tragedy was performed?
> 4. Judging from these fragments and the relief, in what ways does Roman tragedy appear to be similar to serious drama (theatrical, film or television) with which you are familiar? In what ways is it different?

Besides adapting Greek tragedies, Roman tragic poets also created a new dramatic genre with plots derived from Roman history. These plays were called **fabulae praetextae** after the *praetexta*, a toga with a purple border worn by Roman magistrates. Gnaeus Naevius (late third century BC) is credited with the first two *fabulae praetextae*: a play called *Romulus* or *The Wolf*, about the founding of Rome, and one called *Clastidium*, about a victory of the Roman general Marcus Claudius Marcellus in 222 BC. Ennius, Pacuvius and Accius also wrote *fabulae praetextae*.

> Accius' *Brutus* was about the expulsion of Rome's last king, Tarquinius Superbus, in 509 BC. In it Tarquinius consults a seer about a dream he has had. The dream refers to Lucius Junius Brutus, whose brother was murdered by Tarquinius. Brutus protected himself by pretending to be dimwitted until he found an opportunity to lead a successful rebellion against Tarquinius (17–38 Warmington).

5.6   TARQUINIUS When night came and I gave my body over to rest, soothing my weary limbs with sleep, in my **dreams** I saw a shepherd driving towards me a wool-bearing flock of exceptional beauty. From that flock I chose two rams, brothers, and I sacrificed the more splendid of the two. Then the ram's brother exerted himself with his horns and rammed me, and with that blow I was thrown down. And while I was lying there on my back, stretched out on the ground, severely wounded, I saw in the sky a truly great and marvellous thing: the flaming, beaming disk of the sun melted away towards the right in a new course.

   SEER King, it is no wonder if the things in life that men accomplish, think about, worry over, see, do and plan while they are awake also happen in sleep. But in a matter as great as this the gods are certainly not presenting strange things without reason. Therefore be careful that the one you believe is unintelligent as a sheep doesn't in fact have a soul excellently fortified with wisdom and drive you from your kingdom. For what was shown to you regarding the sun, that shows that conditions in Rome will change very soon. May these things turn out well for the Roman people! As to the fact that the most powerful star took its course from **left to right**, this is the most favourable sign that Rome will be the most powerful state.

> 1 Some Romans may have learned parts of their history from *fabulae praetextae*. How does this compare with the role of history in modern dramatic genres?
>
> 2 Tarquinius reports his dream in unaccompanied iambic senarii (see p. 36), but the seer sings in an accompanied metre. Why do you think Accius made these metrical and musical choices?

Both tragedies set in Greece and *fabulae praetextae* continued to be performed regularly in the first century BC. Cicero reveals how actors and audience members could read contemporary significance into verses from tragedy when he reports how the actor Aesopus performed verses by Ennius and Accius during a time when Cicero had been driven into exile (58–57 BC) (*Speech for Sestius* 120–3).

---

dreams a very common feature of Greek and Roman drama, often playing an important role in the plot: compare Philolaches' alleged dream in Plautus' *The Haunted House* (**3.5**).

left to right in omens the Romans considered the left inauspicious and the right auspicious.

5.7 For he [Aesopus] expressed the genius of the greatest poet not only with his skill, but also with his grief. How powerfully he said that I had stood with you, and pointed out all the classes, saying:

'**Who helped and upheld the state** with a sure purpose and stood with the **Achaeans**.'

He was called back by all for an encore of the words:

'**When things were in doubt** he would not hesitate to offer his life, nor did he spare his head.'

What shouts accompanied his performance of these words, when, with the gestures left out, the words of the poet and the zeal of the actor and the anticipation of my return were applauded:

'**The greatest friend** in the greatest war.'

The actor himself, out of friendship for me, added the words, 'and endowed with the greatest character', and perhaps people approved of that addition because of some longing for me. Then how the Roman people groaned when a little later in the same play the same actor performed those words:

'**O father...**'

He considered that I, I, should be mourned while absent like a father. ... With what weeping about the burning and destruction of my property, when he bemoaned the father driven into exile and the fatherland oppressed, did he act out the home burned and destroyed, in such a way that, when he had shown the previous good fortune and had turned to the audience at the line,

'**I saw all these things go up in flames**',

he excited weeping even in those who hate and envy me! By the immortal gods! And then? How the same actor said the following words! ...

Who helped and upheld the state ... When things were in doubt ... The greatest friend ... these verses probably come from Ennius' *Andromache*, which showed events after the fall of Troy. They may have been spoken by Ulysses about Achilles, whose ghost appeared after Troy fell and demanded that the Greeks sacrifice Polyxena, the daughter of Priam, to him.

Achaeans Greeks.

O father ... I saw all these things go up in flames these are verses from Ennius' *Andromache* in which Andromache laments the destruction of Troy. Cicero's house was condemned and destroyed while he was in exile.

'**O ungrateful Achaeans**, indifferent Greeks, forgetful of the kindness you have received …'

The most learned poet wrote that on my behalf, and the actor – the bravest actor, not only the best – performed that about me, when he pointed out all the classes and accused the senate, the *equites*, the entire Roman people:

'**You allow him to be in exile**, you let him be driven out, you endure that he has been banished! …'

The actor wept for my sufferings so many times, when he acted out my case in such a mournful way, that that famous voice of his was blocked by tears… In the *Brutus* I was called upon by name: the words

'**Tullius**, who had established liberty for the citizens'

were encored a thousand times.

123

> 1 What does Aesopus' ability to apply verses from Ennius' and Accius' plays to the political situation of his own day suggest about how Roman audiences responded to plays and about the political significance of theatrical performances? Can you think of modern analogies for such political allusions in dramatic performances?
>
> 2 What does this passage reveal about the acting style of Roman tragic actors?

> **The fragments of Roman tragedy**
>
> The passages quoted in this chapter are among the longest fragments of Roman tragedy that survive. They are primarily from oratorical and philosophical texts, in which authors like Cicero cite verses from tragedy to support their points. Most fragments from Roman tragedy, however, are much shorter passages used by grammarians to demonstrate points of grammar or semantics. The only surviving fragment from Livius Andronicus' *Andromeda*, for example, is in the grammarian Nonius (62.15):
>
> > *Confluences are places into which various streams flow together. Livius writes in his* Andromeda: *'Where the confluences flood the whole plain with their coming together.'*
>
> As a result, it is often very difficult to tell the plots of Roman tragedies, beyond knowing the basic outline of the myth from other sources.

O ungrateful Achaeans … You allow him to be in exile … these verses are from Accius' *Eurysaces*. Eurysaces was the son of Ajax. Originally the lines probably referred either to Ajax's father Telamon or his brother Teucer, both of whom were driven into exile.

equites Rome's second highest social class (the word is sometimes translated 'knights'). *Equites* were often as wealthy as senators but were not usually involved in politics.

Tullius … this is a verse from Accius' *Brutus*, in which someone refers to Servius Tullius, the king of Rome who was murdered when Tarquinius Superbus usurped the throne. Because Cicero's full name is Marcus Tullius Cicero, Aesopus and the spectators interpreted the verse as a reference to Cicero.

6 Mime

The word 'mime' (*mimus*, from Greek *mimos* meaning 'imitator') did not mean to the Romans what it usually means to us. Mime in ancient Rome was not a performance relying on movement without spoken or sung words, but a type of comic play. Mime therefore shared many features with the types of comedy discussed in chapters 2–4, the *fabula palliata* and the *fabula togata*. Like those genres, it included a great deal of farce, a mixture of spoken and sung dialogue, and a significant Saturnalian element. It differed from *palliatae* and *togatae*, however, in several very important respects:

1. Most mimes were probably quite short, with very simple plots: they might better be described as skits than plays.
2. Women, barred from performing in the other Roman theatrical genres, could perform in mimes.
3. Both actors and actresses in mime performed without masks.
4. Mime actors often wore a kind of shawl called a *ricinium* and no shoes (hence one name for a mime actor was *planipes*, meaning 'flatfoot').
5. Mime included a greater element of dance than did *palliatae* and *togatae*.
6. Mime appears to have allowed a considerably higher level of bawdy and even obscene humour than was usual in *palliatae* or *togatae*.
7. Mime included much more improvisation than the other genres: some performances occurred without a formal script, as actors improvised on some basic scenario. Even the mimes that had a script probably included much spontaneous creation within performance.

Greece had a long tradition of mime. Roman mime appears to have developed from a mixture of this tradition with farcical, improvisatory Italian forms of theatre such as the Atellan plays and the Fescennine verses, both discussed in chapter 1. Mime was an official part of at least some theatrical *ludi* as early as the late third century BC (see **6.9**). Early on it became the standard form of theatrical entertainment at the **Ludi Florales** held in the spring in honour of Flora, a vegetation goddess. Mimes were also often performed at private dinner parties and may have been a common form of street entertainment. The popularity of mime continued to increase throughout the last centuries of the Republic, and by the time of the Empire mime, along with pantomime (see chapter 7), had become the most popular form of theatrical entertainment in Rome, practically driving the *palliata* and the *togata* from the stage.

As is the case with Republican tragedy and the *fabula togata*, no full plays of Roman mime have survived. Our most extensive fragments of Roman mimes are in Greek and are from Roman Egypt, where the dryness of the climate has preserved the **papyrus** on which they were written.

The following anonymous mime text is probably a performance script from the second century AD. It appears to be a parody of a tragedy by Euripides called *Iphigenia among the Taurians*. In Euripides' play Iphigenia serves as a priestess for a barbarian king. Her brother Orestes arrives at the kingdom with his friend Pylades, fleeing from the Furies after he killed his mother Clytemnestra. Brother, sister and friend escape from the Taurians' barbarian king by means of a deception. The mime is set in India, and the sister is named Charition. In this fragment, probably from the end of the mime, brother, sister and friend escape. These scenes thus parody not only Euripides' *Iphigenia among the Taurians*, but also other tragedies (e.g. Euripides' *Helen*) and satyr plays (e.g. Euripides' *Cyclops*) in which characters escape from danger through trickery. The mime also echoes the ninth book of Homer's *Odyssey*, in which Odysseus and his men escape from the Cyclops by getting him drunk. The papyrus is in a poor state of preservation and includes some obscure symbols, so some of what follows is guesswork (*Oxyrhynchus Papyri* 3.413, 'Charition').

6.1
ATTENDANT	Lady Charition, rejoice with me! I've escaped!	
CHARITION	The gods are great.	
BUFFOON	What do you mean gods, you fool? (***He farts***.)	
CHARITION	Shut up, you.	5
ATTENDANT	Wait for me here. I will go and anchor the ship.	
CHARITION	Yes, go. Look: the **women** are here again, back from their hunt.	10
BUFFOON	Wow! What long bows they've got!	
WOMAN 1	**Kraunou**.	

Attendant in the papyrus the characters are for the most part not named, but are identified only with single letters. Here and in what follows I have provided what I think are the most likely identifications from what is said in the dialogue.

Buffoon this character may be meant as a parody of Pylades, the friend who accompanies Orestes in Euripides' play.

He farts this is one of many directions in the papyrus regarding what sounds are to be produced in performance. This direction is clear: it is the Greek word *pordē* (fart; I have assumed that the Buffoon himself does the farting). The other directions, however, are abbreviations or symbols, and it is not always clear what sounds they suggest.

women this chorus of Indian women is presumably modelled on the mythical Amazons, women who were both hunters and warriors.

Kraunou throughout the fragment the author of the mime uses nonsense words to represent the words of the Indians. Some correspondences have been noted between these nonsense words and various Indian languages (Dravidian, Kanarese and Sanskrit), but the correspondences may be coincidences. Though there was a good deal of trade between India and the Roman empire, most Romans knew very little of India, and India often serves in Roman literature as the quintessential exotic foreign land.

WOMAN 2	Lalle.
WOMAN 3	Laitalianta **lalle ab** […] **aigm** […]
WOMAN 4	Kotakos anab[…]iosara.
BUFFOON	Greetings! (*crotala*)
ALL THE WOMEN	Laspathia. (*crotala*)
BUFFOON	Lady, help me!
CHARITION	Alemaka. (*crotala*)
ALL THE WOMEN	Alemaka.
BUFFOON	By Athena, there's **no** […] among us.
CHARITION	You poor fool! They thought you were an enemy and nearly shot you!
BUFFOON	I'm always in trouble. Do you want me to drive them to the river **Psolichos** too?
CHARITION	If you want.

(*crash on the tympanum*; *the Buffoon farts*)

WOMEN	**Minei**.
ATTENDANT	Lady Charition, I see the beginning of a wind that will let us escape across the Indian Ocean. Go inside and get your things and carry off whatever you can of the votive offerings to the goddess.
CHARITION	Control yourself! Those who need salvation from the gods should not seek it with temple robbery. Do you think they will listen to appeals for mercy from wrongdoers?
BUFFOON	Don't you touch them. I'll grab them.
ATTENDANT	Well then, you get your own things.
CHARITION	I don't need them. All I need is to see my father's face.
ATTENDANT	OK, go in. You (*to Buffoon*): prepare some food and give them some rather strong wine. Here they come […] [*gap in the text*]
BUFFOON	I think they're piglets' daughters, and I'll drive them away too.

(*crash on the tympanum*; *the Buffoon farts*)

---

lalle ab […] aigm […]   numerous parts of the text have been lost owing to damage to the papyrus, including part of this speech.

crotala   two curved lines appear in the papyrus here and elsewhere. They probably indicate some kind of sound from a percussion instrument, perhaps the **scabillum** (see p. 109) or, as I have proposed here (following earlier editors), clapping on a pair of hand-clappers called **crotala** (see **6.13**).

no […]   the text of the papyrus is unintelligible here.

Psolichos   it is not clear to what river the Buffoon refers.

crash on the tympanum   the papyrus here and elsewhere has the abbreviation 'T', which probably stands for **tympanum**, a flat round drum, similar to a tambourine, but without the brass discs that make a tambourine jingle.

Minei   presumably the chorus of women flees the stage at this point.

ANOTHER GROUP OF WOMEN	Ai arminthi.	45

(*crotala;* **sound from the tibia**; *crash on the tympanum*)

BUFFOON	They've fled to the Psolichos river too.
CHARITION'S BROTHER	Yes, they have. But **let's try to get out of here** […]
CHARITION	If they come here, prepare unmixed wine for them. 55
BUFFOON	What if they don't want to drink?
BROTHER	Don't be silly. In these places you can't buy wine. So it follows that if they get a hold of such a thing they'll want it because it's unfamiliar, and they'll drink it up **unmixed**. 60
BUFFOON	I'll prepare it for them, dregs and all.
BROTHER	Here they are, all bathed, **with** […]

(*crash from tympanum; two moderately loud crashes from tympanum; another crash from tympanum*)

KING	Brathis.
INDIANS	Bratheis.
BUFFOON	What are they saying?
BROTHER	He says, let us draw lots for our portions.
BUFFOON	Yes, let's do that. 65

(*crash from tympanum*)

KING	Stoukepairomellokoroke.
BUFFOON	Get out of here, damn you!
KING	Brathie.

(*crotala; crash from tympanum*)

KING	Bere konzei damun petrekio paktei kortames bere ialero depomenzi petrekio damut kinze paksei zebes lolo bia bradis kottos. 70
INDIANS	Kottos.
BUFFOON	May *kottos* kick you in the butt!
KING	Zopit.

(*crash from tympanum*)

---

sound from the tibia   here and elsewhere the papyrus includes a dash (–). I have followed earlier editors in guessing that this symbol represents a flourish played by the *tibia* player.

let's try to get out of here   after these words the earlier dialogue about taking the goddess' votive offerings is repeated almost verbatim. I have assumed that this is an example of a performance doublet, in which versions of the text used in two different performances have been preserved in the papyrus. Such performance doublets are common in manuscripts of ancient drama.

unmixed   Greeks and Romans usually mixed their wine with water. Drinking wine undiluted was considered typical of barbarians.

with […]   again, part of the text is missing from the papyrus.

BUFFOON	What are they saying?	
BROTHER	Quick. Give them something to drink.	
BUFFOON	So you don't want to talk then? Good day. Hello.	

(*crotala; crash from tympanum*)

KING	Zeisoukormosede.	

(*crash from tympanum*)

BUFFOON	Ah, not while I can help it.	
BROTHER	It's watery. Put in some wine.	75

(*big crash from tympanum*)

INDIAN 1	Skalmakatabapteiragoumi.	
INDIAN 2	Tougoummi. (*crotala*) Nekelekethro.	
INDIAN 1	Eitoubelletra choupteragoumi.	
BUFFOON	Hey! (*crotala*) No funny business. Stop that! (*crash from tympanum; crotala*) Hey! (*crotala*) What are you doing?	
INDIAN 2	Trachountermana.	
INDIAN 1	Boullitikaloumbai platagoulda. (*crotala*) Bi […] apuleukasar. (*crash from tympanum*)	80
KING	Chorbonorbothorba […]	
INDIANS	Toumionaxizdespit platagoulda. (*crotala*) Bi […] seosarachis.	

(*crash from tympanum*)

KING	[…] orado. (*crotala*) Satur.	

(*crash from tympanum*)

KING	Ouamesaresumpsaradara. (*crotala*) Ei. (*crotala*) Ia. (*crotala*) Da […]	
BUFFOON	Martha. (*crotala*) Marithouma edmaimai. (*crotala*) Maitho … Thamouna martha. (*crotala*) Marithouma. (*crash from tympanum*) […] tun.	85
KING	Malpiniakouroukoukoubi. (*crotala; sound from tibia*) Karako […] ra.	
INDIANS	Aba.	
KING	Zabede. (*crotala; sound from tibia*) Zabiligidoumba.	
INDIANS	Aba oun […]	
KING	Panoumbretikatemanouambretououeni.	90
INDIANS	Panoumbretikatemanouambretououeni. Parakoumbretikatemanouambretououeni. Olusadizapardapiskoupiskateman. (*crotala*) Areiman […] ridaou. (*crotala; sound from tibia*) Oupatei … a. (*crotala; sound from tibia; five crashes from tympanum*)	
KING	Goddess **Selene**, I lead a barbaric, boundless dance, stepping forward in rhythm with a wild, barbaric step. Leading men of	95

Selene goddess of the moon.

India, by the mystic sounds […] (*crotala*) Give […] a frenzied **Seric** step, each on your own, […]

(*loud crash from tympanum*; **additional percussion**)

INDIANS	Orkis […]	
BUFFOON	What are they saying now?	100
BROTHER	He says, dance.	
BUFFOON	They're just like real men in all they do!	

(*crash from tympanum*; *Buffoon farts*)

BROTHER   Lift him up and bind him with the sacred belts.

(*loud crash from tympanum*)

Finale

BUFFOON	Now they're all weighed down with wine.	
BROTHER	Well done. Charition, come out here.	
CHARITION	Come here, brother, quickly. Is everything ready?	105
BROTHER	Yes. The ship lies at anchor right nearby. What are you all waiting for? Helmsman, bring the ship over here right away.	
CAPTAIN	If I give the order first […]	
BUFFOON	Are you chattering again, you bungler? Let's leave him behind to kiss the ship's butt.	
BROTHER	Are you all inside?	
ALL	We are.	
CHARITION	Oh poor me, such things I've suffered! I am overcome by a great trembling. Dear goddess, look kindly upon us. Save your servant!	110

> 1 What can you surmise from the text here about the staging of this mime? What personnel were involved? What kind of movement appears to have occurred on stage? What was the musical accompaniment like, and what might have been the effect of all the musical interjections?
>
> 2 What do you think of the content of this mime fragment? Do you see analogies for this kind of plot in any modern genres of entertainment?
>
> 3 How does the humour of this mime fragment work?
>
> 4 This fragment offers both very crude jokes and sophisticated literary parody. What does that combination suggest about mime and its audience?
>
> 5 Why do you think the mime includes such extensive passages of Indian-sounding nonsense words? When the brother translates, do you think he really understands what the Indians are saying, or is he just making things up?

Seric   the meaning of this term is not clear. The word might suggest mystic sounds associated with the religious ritual being performed here.

additional percussion   here the papyrus includes the word *krousis*, which means 'striking'.

We know the names of very few Roman mime authors: most mimes appear to have relied entirely on improvisation or oral transmission, and many of the fragments we have are, like the fragment in **6.1**, anonymous. We do know of two famous authors of mime from the first century BC, however: Publilius Syrus and Decimus Laberius. The fourth-century AD writer Macrobius records a story that Julius Caesar made Laberius compete with Syrus on stage (*Conversations at the Saturnalia* 2.7.2, 4–6, 7–9).

6.2 Laberius was a Roman *eques* with a sharp and free-speaking tongue. Caesar, offering 500,000 *sestertii*, invited him to go on the stage himself and act in the mimes that he was continually writing. **But Caesar's power** was such that even if he 'begged', let alone 'invited', he could not be refused … In his performance Laberius avenged himself as much as he was able. He put on the costume of a Syrian and, acting as if he were escaping after being flogged, he shouted, 'Oh Romans, we are losing our liberty.' A little afterwards he added, 'He whom many fear must also be afraid.' At these words everyone there turned their eyes and faces to Caesar alone, noting that this biting wit was aimed at his lack of self-restraint. Because of this Caesar turned his favour to Publilius.

This Publilius, Syrian by birth, was brought as a boy to his master's patron. He won the patron's favour not less by his wit and his talent than by his beauty … He was freed and educated with great care. When he was writing mimes and had begun to perform to great acclaim in the towns of Italy, he was brought to Rome for the games of Caesar, and he called together all those who at that time had written for the stage, challenging them to present their works in competition against his. No one refused, and he defeated them all, even Laberius. So Caesar smiled and said, 'Laberius, I favoured you, but Syrus beat you just the same.' And at once he gave Syrus the palm of victory and gave Laberius a **golden ring worth 500,000 sestertii**. As Laberius was **returning to his seat**, Publilius said to him,

---

eques a member of the *equites* class.

But Caesar's power the event allegedly occurred during Caesar's dictatorship (49–44 BC). Although the request to perform was framed as a mere invitation, Laberius could not refuse, as Caesar had absolute power in Rome at the time. Because actors were subject to *infamia*, by performing on the stage Laberius would lose his status as an *eques*.

golden ring worth 500,000 sestertii 500,000 *sestertii* was the amount of property one had to possess in order to belong to the class of *equites*. Through the gift Caesar thus restored to Laberius the status he had lost by appearing on the stage.

returning to his seat by this time *equites* had special seats reserved for them near the front of the theatre, behind the senators.

'Support as a spectator the one you competed with as a writer.' But Laberius, at the next opportunity, inserted these words into a new mime: 9

> No one is able to be first all the time. You have come to the highest level of fame, but it will be hard for you to stay there, and you will fall more quickly than you rose. I fell, and the one who follows will fall. Glory belongs to the people.

> 1 What does this story suggest about the relationship between those who wrote and performed in mime and those in power?
> 2 What does the story suggest about interactions between authors of mime?
> 3 Many have doubted the veracity of this story. What do you think?

A number of titles of mimes have been preserved. They give an idea of the wide range of areas that could be the subject of mimes. Here are some of them (from Bonaria).

6.3 *The Bean, Just Now a Pauper But Suddenly Rich, Hot Springs, The Augur, The Prison, The Play about the Puppy, The Fireman, The Flatterer, The Painter, The Festival of the Crossroads, The Hamper, The Fuller, The Courtesan, Speaking Far and Wide, The Wedding, Poverty, The Fisherman, The Rope-Dealer, The Head of the Salt Works, The Bull, The Maiden, The Tree-Trimmers, The Ghost, The People from Catina.*

> 1 What do these titles suggest about some possible subjects and plots of mimes?
> 2 How useful do you think titles are in revealing what a dramatic work is about? What do we learn about modern films, plays and television shows from their titles?

Mimes were known for the extent to which they pushed the limits of acceptable behaviour. One of the most popular varieties of mime appears to have been the adultery mime, in which a woman and her lover, surprised by the woman's husband, devise various ways of hiding the lover. The poet Horace (65–8 BC) appears to describe an adultery mime as he admonishes his readers to avoid affairs with married women (*Satires* 2.7.59–61).

Augur   an official who interpreted signs sent by the gods through natural phenomena such as the flight-patterns of birds.

Festival of the Crossroads   the *Compitalia*, an annual festival that celebrated minor divinities who watched over crossroads.

Fuller   someone who laundered and dyed clothes.

Catina   a town in Sicily.

6.4 Bent over, you would touch your head to your knees, closed up shamefully in a chest, where the mistress of the house, conscious of her wrongdoing, has put you.

> Valerius Maximus, writing in the first century AD, notes that the people of Marseilles objected to the sexual content of mimes (*Memorable Words and Deeds* 2.6.7b).

6.5 The same city [Marseilles] is the most severe protector of stern morality. It does not allow mime performers any approach to its stage, because most of their plots include adultery. They don't want the habit of watching such things to lead to licence in imitating them.

> Elsewhere Valerius Maximus reveals that sometimes mimes could feature naked actresses (*Memorable Words and Deeds* 2.10.8).

6.6 When **Marcus Porcius Cato** was in the audience at the *Ludi Florales*, which the **aedile Messius** was putting on, the crowd was ashamed to demand that the mime actresses perform naked. When Cato learned this from his dear friend Favonius, who was sitting with him, he left the theatre, so that his presence would not interfere with the customary progress of the show. As he was leaving the people gave him loud applause and **brought the old mode of comedy back** to the stage, confessing that they attributed more dignity to him alone than they demanded for themselves all together.

> In spite of these passages, however, it does not appear that mimes were inevitably lascivious or immoral. Our evidence suggests that many adultery mimes ended with apprehension of the adulterers and legal retribution. The first-century AD philosopher and playwright Seneca (see chapter 8) reveals that some mimes contained criticism of luxury (*On the Brevity of Life* 12.8).

Marcus Porcius Cato   (95–46 BC) a leading senator during the last years of the Roman Republic who was known for his integrity and his stern loyalty to traditional Roman ideals.

aedile Messius   Rome had two sets of aediles. The curule aediles, as we saw in chapter 2, were responsible for the *Ludi Megalenses* and the *Ludi Romani*. The *Ludi Florales* (see p. 97) were held by another set of aediles known as the **plebeian** aediles. Messius was plebeian aedile in 55 BC.

brought the old mode of comedy back   that is, they allowed the actresses to remain clothed.

6.7 Go ahead and believe that the mime performers make up a lot in order to criticize luxury. No, by god, I say they pass over more things than they make up. In our time, with its talent for only luxury, such a great abundance of clever variations on unbelievable vices has come to the fore that now you could accuse the mimes of carelessly leaving them out.

> The most extensive remains of ancient mime in Latin are just under 700 moralizing quotations attributed to Publilius Syrus, which were culled from the plays and handed down as a collection. Here are a few.

6.8 Love your father, if he's fair. If he's not, put up with him. (8)

He who judges quickly hastens to repentance. (32)

You've done twice the favour, if you give of your own accord what somebody needs. (44)

It's worse to be despised than to be beaten. (102)

Beware of trusting your friend unless you have tested him with experience. (120)

The poor lack many things, the greedy everything. (236)

When you despise death, you have overcome all fears. (364)

Fortune makes foolish the one she wishes to destroy. (612)

When a fault is swiftly corrected, it is usually forgotten. (694)

> It should also be kept in mind that many mime performances had a religious role as part of *ludi*. The grammarian Sextus Pompeius Festus, who lived in the second century AD, describes an event from the early history of mime that demonstrates what the genre's religious importance could be (*On the Meaning of Words* 326 M = 436, 438 L).

6.9 **Verrius** in his fifth book … explains why the **parasites of Apollo** often say on the stage, 'It's OK: the old man is dancing.' He says they say this because **when Gaius Sulpicius and Gaius Fulvius were consuls**, when the **urban praetor** Marcus

---

Verrius Marcus Verrius Flaccus (c. 55 BC? – c. AD 20?), the grammarian whose work Festus reworked to produce his lexicon. Verrius' own work has been lost.

parasites of Apollo an organization of actors, who considered the god Apollo their patron.

when Gaius Sulpicius and Gaius Fulvius were consuls 211 BC.

urban praetor urban **praetors** were responsible for the **Ludi Apollinares** in honour of the god Apollo.

Calpurnius Piso was holding games, they went suddenly to battle upon learning that **the enemy had arrived**. They won the battle, but when they returned to the theatre they were worried that in stopping the performance they had committed a sacrilege and would have to perform an *instauratio*. They found, however, that Gaius Pomponius, an old freed-slave mime performer, was still there, dancing to the accompaniment of the *tibia* player. The words they said in their relief that the ritual had not been interrupted are still celebrated today.

> Some mime performers were known for daring jokes about those in power, including not only the dictator Julius Caesar, as we saw in **6.2**, but also a number of Roman emperors. Suetonius, for example, reports brazenness on the part of the mime actor Favor (*Vespasian* 19.2).

6.10 Even at Vespasian's funeral the *archimimus* Favor, wearing Vespasian's mask and imitating his deeds and words, **as is customary**, openly asked those in charge of the funeral how much it cost. When they replied that it cost 100,000 *sestertii*, he shouted, '**give me the money** and throw me in the Tiber!'

> Mime was considered the most realistic of the ancient theatrical genres. In fact it could be brutally realistic. The poet Martial (late first century AD) describes a mime that included an actual execution of a criminal (*On the Spectacles* 9.1–10).

6.11 Just as **Prometheus**, bound to the **Scythian** rock, fed the bird large parts of his liver without stop, so did **Laureolus**, hanging on a real cross, offer his naked

---

the enemy had arrived the Carthaginian general Hannibal, who invaded Italy during the Second Punic War (218–201 BC), led his army to within sight of Rome in 211 BC.

instauratio when a performance that was part of a religious festival was not carried out properly, it would need to be repeated, through a practice called *instauratio*, in order to avoid the displeasure of the gods.

archimimus the leading actor in a troupe of mime performers. Mime performers could also be identified by other roles they played, including *secundus* (player of the second role) and *stupidus* (player of the fool).

as is customary it was standard practice at Roman aristocrats' funerals for an actor to wear a mask with the features of the dead person in the funeral procession.

give me the money Vespasian had a reputation for stinginess.

Prometheus because he tricked Jupiter and gave fire to humans, Prometheus was chained to a rock where an eagle continually fed upon his liver.

Scythian Scythia is a region on the north coast of the Black Sea including parts of modern Georgia, Ukraine and Russia.

Laureolus a criminal character in a mime, played by a real criminal.

innards to a bear from **Scotland**. His limbs, torn, still lived while their parts were dripping with blood, and in all his body there was no body. In the end he paid the penalty he deserved for cutting the throat of his parent or master with a sword, or for madly stealing the hidden gold from a temple, or for trying to set fire to Rome with savage torches.

> 1 What do passages 6.4–11 suggest about the subject-matter of mimes?
> 2 How does the content suggested in these passages compare with the content of the mime quoted in 6.1?
> 3 How does mime seem to compare with modern forms of entertainment with which you are familiar?
> 4 How do you think we can account for the apparently contradictory assessments of mime, i.e. that it appears to have been considered both a corrupting influence and a source of moral lessons?

> **Augustus' dying words**
>
> The first Roman emperor, Augustus (ruled 27 BC–AD 14), was fond of theatrical entertainments of all types (remember the theatrical motifs in his house: 2.13), including mime. Suetonius reports the emperor's last words (*Augustus* 99.1):
>
> > He gathered his friends together and asked, 'Do I seem to you to have acted well the mime of life?'

Cicero, arguing that a story told by his opponents in a law case is nonsensical, compares it to the finale of a mime (*Speech for Caelius* 65).

6.12   This is not the finale of a play, but of a mime, where there's no proper ending, but somebody escapes from the hands of his pursuers, then the *scabilla* clap, and the curtain is lifted up.

Scotland   just at the northernmost border of the Roman empire, Scotland was associated with the wild and the exotic.

The passage reveals two elements in the development of the Roman theatre that appear to have become central to the performance of mime by the time Cicero delivered this speech in 56 BC. One is a pair of wooden, or sometimes metal clappers, called a *scabillum*. A *tibia* player, and perhaps sometimes other musicians as well, would stomp upon the clappers to produce a loud percussive sound that helped instrumentalists and singers keep the rhythm. The mosaic in 6.13 gives a good sense of what a mime might have looked like, with a *tibia* player using a *scabillum* and an unmasked woman dancing with *crotala*.

6.13

Cicero also describes a curtain. Roman theatres originally had no curtains, but some time in the late second or early first century BC some Roman stages began to be built with a curtain called an **aulaeum** in front of them. The *aulaeum* was lowered into a slot at the front of the stage to reveal the performers behind it and then could be raised to conceal the performers and signal the end of a performance.

The poet Ovid (43 BC–AD 17) describes figures embroidered on the *aulaeum*, which became visible as the *aulaeum* was raised. He is telling a myth in which soldiers magically spring forth from the earth (*Metamorphoses* 3.111–14).

6.14 In just this way, when curtains are lifted up in the theatre during festivals, figures rise up. First they show their faces, then the rest of themselves little by little, until, brought out by a gently moving rope, they reveal themselves in their entirety and place their feet on the edge of the stage.

> Mime performances also sometimes featured hanging curtains (***siparia***) further back on the stage that served as backdrops or to conceal parts of the stage from view.

> 1 How does Cicero's description of the end of a mime in 6.12 compare with the end of the fragment quoted in 6.1?
> 2 How would the use of the *scabillum* have affected a mime performance?
> 3 How would the presence of a curtain change the nature of a theatrical performance?
> 4 In what ways, if at all, would the effect of a curtain that is lowered to reveal the stage and raised to conceal it be different from that of our theatre curtains, which either rise to reveal the stage or are opened and closed from the sides?

We know about a large number of mime performers from funerary inscriptions, including the following. A vast majority of the names of mimes in these inscriptions are Greek names: this may reflect a preponderance of Greek slaves or former slaves among mime performers, but it may also result from the fact that mime performers often used stage names, many of which were Greek.

6.15 Sleep well in death. Her heirs set this monument up for Claudia Hermiona, the leading **archimima** of her day.

(Corpus Inscriptionum Latinarum (CIL) 6.10106)

Protogenes, the delightful slave of Cloulius, rests here. As a mime he brought much joy to the people with his playful performances.

(CIL 1.1297)

I am Tiberius Claudius Pardalas, freedman of the emperor, a **parasite of Apollo**. I wish the best to you who read this. I was the fellow student of **Apolaustus the Elder** and the teacher of **Apolaustus the Younger**.

(CIL 11.7767)

---

archimima   note that a woman could be the leading performer in a mime troupe.

Apolaustus the Elder, Apolaustus the Younger   mime performers, like other members of the theatrical professions in Rome, often belonged to families of performers.

- What do these inscriptions reveal about mime performers and their own attitudes towards their profession?

> **Female mime performers**
>
> A number of female mime performers gained notoriety. The most famous such performer in the Roman Republic was the freed slave Cytheris. She was the mistress of the general Mark Antony, who supposedly once rode with her in a chariot drawn by lions. The orator Cicero, an enemy of Antony, mockingly called the general 'Cytherius'. But Cicero also reports in a letter to his friend Atticus how he was once very surprised to find Cytheris among the guests at a dinner he himself attended. Another lover of Cytheris was Cornelius Gallus (*c.* 70–27 BC), a pioneer Latin poet. According to Servius, a scholar of the fourth century AD, Cytheris herself performed in the theatre a poem by Rome's greatest poet, Virgil (70–19 BC), in which the poet portrayed Gallus lamenting that Cytheris had left him. Hundreds of years later the mime performer Theodora became the powerful wife of the emperor Justinian (ruled AD 527–65).

7 Pantomime

One of the most popular forms of entertainment from the time of the first Roman emperor on was a form of dance known as pantomime. Besides sometimes being performed in private homes, pantomime was the dominant type of theatrical production offered in the many large theatres found throughout the empire.

Theatres of the Empire

As we have seen, the first permanent theatre in the city of Rome was built in 55 BC by the general Gnaeus Pompey. The reconstruction in 7.1 shows what the theatre may have looked like.

Note the features we have already discussed in connection with earlier temporary theatres: a semicircular *cavea* for spectators attached to the high *scaenae frons*, in front of which was a raised stage. At the back of the *cavea*, at the highest level, was a temple to Venus Victrix, or Venus the Victory Bringer. Pompey allegedly included the temple to counter those who opposed the construction of a permanent theatre in Rome: the *cavea*, he could argue, was in fact a set of steps leading to the temple! Behind the *scaenae frons*, not shown in this reconstruction, was a large portico, at the other end of which was a building where the Roman Senate could meet: Julius Caesar was assassinated there in 44 BC.

7.1

112 *Pantomime*

Although the theatre no longer stands, its foundations have left a pattern covering hundreds of metres in the neighbourhood of Rome where it was built that is still visible in aerial photographs of the city. This is an aerial view of the part of Rome where the Theatre of Pompey once stood.

7.2
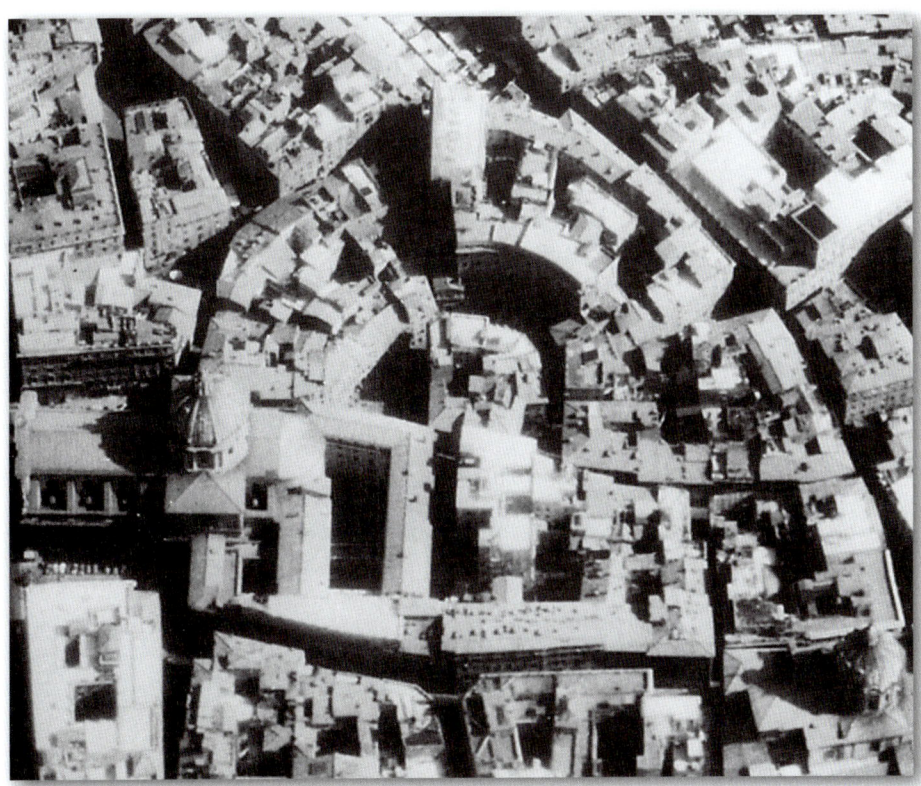

Other cities of Italy – Pompeii, for example – had permanent theatres well before 55 BC. Two more stone theatres, the **Theatre of Marcellus** and the **Theatre of Balbus**, were built in the city of Rome in the last decades BC. During the imperial period, any self-respecting city in the Roman empire had a theatre, so theatres are among the most common monuments that remain from the Roman world. Many theatres of the Empire were quite large, seating thousands of spectators, and some, like the theatre at Aspendos (7.3, second century AD) in what is now Turkey (see map on p. x), are very well preserved.

7.3

The Theatre at Aspendos.

Almost all Roman theatres were built to a very similar design, which included both similarities to and important differences from the Greek theatres that preceded them. Here are basic plans of a Greek theatre and of a typical Roman theatre (based on the plan of the theatre at Aspendos).

7.4

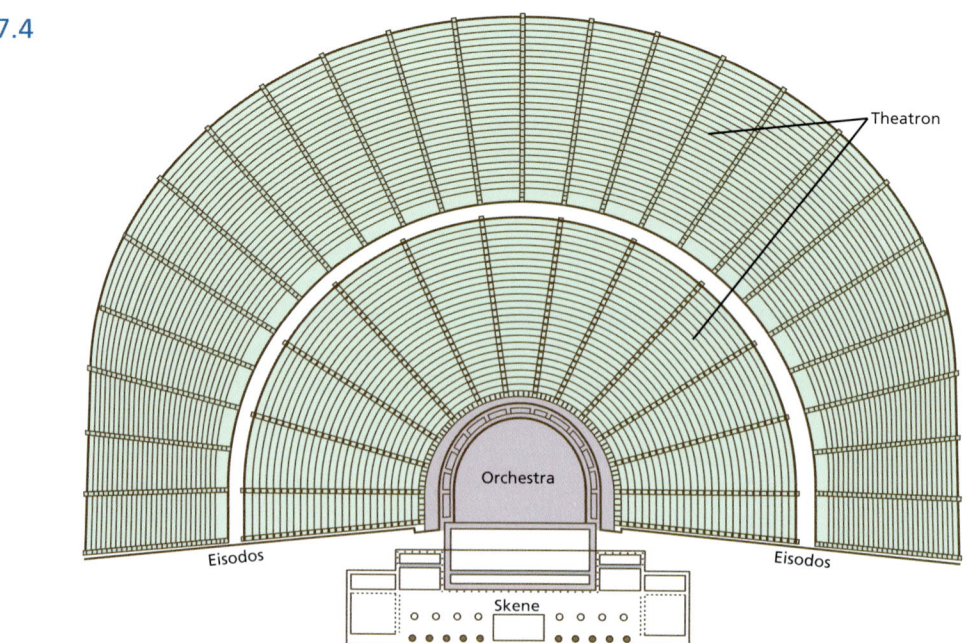

Plan of a Greek theatre.

114 *Pantomime*

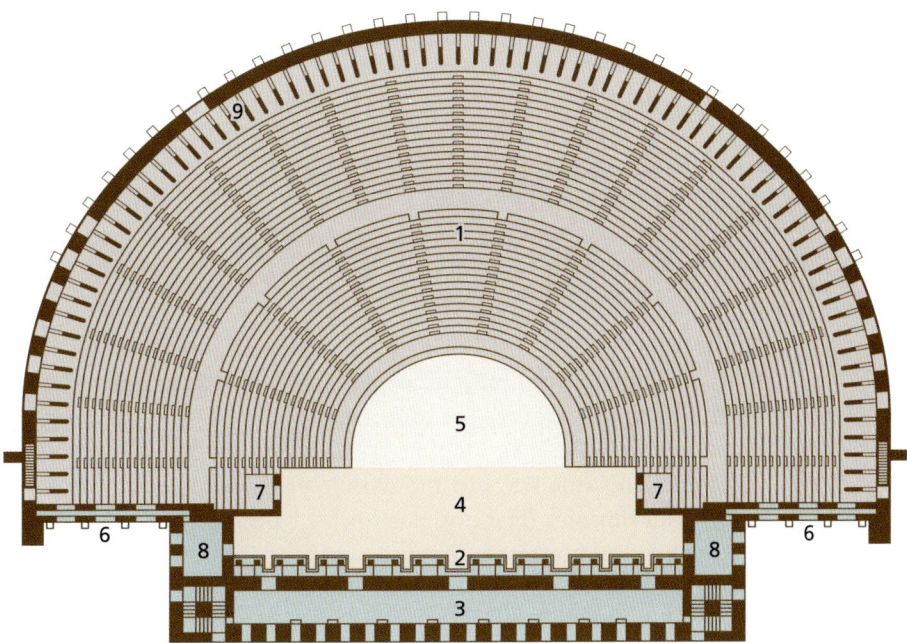

Plan of a Roman theatre.

Greek theatres usually consisted of seating carved out of the natural stone of a hillside and wrapping around a circular space. Roman theatres, on the other hand, were usually semicircular buildings constructed above the ground. The semicircular seating section, called the *cavea* (**7.4**, 1), was enclosed on one end by a high wall called the *scaenae frons* (2). Behind the *scaenae frons* was a narrow room, which in some theatres served as the dressing area (3). In front of the *scaenae frons* was a wide stage (*proscaenium*, 4). Temporary seating for the most distinguished spectators was placed on the ground in front of the stage (5). Vaulted entranceways underneath the seats closest to the stage allowed entrances from the sides of the theatre (6). Actors could also enter through doorways in the *scaenae frons*. In front of the stage on both sides of the *cavea* were boxes for magistrates or other important persons (7). On both sides of the stage were narrow tall buildings, built into the theatre (8): perhaps equipment was stored here. Around the upper perimeter of the *cavea* was a covered walkway, where spectators could walk about before and after performances (9). Much of the stage was covered by a wooden roof, which extended forward from the *scaenae frons* at a raised angle. Systems of poles and hooks at the top of this roof and over the walkway allowed a large awning, called a **velarium**, to be placed over the entire theatre during performances.

> 1 What are the most important similarities and differences between Greek and Roman theatres?
> 2 How do the theatres of the Roman imperial period compare with modern theatres?
> 3 How do the theatres of the Empire compare with the earlier Roman theatre spaces described on pp. 9–11?
> 4 What kinds of performances do you think would be most effective in these theatres? What effect would the theatre space have on how performances were presented and received?

The word 'pantomime' comes from the Greek *pan* (all) and *mimos* (imitator), for the main performer in pantomime told stories entirely through dance and gesture, without speaking or singing. The name thus describes a kind of performance similar in some ways to the wordless performance we today call either 'mime' or 'pantomime'. The popular form of British farcical Christmas entertainment known as pantomime, on the other hand, has no direct connection with ancient pantomime aside from its name.

Like its name, pantomime had roots in the Greek world, and ancient authors state that pantomime was introduced to Rome by Pylades of Cilicia (see map on p. x) in the late first century BC. In fact, forms of pantomime almost certainly existed in Rome long before that. The mimed songs attributed by Livy to Livius Andronicus, for example (**1.1**), may reflect a tradition of pantomime. What Pylades probably did was to make one or more innovations that contributed to the most common form of pantomime under the Roman Empire, in which a single masked dancer danced scenes from mythology, accompanied by one or more instrumentalists and a chorus, and sometimes by one or more supernumerary performers. Pylades was known for his tragic pantomimes. His contemporary and rival, Bathyllus from Alexandria in Egypt, is credited with inventing a comic form of pantomime.

> Without videos, scores, or even texts, it is difficult to reconstruct exactly what happened during a pantomime performance, but a number of ancient descriptions of the genre give us some idea. One of our best sources on pantomime is the treatise 'On the Dance' by Lucian, a Greek author of the second century AD. The work is a dialogue between two interlocutors: Lycinus (the speaker in all the passages quoted here) defends pantomime, which he calls simply 'dance', against Crato, who charges that pantomime is vulgar and morally corrupting. In one section of the work Lycinus argues that pantomime is superior to tragedy and comedy (29–31).

7.5 There is no need for me to say how beautiful and glorious the appearance of the dancer is, for that is clear to everyone who is not blind. His mask itself is as beautiful as possible and suitable for the drama being performed. It is not gaping open like the masks of comedy and tragedy, but has its mouth closed, since the dancer has **many others** to do the shouting for him. In the old days they both 30 sang and danced. But then, since the breath required for dancing interfered with the song, it seemed better for others to sing in accompaniment to their dance.

Tragedy and the dance have the same plots, except that the plots of dance are 31 more varied and more learned, having thousands of changes of fortune in them.

- On what grounds does Lycinus claim that pantomime is superior to tragedy and comedy? What do you think of his arguments?

On this ivory plaque from Trier in Germany, carved in late antiquity, a pantomime dancer holds three pantomime masks, along with other accoutrements for the performance: a crown, a sword and a lyre. Note the closed mouths on the masks. The gender of the person portrayed here is not certain, and we do have other evidence for female pantomime dancers.

7.6

many others that is, the chorus.

Pantomime 117

Later, Lycinus tells a story about how effective pantomime dancers could be at relaying stories (Lucian, 'On the Dance' 62–3).

7.7 Since [the dancer] is imitative and professes to show with movements what is being sung, it is necessary for him to practise clarity, just as orators do, so that each of the things he represents is made clear by him, with no explanation missing. Just as the **Delphic oracle** said, the one watching the dance must be able to understand the mute and hear the dancer though he is silent. 62

That's what they say **Demetrius the Cynic** experienced. He himself spoke against the dance just as **you** do, saying that the dancer was just an adjunct to the *tibia* and the pan-pipes and the clapping of the *scabillum*, and that the dancer himself added nothing to the performance, but vainly made meaningless and foolish movements, to which no thought was given. He said those who liked pantomime were spellbound by the things that went along with the performance: the silk costumes and the lovely masks, the *tibia* and its musical flourishes, and the sweet singing of the chorus, adornments to which the performance of the dancer contributed nothing. In response, a **well-known dancer** of the time of Nero, a man not without intelligence, so they say, who excelled as no one else did in his ability to recount stories and in the beauty of his movements, made of Demetrius what I think was a very reasonable request: he asked him to watch him dance before he found fault with him. And he promised that he would perform for him without the *tibia* or any singing. 63

And that's just what he did. He demanded silence from the *scabillum* players, the *tibia* players, and even the chorus. Then, completely on his own, he danced the **affair between Aphrodite and Ares**, Helios reporting it, Hephaestus plotting and catching both of them, Aphrodite and Ares, in chains, and each one of the gods who stood around them, and Aphrodite being ashamed, and Ares trying to hide and begging for mercy, and everything that belongs in the story. Demetrius, utterly delighted with what he had seen, gave the highest possible praise for a dancer. He shouted out in a loud voice: 'My good man, I hear what you are doing! I don't just see it, but you seem to me to be speaking with your hands.'

Delphic oracle an allusion to a famous story in which the prophetess of Apollo boasted that she could hear the mute and the silent (Herodotus 1.47).
Demetrius the Cynic the Cynics were a philosophical school known for their rejection of the trappings of civilization. Demetrius was a leading Cynic of the first century AD.
you Crato, Lycinus' interlocutor, who had spoken against pantomime.
well-known dancer this was probably a pantomime dancer named Paris.
affair between Aphrodite and Ares according to Homer's *Odyssey* (8.266–366), Aphrodite, the goddess of love, who was married to the craftsman god Hephaestus, once had an affair with the war god Ares. Helios, the sun god, told Hephaestus. Hephaestus crafted a metal net so thin that it could not be seen and ensnared Aphrodite and Ares in it while they were in bed together. He then called all the gods together to witness the sight, and the gods had a good laugh.

1 What does this passage suggest about the nature of a pantomime dancer's performance?
2 What do we learn here about the musical accompaniment of pantomime?
3 Do you think such exact imitation through dance is possible, or is Lycinus exaggerating?
4 Do the dance traditions of our society (e.g. ballet, modern dance) tend to be imitative in this way?

A relief from the first century AD shows what is probably a 'curtain call' after a pantomime performance. Note the niches and statues in the *scaenae frons*, and the *velarium* over it. Among those identifiable on stage are a *tibia* player with a *scabillum*, a player of the pan-pipes and the chorus.

7.8

Lycinus claims that pantomime is the best form of entertainment (Lucian, 'On the Dance' 67–9, 71–3).

7.9 It is not at all unfitting that the **Italians** call the dance pantomime, because of what the dancer does. The good advice of the **poet**, 'In your dealings with all cities, be like the sea creature who keeps close to the rocks', applies to the dancer as well. For he must cling closely to the material he presents and adapt himself to each of his plots.

The dance promises to present in action characters and emotions in their entirety, offering now a lover, now someone angry, and another insane, another in grief. And all of this must be done in time with the music. What is most amazing is that on the same day the same dancer can be **Athamas** in his insanity, **Ino** in terror, **Atreus**, and a little later **Thyestes**, then **Aegisthus** or **Aerope**. All of these characters presented by the same person!

Furthermore, the other forms of spectacle or concerts each present just one activity. Either there is a *tibia* or a **cithara** or singing or the drama of tragedy or the laughter of comedy. But the dancer brings everything, all mixed together with great variety: the *tibia*, the pan-pipes, the stamping of *scabilla*, the noise of hand cymbals, the lovely voice of the actor, the rich sounds of the chorus.

In addition, the other forms of entertainment exercise one of the two parts of a human being: the soul or the body. But in dance the two parts are both mixed together. For the things that happen in dance display the workings of the mind as well as the training of the body. And the greatest thing in the dance is the wisdom of what is presented and the fact that nothing is done irrationally. Indeed, **Lesbonax of Mytilene**, a most excellent man, called dancers 'the ones who are wise with their hands', and he went to their performances so that he could come home from the theatre a better person. And Timosthenes, his teacher, seeing a dancer perform just once by chance, said, 'What a wonderful spectacle I have deprived myself of because of my reverence for philosophy!'…

Furthermore, of the other pursuits in life some promise pleasure and some utility, but only the dance offers both. Indeed the dance is much more beneficial because of the pleasure it brings. It is so much more pleasant to watch than young men boxing, streaming blood, or others wrestling in the dust. In fact, the dance

---

Italians   the name 'pantomime' was first used by Greeks living in southern Italy.

poet   Pindar, a Greek lyric poet (c. 518–c. 446 BC).

Athamas, Ino   a married couple of mythology, driven mad by Juno because they had taken care of her husband Jupiter's bastard son Bacchus.

Atreus, Thyestes   see p. 130 for the story of Atreus and Thyestes.

Aegisthus, Aerope   Aegisthus was Thyestes' son, Aerope Atreus' wife, whom Thyestes seduced.

cithara   a large lyre.

Lesbonax of Mytilene   a philosopher of the first century BC.

often shows these same activities in a way that is safer, more beautiful and more pleasurable to watch than the activities themselves. And the tense movement, the twisting and turning, the leaps and backwards stretching of the dancer both bring pleasure to those watching and are extremely healthful for the dancers themselves. In fact I would say that dance is the finest and most graceful form of exercise. It trains the body to be supple, flexible, lithe and nimble, and at the same time brings it considerable strength.

How could you deny that the dance is completely harmonious? It sharpens the soul, trains the body, gives pleasure to spectators and teaches many things of antiquity to the accompaniment of *tibiae*, finger cymbals, well-ordered songs and enchantment for both the eyes and the ears. If you are looking for the blessed sound of the human voice, where else would you find it? Or where would you find a set of sounds more varied or melodious? Or if you are after the bright high sounds of the *tibia* or the pan-pipes, you can enjoy those instruments in abundance in the dance. Not to mention how taking part in such a spectacle will improve your character, as you see everyone in the theatre hating crimes, weeping at injustice and in fact being completely trained in ethics. And now I will tell you what is especially praiseworthy in the dancers: the way they exercise both strength and delicacy in their bodies seems as amazing to me as if someone were to demonstrate in the same body both the strength of Heracles and the daintiness of Aphrodite.

> 1 What does this passage add to your knowledge of what pantomime performance was like?
> 2 What grounds does Lycinus give for the superiority of pantomime to other forms of entertainment? What do you think of his arguments?
> 3 Are there any reasons why we might be sceptical about Lycinus' assessment of pantomime?

Lycinus observes, however, that the pantomime dancer's quest for accurate imitation can be taken too far (Lucian, 'On the Dance' 82–4).

7.10 What is generally called poor taste can occur among dancers just as it occurs in orators, when they exceed the proper measure in their imitation and make an effort beyond what is necessary. That is, if they need to show something big, they make it enormous; something delicate they make overly feminine; and they perform manliness to the point of bestial savageness. I remember seeing a dancer do something like this myself once. He was very well thought of before this, for he was both intelligent in other respects and he deserved the great admiration he got from those who watched him. But by some bad luck he fell into a shameless performance through exaggeration in his imitation. For when he was dancing the role of **Ajax** going mad after his defeat, he went so far beyond all bounds that someone might have thought he was not feigning madness but was himself insane. He tore the costume off one of the men who was beating time with the iron *scabillum*. Then he grabbed the *tibia* from one of the accompanying *tibia* players, clobbered Odysseus, who was standing near boasting of his victory, and cracked his head open. If it hadn't been for his helmet, which received the brunt of the blow, poor Odysseus would have perished, falling down right in front of the crazed dancer.

But the whole theatre went mad along with Ajax: they leapt and shouted and ripped off their clothing. The most vulgar spectators, who knew nothing of this type of performance and who had no thought for what was proper or discernment between good and bad, thought that such things represented the greatest skill in the imitation of emotion. Those who were more sophisticated recognized what was going on and were ashamed at it, but they did not express their disapproval through silence. Instead, they themselves tried to conceal the foolishness of the dance through their applause, although they could see clearly that what was happening reflected the madness of the dancer, not of Ajax.

Not satisfied with all this, the fine fellow did something else far more laughable: going down into the audience he sat down among the senators, between two former consuls, who were very afraid that he would grab a hold of one of them and beat him like one of the sheep.

Some marvelled at this, some laughed, and some suspected that from excessive imitation the dancer had been carried off into true madness. And indeed they say that he himself, after he regained his senses, regretted so much what he had done that he became ill from grief and was pronounced truly insane. In fact he himself showed this clearly. For when his fans begged him to dance Ajax for them again, he begged to be let off and said to the audience, 'It is enough for an actor to have gone mad once.' What most distressed him was that his competitor and rival, when the same part of Ajax was assigned to him, presented the madness with such refinement and moderation that he won praise as one who remained within the limits of the dance and did not insult the art of acting.

84

> 1 What does this passage suggest about the nature of pantomime dancing and its audience?
> 2 Does this story seem believable to you? Do you know modern examples of performers getting carried away in their imitation?

Ajax a hero of the Trojan War. When Achilles died, a contest was held between Ajax and Odysseus to determine who would inherit Achilles' armour. After Odysseus won the contest, Ajax went mad and slaughtered a flock of sheep, thinking they were Odysseus and his allies, then committed suicide out of shame.

Pantomime was immensely popular. In the mid-first century AD Seneca complains that his contemporaries have become obsessed with it (*Questions about Nature* 7.32.3).

7.11 But how hard they work to make sure that the name of no pantomime falls into oblivion! The names of Pylades and Bathyllus **survive because of their successors**, and there are many students and many teachers of this art. Private stages resound throughout the city. On this one men are dancing, on that one women. Men compete among themselves and with their wives to see who can make more effeminate moves.

The satiric poet Juvenal (early second century AD) claims that women became inordinately enamoured of pantomime performers (*Satires* 6.63–6).

7.12 When effeminate Bathyllus dances the part of the gesturing **Leda**, Tuccia can't control her bladder, Apula yelps and Thymele watches intently.

Repeatedly throughout the history of the Empire, the enormous popularity of pantomime led to riots between groups of fans loyal to rival performers. The historian Tacitus (*c*. AD 56–*c*. 120) describes how under the emperor Tiberius in AD 15 such riots led to debates in the Senate (*Annals* 1.77).

7.13 But the disturbances in the theatre, which had begun in the previous year, broke out even more violently this year, leading to the deaths not only of common people but of soldiers and of a centurion; and a tribune of the **praetorian guard** was wounded when he tried to prevent the mob from fighting and insulting the magistrates. The riots were debated in the Senate, and it was proposed that the **praetors** get the power to beat stage performers. The **tribune of the plebs** Haterius Agrippa vetoed this proposal … The veto held because the divine Augustus had once decreed **actors immune from beatings**, and Tiberius considered it sacrilege to go against his decrees. Many measures were taken concerning the tax used to pay

---

survive because of their successors many pantomime dancers took the names Pylades or Bathyllus after the alleged founders of the genre.

Leda in Greek mythology Leda, raped by Jupiter, became the mother of Helen, the beautiful woman over whom the Trojan War was fought.

praetorian guard a cohort of soldiers stationed in Rome to protect the emperor.

praetors magistrates responsible for maintaining order in the city of Rome.

tribune of the plebs a magistrate who had veto power over all legislation.

actors immune from beatings under traditional Roman law magistrates could beat stage performers at will. Augustus had restricted somewhat the freedom with which magistrates could beat actors.

actors and against the unruliness of the fans. Among these the most conspicuous measures were that no senator could enter the homes of pantomime dancers, that groups of *equites* should not escort the pantomime dancers when they went out in public, that they should not be watched except in the theatre, and that the praetors gained the power to punish spectators' unruliness with exile.

> Many Roman writers, like Lucian's Crato, expressed disdain for pantomime, suggesting that it degraded the morals of both its performers and its spectators. The leading senator Pliny the Younger (*c.* AD 61–*c.* 112), for example, writes in a letter about how one of his friends failed to be corrupted by his aunt's pantomime troupe (*Letters* 7.24).

7.14 Ummidia Quadratilla has died … I am very good friends with her nephew Quadratus… He lived with his pleasure-loving aunt but he remained very virtuous even while he remained most dutiful to her. She had a troupe of pantomime dancers that she cherished more enthusiastically than suited a woman of her high status. Quadratus never watched these, either in the theatre or at home, and she did not make him watch. I once heard the woman herself, when she was praising her nephew's studies to me, say that she, having a woman's leisure, often relaxed with a board game and watched her pantomime dancers, but when she was about to do either thing, she always ordered her nephew to go away and study. It seemed to me she did this because she both loved and esteemed him.

You will marvel at the following story, just as I did. In the most recent religious games, when the pantomime dancers had been entered in the competition, I came out of the theatre together with Quadratus, and he said to me: 'Do you know, today is the first time I have ever seen my aunt's **freedman** dancing?' This from her nephew! But by god, others, who hardly knew Quadratilla, in order to honour her – I am ashamed to say 'honour' – used to run into the theatre time and time again to perform their duties as flatterers, jumping about, applauding, expressing their admiration, and then matching her movements as she gestured in time with the song.

> This funerary inscription from Timgad in what is now Algeria commemorates a pantomime dancer. The author of the inscription is clearly eager to combat the stereotype that pantomime dancers were immoral (J. Bayet, *Libyca* III 1 (1955), p. 104).

---

equites bands of young *equites*, supporting rival pantomime dancers, appear to have been the primary instigators of the riots.

freedman many pantomime performers, like many actors and others involved with the theatre, were freed slaves. Other evidence suggests that Quadratilla was by no means unique in having her own private troupe of pantomime performers. We read elsewhere of such troupes performing at dinner parties.

7.15 To the sacred memory of Vincentius, the glory of the pantomime performers, who was talked about year in and year out, and who was loved by all, not only for the skill he showed on stage, but also because he was a good man if there ever was one, temperate and free from blame. Whenever he danced the famous stories, he kept the attention of the entire theatre into the evening. Buried, he dwells here **in front of the walls**. He lived for twenty-three years, strong in body; but the purity of his life was more eloquent than his gestures.

> 1 What do passages 7.11–15 suggest about the effects of pantomime on those who watched it? Can you think of modern performance genres that have had effects on their fans like those described in these passages?
> 2 What do you think it is about pantomime that caused it to have such a powerful effect on so many Romans?
> 3 To what extent do you think we should believe these authors regarding pantomime and its effects?

> ### Caligula and pantomime
>
> Eventually Tiberius exiled all pantomime performers from the city of Rome. Tiberius' successor Caligula (emperor AD 37–41) was a great fan of pantomime and allowed the dancers to return. Caligula was notorious for his erratic behaviour: many ancient writers believed he was insane. Like several other 'bad emperors', Caligula had close relations with pantomime performers, whose sexual allure was notorious (see **7.12**). Suetonius reports that Caligula became obsessed with the pantomime dancer Mnester (*Caligula* 55):
>
>> He used to kiss the pantomime actor Mnester even in the middle of the performance, and if anyone made even the slightest noise while Mnester was dancing, he ordered the culprit dragged from his seat and whipped him with his own hands.
>
> Caligula is even said to have done pantomime dances himself (Suetonius, *Caligula* 54):
>
>> Moreover, sometimes he even danced at night. One time in the middle of the night he summoned three ex-consuls to his palace and made them sit in stands overlooking a stage. They were fearing the worst, when suddenly there was a loud sound of tibiae and scabilla, and the emperor leapt out with a dancer's cloak and tunic, danced a number, and left.

---

in front of the walls Romans buried their dead outside the city walls.

Apuleius (born *c.* AD 125) describes in his novel *Metamorphoses* a variation of pantomime that included several dancers (10.29–32, 34).

7.16 The front curtain was lowered, the back curtains were rolled up, and the stage was arranged. There was a mountain made out of wood, like that famous **Mount Ida** the poet Homer sang about. It had been **crafted with supremely fine workmanship** and was planted with areas of greenery and live trees, and at its summit a river of water poured forth from a spring produced by the hands of a workman. A few little she-goats were grazing on short grass, and someone dressed just like Paris, the **Phrygian** shepherd, in a fine tunic, an exotic cloak flowing from his shoulders, and a golden turban on his head, pretended that he was watching over them. 30

Near him was a splendid boy, naked except for an **ephebe**'s cloak covering his left shoulder. He had a fine head of blond hair, from which protruded little golden wings, fastened symmetrically on each side. His herald's staff and wand indicated that he was Mercury. Running forward dancing and carrying in his right hand an apple gilded with gold leaf, he offered it to the boy playing Paris, indicating with a nod what **Jupiter had ordered**. Then immediately he withdrew from the stage with graceful steps.

Then a girl with a fine-looking face entered, looking like the goddess Juno. She had a bright crown around her head, and she carried a sceptre. Another girl burst onto the stage, looking just like Minerva. A shining helmet, adorned with a crown of olive leaves, covered her head. She lifted up her shield and shook her sword, as Minerva does when she enters a battle.

After these another girl entered, more beautiful than the others, indicating Venus with her graceful, ambrosia-like complexion. She looked like Venus did when she was still unmarried, showing her perfect beauty with a body naked and uncovered except for a thin silk cloth that shaded her lovely private parts … The goddess presented contrasting colours: she had a shining white body since she comes down from the heavens, and a dark blue cloak because she also **comes from the sea**. 31

Mount Ida a mountain near Troy, where Paris is said to have judged between the goddesses Juno, Minerva and Venus to determine who was the most beautiful.

crafted with supremely fine workmanship throughout Apuleius' description we find an obsession with verisimilitude, or the accurate depiction of nature. Such verisimilitude was a goal of much Roman art.

Phrygian Troy was in the same region of modern Turkey as Phrygia (see map on p. x).

ephebe a youth of about 18–20 years old.

Jupiter had ordered Jupiter had assigned Paris to judge between the goddesses.

comes from the sea according to mythology, Venus was born from the sea.

Each of the maidens had her own attendants. **Castor and Pollux** accompanied Juno, wearing on their heads egg-shaped helmets covered with stars. They were boys of the theatre. The girl playing Juno, moving forward with calm and restrained movement while the *tibia* player played varied melodies in the Ionian **mode**, promised the shepherd with graceful signs that, if he gave her the prize for beauty, she would give him rule over all Asia.

The girl whose armour indicated she was Minerva was accompanied by two boys, the arm-bearing companions of the goddess of war, Fear and Terror, each leaping about with their swords drawn. Behind them a *tibia* player, playing in the warlike Dorian mode, mixing high ringing sounds like a trumpet's with deep tones, boosted the energy of their agile dance. She, moving her head restlessly, giving a threatening look with her eyes, and making vehement and complex gestures, showed Paris in an excited manner that, if he handed over the victory in beauty to her, he would be a courageous warrior, famous for the trophies of war he would win with her aid.

But there stood Venus, right in the middle of the stage, to the delight of the spectators, smiling pleasantly, surrounded by a crowd of the happiest children. You would swear that those boys, with their smooth, milky-white skin, were real Cupids, who had just flown down from the sky or up from the sea. For they excellently matched Cupid with their little wings and arrows and the rest of their costumes, and with flashing torches they lit the way for their mistress, as if she were going to her **wedding banquet**. And beautiful groups of unwed girls flowed onto the stage as well. From this side came the most graceful **Graces**, from that side the most beautiful **Seasons**. Propitiating their goddess by tossing flowers, both woven together and singly, they made up a very elegant chorus, flattering the mistress of pleasures with the foliage of spring. A *tibia* **with many holes** played along sweetly in the Lydian mode. While they were charmingly caressing the spectators' hearts, Venus herself, by far more delightful, began to move forward gently and slowly, with hesitating steps, with her back moving smoothly back and forth and her head nodding slightly, responding with delicate gestures to the soft accompaniment of the *tibia*. Her eyes would blink gently at one moment, and at another they would threaten fiercely: she seemed sometimes to be dancing

32

Castor and Pollux   two brothers, half-divine, half-mortal, brothers of Helen.

mode   the various modes of Greek music, which represented different kinds of melodic and rhythmic structures, were associated with different emotional effects. The exact differences between the modes are not clear to us.

wedding banquet   torches were a standard part of Roman wedding processions.

Graces, **Seasons**   groups of minor divinities often associated with Venus.

with many holes   the most sophisticated *tibiae* had more holes than could be covered with the fingers of each hand. Unused holes were covered with rotating metal bands so that the instrument could play in several different keys.

with only her eyes. As soon as she was within Paris' sight, with movement of her arms she seemed to promise that if she were preferred to the other goddesses, she would give Paris a bride exceptionally beautiful, like herself. Then the Phrygian youth eagerly handed over to the girl the golden apple he held, like a token of victory …

After that judgement of Paris was completed, Juno and Minerva, unhappy and angry, left the stage, showing the indignation of the rejected with their gestures; but Venus, rejoicing brightly, showed her happiness by dancing with the entire chorus. Then from the highest peak of the mountain, through a hidden pipe, **saffron mixed with wine burst forth** into the heights and, spraying about as it flowed down, showered the grazing goats with sweet-smelling rain, until, sprinkled, they took on a more beautiful colour, replacing their native grey with yellow. And then, when the whole theatre was filled with the sweet smell, the earth opened up and swallowed that wooden mountain. 34

> 1 What does the rich detail of this passage reveal about such elements of the performance as the stage set, costumes, masks (are there masks?), personnel and movement?
> 2 How does this performance compare with the kind of pantomime performances described by Lucian (7.5, 7.7, 7.9–10)?
> 3 Apuleius' *Metamorphoses* is a work of fiction. Does it seem likely to you that the description here reflects actual performance practice in Apuleius' day, or does it seem like a fantasy?

saffron mixed with wine burst forth special effects like this were common in Roman performances.

Tragic singing

Another very popular form of theatrical entertainment under the Roman Empire was a practice known as **tragoediam cantare** or tragic singing. In this type of entertainment a masked performer, known as a *tragoedos*, would sing excerpts from tragedies, accompanied by a *tibia* and/or other instruments, and sometimes with other performers assisting. *Tragoedoi* were like pantomime dancers, then, except that they sang instead of danced. Also like pantomime dancers, successful *tragoedoi* could win passionate fans and demand high fees. *Tragoedoi* performed in theatres throughout the empire, and their performances, along with pantomime, appear to have for the most part replaced performances of whole tragedies. Some of the very few (about 65) pieces of music with notes that survive from the ancient world may have been intended for performance by *tragoedoi*.

Rome's most famous *tragoedos* was the emperor Nero (emperor AD 54–68). Suetonius describes his career (*Nero* 21, 24):

> He also sang tragedies, donning the masks of heroes and gods, and likewise of heroines and goddesses, with masks made to look like himself or whatever woman he was in love with at the moment. Among the roles he sang were Canace giving birth, Orestes the matricide, the blinded Oedipus, and Hercules in his madness. There is a story that when he was singing the mad Hercules a newly recruited soldier, placed at the entrance of the theatre as a guard, when he saw the emperor in his costume and bound in chains, as the plot required, ran to help him …

> But when he competed he followed the rules so diligently that he never dared to clear his throat or wipe the sweat from his brow with his arm. Indeed, in the middle of a tragic act, when he had quickly picked up his staff, which had slipped out of his hands, he grew pale, fearful that he would be disqualified from the contest on account of that fault, and he did not take heart until his assistant swore that the fault had not been noticed in the midst of the clamour and applause of the people.

8 Seneca

As was noted in chapter 5, no tragedies from the Roman Republic have survived in their entirety. We do, however, possess several tragedies from the Empire, each attributed to the philosopher and playwright Lucius Annaeus Seneca (*c.* AD 1–65).

Seneca's *Thyestes* presents one episode in the gruesome saga of the house of Tantalus. The gods so favoured Tantalus, a mortal son of Jupiter, that they dined in his home. Tantalus wanted to prove he was superior to the gods, so he chopped up his own son, Pelops, and tried to feed him to them. The gods recognized the ruse, restored Pelops to life, and condemned Tantalus to spend eternity in the underworld above a pool of water and below a fruit tree. Every time Tantalus reached for the fruit it was lifted out of his reach, and the water receded every time he tried to drink (see the illustration below; our word 'tantalize' comes from Tantalus). Pelops gained control over much of southern Greece, which got the name Peloponnesus from him (see map on p. x). Among Pelops' children were Atreus and Thyestes. It was determined that the brother who had control of a ram with a golden fleece would succeed to Pelops' kingdom. With the help of Atreus' wife, whom he seduced, Thyestes acquired the ram and hence the kingdom. When the play begins, however, Atreus has regained the throne and driven Thyestes into exile. Seneca's audience would know what is going to happen: Atreus will kill Thyestes' sons and feed them to their father.

Tantalus, *by Giulio Santo (c. 1565).*

The play takes place in front of the palace at Argos, the capital of Atreus' kingdom (see map on p. x). Tantalus enters, called up from the underworld (Seneca, *Thyestes* 1–39, 52–121).

8.1 TANTALUS Who is it that drags me up from the unhappy land of the dead, where, with eager lips, I try continually to grasp food that is always just out of reach? Who shows Tantalus the sky again, under which he once wreaked such havoc? Has some punishment been found even worse 5 than parched thirst in the midst of water, or hunger that yearns without end? Will I, like **Sisyphus**, have to carry a rock that slides off my shoulders? Will my limbs, like **Ixion**'s, be wrenched apart on a turning wheel? Or will I be like **Tityus**, who lies spread out, a gaping hole in his stomach, feeding the black birds who dig out his entrails, 10 regaining at night what he has lost during the day, so that every day he offers ample fodder for a new flock of birds? What fresh torture awaits me?

Whoever you are, harsh judge of the shades, you who assign new punishments to the dead: if you have a punishment that would 15 frighten even **Cerberus**, or **Acheron** – or even me – find it. For now my descendants plot to commit crimes that make me seem innocent. 20 They dare what no one has ever dared. Whatever room remains in the place where the impious are punished, I will fill it up with my family. **Minos** will never lack cases while the house of Pelops stands.

FURY Go on inside, you detestable shade, and torment your **household gods** with madness. Let the struggle be carried on with every crime 25 imaginable. Let one attack lead to another. Let there be no limit to anger, or shame at the acts anger will cause. Let blind madness drive

---

Sisyphus for his crime in trying to cheat death, Sisyphus spent eternity pushing a boulder up a hill. Whenever he neared the hill's peak the boulder rolled back.

Ixion he tried to rape the goddess Juno and was therefore tied to a wheel for eternity.

Tityus for attempting to rape Leto, mother of the god Apollo, Tityus spent eternity chained to a rock while vultures ate his continually renewed liver.

Cerberus a three-headed dog that guarded the gates of the palace of Pluto, the god who ruled the underworld.

Acheron a river in the underworld.

Minos judge of the dead in the underworld.

Fury the Furies were hideous goddesses of the underworld who insisted upon vengeance and drove people to madness.

household gods every Roman household was believed to have its own set of protective divinities, called Lares and Penates. Here the household gods stand for the household as a whole.

Seneca

them on. Let the insanity of parents endure, and let long-lasting abomination continue down through the generations. Let no one have time to hate an old crime, as new crimes continually rise up, many at a time. And let wrong increase as wrong is punished. Let the arrogant brothers lose their kingdoms and then regain them from exile. Let the fortune of this violent house totter in uncertainty between two kings. Let the downtrodden one become powerful, the powerful one downtrodden. Let chance determine the kingship in continual flux. Let those who have been driven out because of their crimes, when a god returns them to their country, return to more crimes, and let them be as hateful to all as they are to themselves. Let their anger consider nothing forbidden … 30

Throw the household gods into confusion. Summon hatred, slaughter, and death and fill the entire house with Tantalus. Let the high column be adorned, and let the doors be splendid with **fresh laurel**. Let a bright fire burn, as befits your homecoming. But then let the **Thracian crime** be repeated, but in greater number. Why is the uncle's right hand empty? Will he ever raise it up? Let the bronze cauldrons boil over on the fire. Let the dismembered limbs go into the pots in pieces. Let blood pollute the ancestral hearth. Let the banquet be prepared. You will be guest at a crime you know well. We have given you a holiday for this dinner, relieving you of your hunger. End your fast, let the blood, mixed into the wine, be drunk while you watch. I have found a feast that would disgust even you. Hold on there, where are you rushing off to? 35

55

60

65

TANTALUS To the pools and rivers and waters that recede from me, and to the tree, full of fruit, that flees from my lips. Please, let me go off into my gloomy prison, or, if that doesn't seem painful enough, let me change rivers. **Phlegethon**, let me stand chained in the middle of your streambed, surrounded by your flaming waters. All you who suffer punishments by the order of the Fates: you who live in fear in a hollow cave, always expecting the collapse of a mountain looming over you; you who, unable to escape, bristle in terror at the savage jaws of hungry lions and the troops of baneful Furies; you who, half burnt, try to push away torches that have been thrust upon you. Listen to the voice of Tantalus as he rushes towards you. Trust me, I know: embrace your punishments. When will I be allowed to escape from the world of the living? 70

75

80

---

fresh laurel   Romans hung laurel on their doors to commemorate homecomings.

Thracian crime   the Thracian Tereus raped his wife Procne's sister. In vengeance Procne killed her son by Tereus and fed him to him.

Phlegethon   a river in the underworld that was believed to flow with flames.

FURY	First bring confusion upon your house: bring warfare, inspire in the kings a wicked love of violence, and strike their savage breasts with mad chaos. 85
TANTALUS	It is fitting for me to endure punishments, not to be a punishment. Am I being sent like a poisonous vapour rising from a fissure in the earth, or a plague, to scatter harmful pollution on the peoples of the world? Shall I, their grandfather, lead my grandsons into horrible 90 abomination? Oh great **father of the gods** (and my father, though you may be ashamed of it): though my tongue may suffer the worst of torments, I won't be **silent about this either**. I warn you, my offspring: don't pollute your hands with cursed slaughter. Don't shower the altars with evil and madness. I will stand here and prevent 95 the crime. Why do you threaten me, savagely lashing out at me with twisted snakes? Why do you stir up the hunger that lies deep inside of me? My breast burns, enflamed with thirst, and flames flicker in my scorched entrails. All right: I follow you. 100
FURY	Now! Now! Spread insanity throughout the house. Yes! Yes! Let them be carried off in madness and thirst for each other's blood. The house senses your arrival and shudders at your abominable touch. Enough 105 now: you have done well. Go back to the infernal caves and the river you know well. **The lands of the earth are already oppressed by your touch**. Do you see how the water of the spring flows backwards, driven within the earth? How the riverbanks are empty? How the fiery wind, desiccating all, leaves only a few clouds? All the trees turn 110 brown, their branches denuded of fruit. The **Isthmus of Corinth**, which usually has raging waters on either side of it as it divides the sea with a graceful sliver of land, now hears waters only from a great distance. Now the **Lernaean marsh** has receded, the river 115 **Inachus** lies hidden, the sacred **Alphaeus** does not offer its waters. The ridges of **Mount Cithaeron** stand without any snow, and

---

father of the gods   Jupiter.

silent about this either   another version of the Tantalus myth held that he was punished because he revealed one of the gods' secrets.

The lands of the earth are already oppressed by your touch   here and later in the play Seneca uses an extreme version of what literary critics have called 'the pathetic fallacy', in which natural phenomena appear to respond to events occurring in the plot.

Isthmus of Corinth   see map on p. x.

Lernaean marsh, **Inachus**, **Alphaeus**   bodies of water in the Peloponnesus.

Mount Cithaeron   a mountain near Thebes, in Greece (see map on p. x).

Seneca

Argos fears a return of the drought it once knew. Look! Even **Helios** 120
hesitates to drive his horses to bring a day destined to perish.

> 1 Why do you think Seneca begins his play with Tantalus, though Tantalus plays no direct role in the plot?
> 2 What appears to be the role of the Fury in the lives of Tantalus' family, judging from this opening scene?
> 3 What do you notice about the way Tantalus and the Fury express themselves? Do they use succinct expressions, or superfluous words? Do they speak literally or metaphorically? Is their train of thought easy or difficult to follow? How do you think their mode of expression would have affected an audience?
> 4 What images do Tantalus and the Fury use in their speeches? What do those images contribute to this opening scene?

Seneca's tragedies all have the same structure: a prologue (here the scene between Tantalus and the Fury), followed by alternation between choruses and scenes of dialogue. After the prologue of *Thyestes*, the chorus enters and sings about the recurring violence in Tantalus' household, begging the gods to prevent Atreus and Thyestes from continuing it. Atreus then enters, joined by an attendant, and plots how he will get revenge against Thyestes now that the tables have turned and Thyestes is in exile. Part of their dialogue is quoted below (244–66, 277–94).

8.2 ATREUS   Tell me, how should I destroy that wicked man?
ATTENDANT Let him, slain with a sword, spit out his hated breath. 245
ATREUS   No! It's punishment I want, not an end to punishment. It's a gentle tyrant who kills people: in my kingdom people beg to be killed.
ATTENDANT Have you no sense of **family duty**?
ATREUS   Family duty, I dismiss you, if you ever were in this household. 250
Come to me, savage flock of Furies, strife-bringing **Erinys**, and **Megaera**, brandishing twin torches. The madness blazing in my breast is not great enough: I want to be filled with something more horrible.

Argos fears a return of the drought it once knew   there was a myth that Argos had no water until someone dug wells there.

Helios   god of the Sun. According to Greek and Roman mythology he drove the sun across the sky in a chariot.

family duty   this phrase translates the Latin word *pietas*, a virtue of great importance to the Romans, which actually includes duty not just to one's family, but also to the gods (our 'piety') and to the state (our 'patriotism').

Erinys, **Megaera**   two of the Furies.

Seneca's life

Seneca was born into a wealthy family in Cordoba in Spain. He moved to Rome as a very young boy and studied rhetoric and philosophy. As an adult he became a successful orator and began a political career. Poor health, which would plague him throughout his life, interfered with this career, as did disputes with two emperors. Seneca withdrew from public life because Caligula (emperor AD 37–41) allegedly wished to have him executed, and under Claudius (emperor AD 41–54) Seneca was accused of adultery and exiled to the island of Corsica (see map on p. x). During his time in exile Seneca began in earnest his career as a **Stoic** philosopher (see p. 141), writing works on how one can control irrational passions and endure suffering. He also probably wrote some of his tragedies during this period.

Seneca's troubles with Claudius most likely resulted from the machinations of Claudius' wife, Messalina. After Messalina was executed and Claudius remarried, the emperor's new wife, Agrippina, arranged for Seneca to be brought back from exile and serve as tutor to her son, Nero. When Nero succeeded Claudius in AD 54, Seneca became one of the new emperor's chief advisers and one of the wealthiest men in Rome. After ruling moderately in his first years, Nero became increasingly cruel and wilful: among his other crimes, he murdered his mother Agrippina. After 62 Seneca distanced himself from Nero's court and spent most of his time writing further works of philosophy, and perhaps more tragedies. Nero grew hostile to his former tutor, and when a conspiracy against the emperor was discovered in 65, Seneca was accused of complicity and forced to commit suicide. Seneca's tragedies, with their emphasis on violence, cruelty and subjection to forces beyond one's control, may well reflect the brutality of the emperors whose reigns he experienced at first hand.

Ancient bust of Seneca.

ATTENDANT	What are you devising now in your madness?	
ATREUS	Nothing within the limits of normal suffering: I will leave nothing undone, and nothing will be enough.	255
ATTENDANT	A sword?	
ATREUS	Not good enough.	
ATTENDANT	How about fire?	
ATREUS	Still not good enough.	
ATTENDANT	With what weapon, then, will you produce such suffering?	
ATREUS	With Thyestes himself.	
ATTENDANT	This is an evil greater than your anger.	
ATREUS	It is, but a frenzied storm stirs up my soul deep within me. I'm possessed, and I don't know where it's leading me. The earth groans under my feet, it thunders though the day is calm. The whole palace rumbles as if its walls were being shattered, and the household gods have turned their faces away. Gods, even you fear this crime. But I say, let it happen.	260 265
ATTENDANT	So what are you planning to do?	
...		
ATREUS	Let the hungry father happily chew up his children and eat their limbs! Yes! That will be great! I like this method of punishment: at least for now. Where is he? Why is Atreus kept innocent for so long? Now I see flashing before me the entire massacre, the missing sons stuffed into their father's mouth. But why are you afraid, my soul? Why do you hesitate before the event? Come on, you must have courage for this. The most atrocious part of the deed he will do himself.	280 285
ATTENDANT	But with what trick will you get him to step into our net? He believes everything here is hostile to him.	
ATREUS	He couldn't be captured unless he wanted to be. But he wants my kingship. For that, he will plunge into a swirling whirlpool. For that, he will enter the treacherous straits of the **Libyan Syrtes**. For that, he will rush against Jupiter's thunderbolt. For that, he will even do what he believes is the worst fate imaginable: he will look upon his brother.	290

> 1 Evaluate Atreus' train of thought here. To what extent do you think he is thinking rationally, and to what extent has his desire for vengeance driven him insane?
> 2 Why do you think Seneca has Atreus hesitate midway through his planning?
> 3 What assumptions does Atreus make about Thyestes here?

Libyan Syrtes sandbars off the coast of North Africa, known for the many shipwrecks they caused.

> **Declamation**
>
> A central feature of education in Seneca's time was a practice known as *declamatio* (**declamation**). To hone or demonstrate their speaking skills, students and others would make arguments for one or both sides in debates from mythology or history or in imaginary lawsuits. In one exercise, for example, a husband and wife have agreed that if the other dies, the surviving spouse will commit suicide. The husband falls in love with another woman and has a message sent to his wife that he is dead. She tries to kill herself but fails. Later, the husband wants his wife back. She wants to return to her husband, but her father forbids her from remarrying him. Students would argue in favour of the wife and/or her father. Seneca's father, known as Seneca the Elder, published two books in which he recorded a large number of declamations he remembered from his own youth. The emphasis in these exercises was on finding ways as clever as possible to express a wide variety of arguments.
>
> Seneca's training in declamation had a profound effect on his tragedies. His characters, both in debates and in monologues, often give the impression that they are performing variations on a theme, working their way through different ways of arguing for a position; and Seneca frequently uses what are called *sententiae*: pithy, clever ways of making a point, as when Atreus says in the passage above that he will use Thyestes himself to punish Thyestes.

Atreus sends his own sons, Agamemnon and Menelaus, to tell Thyestes that if he returns to Argos he can share in the kingship. The chorus, unaware of Atreus' treachery, rejoices that Atreus and Thyestes have ended their quarrel (336–52, 363–8, 390–403).

8.3 At last the royal household, the race of ancient **Inachus**, has settled the violent dispute between the brothers. What madness drives you to spill blood in turn 340 and to seek the sceptre with crimes? You don't know, you who so desire citadels, where kingship really lies.

Wealth and power do not make a king, nor garments of **Tyrian purple**, nor a 345 crown on a royal brow, nor roof beams shining with gold: a king is one who has put aside fears and the evils of a cruel heart. One who is unmoved by uncontrolled 350 ambition or the rash and unstable favour of the people … whom neither the soldier's spear nor the drawn sword frightens, who, rising up over everything, 365

Inachus the river god Inachus, who was believed to have been the first king of Argos.

Tyrian purple the city of Tyre in what is now Lebanon was famous for its expensive purple dye, produced from a shellfish.

approaches death willingly and without complaint … This kingship is a gift everyone can give to himself.

Let whoever so desires stand on the slippery summit of royal power. Let me be satisfied with sweet peacefulness; let me enjoy gentle tranquillity from my obscure position; let me pass my life in silence, unknown to the Roman citizens. Thus, when my days have passed with no commotion, let me die an old **plebeian**. Death weighs heavily upon him who, all too well known to everyone, dies unknown to himself.

> 1 How does the approach to life of the chorus differ from that of Atreus in 8.2, and what does the comparison between these two world views contribute to the play? What do you think of the chorus' philosophy?
> 2 Though the play is set in mythical Argos, Seneca has the chorus refer to Roman citizens and the Roman social class of plebeians. Why do you think he does that?
> 3 What do you think the chorus means by its last sentence about death and knowledge?

Seneca's metres

Most of Seneca's verses except the choruses are written in iambic trimeters, a variation of the iambic senarii used by earlier Latin playwrights (see p. 35). Most of Seneca's choruses are in very simple lyric metres, in which the same metrical pattern occurs in almost every verse. The chorus translated above, for example, is in a metre called glyconic. Every verse has the following pattern of long and short syllables: – – – ⏑⏑ – ⏑ –. An equivalent in English, using our metre based on stress, would be something like, 'I don't know what to do with you'. Read the first three verses of the chorus aloud and you will get a feel for the metre, even if you do not pronounce all the Latin words correctly:

> Tandem regia nobilis,
>
> antiqui genus Inachi,
>
> fratrum composuit minas.

The lyric metres may have been sung to the accompaniment of a *tibia*, as is the practice in other Roman drama.

---

plebeian the lower of Rome's two most basic social divisions, plebeians and patricians.

> The only character in *Thyestes* besides the chorus to deliver a lyric metre is Thyestes, when he is seen rejoicing, unaware that he has devoured his children (**8.6**). He delivers anapaests, in which long syllables alternate with pairs of short syllables. Read the first four lines of his song aloud, and you will get a feel for the metre (920–3):
>
> Pectŏră longīs hĕbĕtātă mălīs,
>
> iām sōllĭcĭtās pōnĭtĕ cūrās.
>
> fŭgĭāt māeror fŭgĭātquĕ păvōr,
>
> fŭgĭāt trĕpĭdī cŏmĕs ēxĭlĭī.

Thyestes returns to Argos with his three sons, the youths Plisthenes and Tantalus (named after his great-grandfather), and an unnamed young boy (404–54, 471–89).

8.4 THYESTES I see the fatherland I longed for, and the wealth of Argos, and – the thing unhappy exiles want most – my native soil and my paternal gods (if there are any gods), and the sacred **towers of the Cyclopes**, a glory greater than human labour, and the **stadia** thronged with youth, in which more than once I won fame and the crown of victory with my father's chariot. The people of Argos will run to meet me, rushing out in a crowd. But so will Atreus! Instead of that, Thyestes, go back to your exile in the dense forest, to your savage life among the beasts. There is no reason why this glimmering kingship should entice your eyes with its false light. When you behold what is given, look also at the one giving it. A short time ago, living a life that anyone would consider harsh, I was brave and happy. But now I am beset by terror. My soul stops in its tracks and tries to drag my body back; my steps resist as I move. 405 410 415 420

towers of the Cyclopes several towns in the Peloponnesus were surrounded by walls made out of huge stones, built during the Bronze Age (c. 2800–c. 1100 BC). After accurate memories of the Bronze Age were lost, a myth developed that these stones were too large for humans to move, and that the walls were made by Cyclopes, giants (like Polyphemus in the *Odyssey*) known for their craftsmanship. The building material of these walls is still known as 'Cyclopean masonry'.

stadia among the stadia in the Peloponnesus was that at Olympia (see map on p. x), where the Olympic games were held. Chariot-racing was one of the most popular athletic contests at the Olympic games and elsewhere.

TANTALUS   What's this? My father stands gaping, hardly moving. He shakes his
           head, uncertain what to do.
THYESTES   Why, my soul, do you hesitate? Why do you keep turning about in your
           mind what should be obvious? Do you trust in those most uncertain
           things, your brother and the kingship, and fear the hardships that you   425
           have already mastered? Do you flee from things that by now are easy
           for you, and from troubles that have actually been good for you? By
           now you are perfectly happy in your poverty. Turn back while you can,
           and snatch yourself away from all this.
TANTALUS   Father, what has caused you to turn back at the sight of your
           fatherland? Why do you put up barriers to your happiness? Your   430
           brother has given up his anger, and he gives you part of the kingship.
           He repairs the limbs of the house, torn apart, and he restores you to
           yourself.
THYESTES   You ask me why I am afraid, but I myself don't know. I see nothing to   435
           fear, but still I'm afraid. I want to go, but my limbs fail me. My knees
           buckle, and I am carried off in the opposite direction from where I'm
           trying to go. I'm like a ship, struggling forward with both its oars and
           its sails, but driven back by the wind.
TANTALUS   Whatever is holding you back, stifle it, and consider what great rewards 440
           await you when you return. Father, you can be king.
THYESTES   **I can, since I am ready to die.**
TANTALUS   The greatest power …
THYESTES   Is nothing, if you desire nothing.
TANTALUS   You will leave the kingdom to your sons.
THYESTES   Kingship cannot endure two rulers at once.
TANTALUS   Does anyone prefer to be miserable when he can be fortunate?   445
THYESTES   Trust me, the pleasures of being great are false, and it is foolish to fear
           difficulties. When I was at the pinnacle of power, I never stopped being
           afraid, fearing even the sword I carried at my own side. Oh, how good
           it is to stand in no one's way, to eat your meals in safety, reclining on   450
           the ground! Small houses are free of crimes, and at a meagre meal the
           drinking cup is safe. Poison is drunk from a golden cup. I speak from
           experience. One can prefer bad fortune to good …
TANTALUS   One should not seek the power to rule, but if a god gives it, it should
           not be refused. Your brother asks you to rule.
THYESTES   He *asks* me? That's what we should fear. There's some trick.
TANTALUS   Family duty, when it has gone, generally comes back, and proper love   475
           regains its lost strength.

I can, since I am ready to die.   Thyestes echoes the chorus' view that true kingship is mastery of one's fears and passions.

THYESTES   Is Thyestes loved by his brother? That will happen when the **two Bears** are submerged in the sea, when the voracious **Sicilian waters** stand still, when grain grows in the middle of the **Ionian Sea**, when black night shines a light upon the earth, and when lasting peace is made between water and fire, life and death, the wind and the sea.   480

TANTALUS   What trick are you afraid of?

THYESTES   Every trick. What limit should I place on my fear? He has as much power as he has hatred.

TANTALUS   What power does he have against you?

THYESTES   I'm not afraid for myself. It's you and your brothers that make me fear Atreus.   485

TANTALUS   Are you afraid of being deceived even though you're cautious?

THYESTES   In the midst of evils it's too late to be cautious. All right, let's go. But as your father I say this: it is you and your brothers who lead; I just follow.

---

1 What aspects of his homeland does Thyestes most anticipate as he enters? What might his attention to those aspects suggest about his state of mind?
2 What does Thyestes debate with himself and his son? How does that debate compare with the thoughts of the chorus in 8.3?
3 Why do you think Seneca chose the son named Tantalus to argue with his father here?
4 What persuades Thyestes to continue his return home instead of returning to exile? What does that suggest about Thyestes?

Stoicism

Seneca was an adherent of **Stoicism**, the most popular philosophy among Roman thinkers. Stoics believed that the highest good was virtue, attained through the domination of reason over emotion. Seneca's tragedies are full of negative examples from a Stoic point of view. Many characters, like Thyestes, attempt to gain control over their emotions but fail. Others, like Atreus, allow themselves to be completely controlled by their passions, offering powerful counter-examples to the Stoic ideal. In addition, Seneca's characters and choruses often express sentiments consistent with Stoicism, such as the chorus' thoughts, echoed by Thyestes, about gaining a kind of kingship through rule over oneself.

---

two Bears the Romans called the Big Dipper and the Little Dipper *Ursa Maior* and *Ursa Minor*, the Greater Bear and the Lesser Bear (they are still called that by astronomers). Unlike other constellations, these two clusters of stars never set below the horizon. With this reference Thyestes begins a series of *adynata*, or expressions of impossibilities (e.g. 'When pigs fly').

Sicilian waters Thyestes refers to the strait of Messina, between Italy and Sicily, which was notorious for the danger it posed to ships.

Ionian Sea the sea between southern Italy and Greece (see map on p. x).

Atreus greets Thyestes, who confesses he has grievously wronged his brother and begs for mercy. Atreus feigns forgiveness and offers Thyestes a share in the kingship. Thyestes accepts. The chorus rejoices at the reconciliation and sings about the changeability of fortune. A messenger then enters and describes how Atreus led the three sons of Thyestes to an altar in the recesses of his palace (684–95, 713–18, 726–46, 755–84).

8.5 MESSENGER How can I even say it? He binds the noble youths' hands behind 685
their backs and ties **purple ribbons** around their poor heads.
There is **incense**, too, and **the sacred liquid of Bacchus**, and a
knife, touching its victim with **salted meal**. Every part of the rite is 690
followed.

CHORUS Who stretches his hand out to the knife?

MESSENGER *He* does! *He* plays priest. *He* sings furiously the fatal **incantation**.
He stands at the altar. *He* examines those dedicated to slaughter,
arranges them in order, and prepares them for the knife. *He* watches
to make sure all is done according to ritual. Nothing is left out ... 695
He hesitates, pondering which he should sacrifice to himself first. It
makes no difference, but still he hesitates, and he takes pleasure in 715
putting his accursed crime in order.

CHORUS Which one does he strike first?

MESSENGER He dedicates the first place to his grandfather (you'd think he had
some sense of familial duty!): Tantalus is the first sacrificial victim
... Then he savagely drags Plisthenes to the altar and adds him to
his brother. He cuts through his neck. The trunk falls straight down,
but the head rolls away, murmuring a garbled lament.

CHORUS What does he do then, when he has completed this twin slaughter? 730
Does he spare the boy, or does he pile crime upon crime?

MESSENGER Imagine a lion in the Armenian forest has defeated a herd of cattle
with great slaughter. His mouth drips with gore, his hunger is
satiated, but that does not calm his wrath. Tirelessly harassing the 735
bulls from all sides, he threatens the calves even though his jaws
are tired. That's what Atreus was like. Raging, puffed up with fury,
holding his sword drenched with twin blood, forgetting even who
his victim is, he pierces the body, and in a moment the sword, 740
thrust into the boy's breast, protrudes from his back. The boy falls
dead, the blood from his front and back putting out the fire on the
altar.

CHORUS How horrifying!

---

purple ribbons, **incense**, **the sacred liquid of Bacchus** (i.e. wine), **salted meal**, **incantation** these are all standard features of Roman animal sacrifice.

MESSENGER	You find that horrifying? This is pure virtue compared to his next actions.	745
CHORUS	What? Does nature allow a crime more horrible than this?	
	...	
MESSENGER	His victims' organs quiver, snatched from breasts still warm with life. The veins pulse and the hearts, still trembling, beat. But he **draws out the entrails and reads the fates**, noting their markings. After he has found the victims satisfactory, he dedicates his full attention to his brother's banquet. He himself removes their limbs, cutting off the wide shoulders up to the trunk and the muscular upper arms. Fiercely he cuts the flesh off the bones: he keeps only the faces, and the hands that were given to him in good faith. Some of the organs cling to spits and drip as they are heated over slow-burning fires. Some move to and fro in the boiling water of a heated pot. The fire leaps right over the food that has been placed over it, and only after it has been drawn back to the flickering hearth six times does it reluctantly obey its orders. A liver hisses on the spits: it's hard to tell whether the bodies or the flames groan more. The fire disperses into pitch-black smoke. Gloomy, in big black clouds, the smoke did not rise up into the rafters, but settled around the household gods in a shapeless mass.	755 760 765 770 775
	Oh Helios, you too suffered. You fled backwards, snatching this day from the middle of the sky and plunging it into the sea. But you set too late: the father is tearing off pieces of his sons, and he chews their limbs with his baneful mouth. His hair shines, anointed with flowing perfume, and he is heavy with wine. Often one piece of flesh, not yet swallowed, blocks the next in his throat. Thyestes, there is only one blessing in your troubles, and that is that you are unaware of them. But this blessing too will soon pass.	780

> 1 What does his parody of an animal sacrifice contribute to our understanding of Atreus?
> 2 What does the messenger imply when he says Atreus sacrifices the children 'to himself'?
> 3 How would an audience respond to the messenger's own reaction to the events he reports?
> 4 Seneca has often been criticized for the gruesomeness of passages like this one. What do you think? Are the vivid details of slaughter and cooking gratuitous? If not, what do they contribute to the play?

draws out the entrails and reads the fates   Romans regularly read the will of the gods in the organs of sacrificed animals, following an elaborate code that determined what different marks on the organs meant.

> **Seneca in performance?**
> The theatres of Seneca's day, as we saw in the previous chapters, appear to have featured primarily mime, pantomime and tragic singing rather than comedy and tragedy; and some features of Seneca's plays would appear to present unusual challenges to actors and directors. Note, for example, the chorus' ignorance of Atreus' plans in **8.3**, though they would presumably have been on stage while he made those plans in **8.2**. Elsewhere characters sometimes appear and disappear without notice, and the settings of plays seem to change arbitrarily. Some scholars have concluded that Seneca's plays were not written for performance in theatres: rather, such scholars argue, the plays were meant to be read, either in public recitation (perhaps by Seneca himself) or in private. On the other hand, the plays contain moments that would have been exceedingly effective if presented in live performance, as, for example, when Atreus shows Thyestes his sons' heads, hands and feet in the next passage. Other scholars, therefore, argue that Seneca meant his plays for performance, if not in the large public theatres, then perhaps in performances for private parties. The question remains fascinating and – at least with the evidence now available – unanswerable.

The chorus sings of its horror at Atreus' deed, fearing the end of the world. Atreus enters exulting. He remains on stage and watches as Thyestes is revealed at the banquet table (920–1112).

8.6 THYESTES Oh my heart, made dull by such long troubles, put aside your cares and distress. Away with grief, away with fear, away with miserable poverty, the companion of frightened exile, and the burdensome shame that comes with it. Where you fall from is more important than where you fall to. It is a great accomplishment, after you have slipped from a high peak, to walk on the plain with a steady step. It is a great accomplishment, when you have been oppressed by a huge avalanche of troubles, to endure the burden of a broken kingship with your neck unbent, and to bear upright the ruin that has been placed upon you, neither weakened nor overcome by your troubles. But now, Thyestes, away with the clouds of your savage fate and all remembrances of that unhappy time. Let cheerfulness return along with this new good fortune. Dismiss the old Thyestes from your mind.
    The unfortunate have a peculiar fault: they never trust good fortune. Even if prosperity returns, those who have been miserable don't want to rejoice. Grief, rising up for no reason, why do you call me back and keep me from celebrating this festive day? Why do you make me weep? Why do you prevent me from binding my head with a seemly garland? Yes, it holds me back, it does! The garland has fallen off my

head! My hair, dripping with rich perfume, suddenly stands on end. A shower of tears falls unbidden from my face, and in the middle of my words I begin to groan. Grief loves its familiar tears. A harsh longing to weep takes hold of those who have been unhappy. I want to cry out inauspicious laments, to tear these garments soaked with Tyrian purple, to let out a wail.

My mind, foretelling evil to come, sends forth signs of future grief: when the tranquil seas swell without a wind, a savage storm threatens sailors. You're mad: what grief, what crisis do you imagine for yourself? Offer your brother a trusting heart: whatever this is, your fear is either without cause or too late. A vague terror wanders inside me against my will. My eyes pour out sudden tears, for which there is no cause. Is this grief or fear? Or are these tears of great joy?

ATREUS Brother, let us celebrate this festive day in harmony. This day will confirm my kingship and bind us together in solid trust and certain peace.

THYESTES I am now filled to contentment with your fine food and the gift of Bacchus. I ask just one thing more to make my joy complete: let me share my happiness with my children.

ATREUS Trust me: **your sons are here**, in the embrace of their father. Here they are and here they will remain. No part of your offspring will be taken away from you. The faces you wish for I will present to you, and I will fill the father and make him complete with his crowd of offspring. Don't worry: you will be filled to satiety. Now your sons are performing the pleasant rites of a youthful feast, together with my own sons. But they will be summoned. Take up the family cup, filled with wine.

THYESTES I receive the gift of my brother's banquet. Let the wine be poured in libation to our paternal gods, then drunk down. But what is this? My hands will not obey me. The weight of the cup grows and weighs down my arm. The wine, moved towards my lips, flees from them and flows around my mouth. The earth shakes and knocks the dinner off the table. The torches give almost no light. Even the **upper air** stands stunned and immobile between day and night, abandoned by the heavenly bodies. And what is this? The vaulted sky, with ever increasing trembling, begins to collapse. A mist, thicker than dense shadows, surrounds me, and night has concealed itself in night. All the stars flee from the sky. Whatever this is, let this entire storm spend

---

your sons are here   note throughout Atreus' gruesome *double entendres*, which Thyestes fails to grasp until well into the scene.

upper air   the stars and planets were thought to revolve around the earth in the uppermost part of the atmosphere, called *aether*.

	itself on my own cheap life, and spare my brother and children. Give me back my sons!	
ATREUS	I will give them back, and no day will ever take them from you.	
THYESTES	What is this upheaval in my stomach? What is trembling within me? I feel a restless weight, and my breast groans with a groaning not my own. Sons, come here. Your poor father calls you. Come here: this suffering will go away at the sight of you. They seem to interrupt me. But from where?	1000
ATREUS	Prepare your embrace, father. **Here they are**. Don't you recognize your sons?	1005
THYESTES	I recognize my brother. Earth, can you bear to have such an abomination upon you? Why do you not open up and drag us down to the **Styx**? Why do you not plunge king and kingdom into the depths of the underworld through a huge chasm? Why do you not rend all the buildings of **Mycenae** from their foundations in a great upheaval? We should both be standing at the side of Tantalus. Let whatever joins the upper and lower worlds split apart and, if anything lies below **Tartarus** and our ancestors, reveal it through an enormous cavity and let us be buried beneath all of Hades. Let our guilty souls wander over our heads, and let fiery Phlegethon, carrying along all its burning sands in a violent whirlpool, flow over our place of exile. Earth, do you remain unmoved, nothing but a sluggish weight? Then the gods have abandoned us.	1010 1015 1020
ATREUS	Receive now gladly those you have yearned for for so long. Your brother is not stopping you. Enjoy their presence, kiss them, share your embraces with all three of them.	
THYESTES	Is this reconciliation? Is this the goodwill and good faith of a brother? Is this the way you put aside your hatred? Please, I no longer ask to see my children unharmed. But as a brother I beg you: let me bury them. That will not undermine your crime or your hatred. Give me them, so you can see them burned immediately. As their father I ask not to have them, but to destroy them.	1025 1030
ATREUS	Whatever remains of your sons, you already have it. And whatever does not remain you have too.	

Here they are Atreus has the heads, hands and feet of the sons brought in. The scene is an especially dramatic example of the recognition scene, a standard feature of ancient tragedy. Aristotle in his *Poetics* noted the tragic effectiveness of recognitions like this one, which bring about a change from good fortune to bad.

Styx a river in the underworld. The Greek word *styx* means hatred.

Mycenae the Bronze Age city of Mycenae (see map on p. x) was often conflated with Argos, six miles away.

Tartarus the lowest part of the underworld, where the worst sinners were punished.

THYESTES What? Have they been made fodder for savage birds? Are they being torn apart by beasts? Are they feeding wild animals?

ATREUS You yourself have dined on your sons in a wicked banquet.

THYESTES Oh! So this is what shamed the gods! This is what drove the sun back in disgust to where it rose. What cries, what laments can I make in my wretchedness? What words will be sufficient? I see their heads, hands and feet, cut off. Those were what their greedy father was unable to consume. Their organs turn about inside me and, shut in without an escape, struggle and seek to flee. Brother, give me your sword, already soaked in my blood, so I can make a path for my children. Do you deny me a sword? Then let my breast resound, smashed with my own hands. No! Restrain yourself. Spare the dead. Whoever saw such an abomination? Not even a stranger-killing barbarian, living on the rugged cliffs of the **Caucasus**. Not even **Procrustes**, terror of Attica. Look! I am a weight upon my sons, and they are a weight on me! Every crime has to have some limit!

ATREUS There ought to be a limit to crime when you do it, but not when you avenge it. Even this is but a small **revenge** for me: I should have poured their blood, warm from their wounds, right into your mouth, so you could drink it while they were still alive. In my hurry I didn't do justice to my anger. *I* stabbed them with the knife, slaughtered them at the altar, poured their blood on the hearth, cut apart their lifeless bodies into small pieces and plunged them into pots of boiling water. *I* let them simmer over a slow flame. *I* cut off their limbs and sinews, warm with life. *I* watched their entrails sizzle on slender spits, feeding the fires with my own hands. I should have made *him*, their father, do all this. The whole punishment has proven fruitless. He chewed up his sons within his impious mouth, but he did it without knowing it, and they were unconscious.

THYESTES Hear me, you seas, hemmed in by wandering shorelines. Hear me, you gods, wherever you have flown to. Hear me, souls of the dead, and all lands. Hear me, Night, dark and gloomy as Tartarus: I have been abandoned to you alone, just as you have been abandoned by the stars. I shall make a prayer that is not unjust. I will ask nothing on my own behalf: what is left for me to ask? My prayers will look out for your interests.

Caucasus the peoples of the Caucasus, on the eastern coast of the Black Sea, were known for piracy and brutality.

Procrustes a monster who lived in Attica (the region around Athens, see map on p. x). He stretched or chopped off the legs of his guests to make them fit into his bed until he was killed by the hero Theseus.

revenge that is, revenge for Thyestes' earlier seduction of Atreus' wife.

	You, greatest **ruler of the sky**, master of the heavenly palace, engulf the entire world in terrible clouds, send everywhere a conflagration of raging winds, let your thunder crash violently in every part of the world. Send down your fiery weapons, not with your weaker hand, the one you use to smite buildings and homes that don't deserve it, but with the hand under which the threefold mass of mountains fell, and with it the **Giants**, who stood level with the mountains. Avenge this day, which has lost its light. Hurl flames! Replenish with lightning the light snatched from the world. Don't hesitate: let us both be proclaimed guilty; or, if not, condemn just me. Strike me! Send your flaming three-pronged torch through my breast. If my sons are to be burned with a proper funeral, I need to be burnt up myself. If nothing moves the gods, and no divine power goes after the impious with its weapons, let this night remain for ever and cover up these heinous crimes with its long shadows. Helios, keep your present course: I do not object.	1080 1085 1090 1095
ATREUS	*Now* I'm happy with my deed. *Now* I have won the true prize. My crime would have failed, if you weren't suffering like this. Now I believe my children are my own, and I have regained faith in my marriage bed.	
THYESTES	How did my children earn this?	1100
ATREUS	They were yours.	
THYESTES	Children, into their father …?	
ATREUS	Yes! And, what pleases me most, they were most certainly yours.	
THYESTES	I call upon the gods, protectors of the pious.	
ATREUS	Which ones? The ones who protect marriage?	
THYESTES	Who repays crime with crime?	
ATREUS	I know why you're so unhappy: it's because I committed the crime first. You suffer not because you devoured this abominable feast, but because you didn't prepare it! You had in mind to prepare similar food for your brother, and to treat his children in the same way, with the help of their mother. Just one thing stood in your way: you thought they were yours!	1105 1110
THYESTES	The gods will be here as avengers. My prayers hand you over to them for punishment.	
ATREUS	I hand you over to your children for punishment.	

---

ruler of the sky Jupiter.

Giants according to myth, giants once attempted to storm Mount Olympus, home of the gods, by piling mountains on top of one another.

1. What is Thyestes' state of mind when he is first seen here? How does that compare with his previous attitude?
2. What echoes do you notice in this passage of earlier scenes in the play? How might an audience have responded to those echoes?
3. How do Atreus and Thyestes react when Thyestes learns what has happened? What do those reactions reveal about the two brothers?
4. Do you think Atreus is justified in the assumptions he makes about Thyestes at the end of the scene?
5. What do you think of Seneca's decision to end the play the way he does?
6. What kinds of decisions would you make if you were given the opportunity to direct Seneca's *Thyestes*?

Other plays attributed to Seneca

In addition to *Thyestes*, nine other plays attributed to Seneca have been preserved in manuscripts of the Middle Ages. Eight of the plays – *The Trojan Women*, *The Phoenician Women*, *Medea*, *Phaedra*, *Oedipus*, *Agamemnon*, and two plays entitled *Hercules* (one of these, sometimes called *Hercules at Mount Oeta*, may not be by Seneca) – present mythological events that had already been put on the stage by Aeschylus, Sophocles and Euripides, the great tragedians of fifth-century-BC Athens (Sophocles and Euripides had also written plays, now lost, about Atreus and Thyestes). Unlike many earlier Roman comedies and tragedies, however, Seneca's tragedies are not adaptations of earlier plays. Seneca generally follows the basic plot of the earlier plays but also introduces interesting new 'twists' to the story. Seneca's *The Trojan Women*, for example, provides a considerably more sympathetic portrayal of Helen and Ulysses (Odysseus) than Euripides does in his *The Trojan Women*, and Seneca adds a sequence in which Andromache tries to hide her son Astyanax from the Greeks.

A tenth play, *Octavia*, is almost certainly not by Seneca (it appears to refer to events that occurred after Seneca's death), but it is nevertheless one of the most fascinating works of Roman drama, for it is our only extant *fabula praetexta*, or tragedy in Roman dress. It describes how Nero brought about the death of his wife Octavia, daughter of Claudius. Seneca himself appears as a character in the play.

9 The legacy of Roman theatre

Roman theatre has had a profound impact on the development of theatre, literature, film and television.

Mime, pantomime and theatre architecture

The influence of Roman mime on later comedy is difficult to assess. State-sponsored performances of mime, as of all theatre, faded in the last centuries of antiquity and disappeared in the early Middle Ages. Throughout the Middle Ages, however, travelling players provided comic entertainment informally in many parts of Europe. The antics of these players were often similar to those of Roman mime performers, and there may well have been an element of continuity in these improvised farcical traditions. The medieval travelling performers are among the ancestors of **commedia dell'arte**, a type of improvisational comedy that had developed in Italy by the sixteenth century. *Commedia dell'arte*, built upon stock scenes and characters (e.g. the clever *Arlecchino*, and *Il Capitano*, the braggart soldier), influenced in turn many of the modern world's informal and improvisational traditions of farce.

The performance traditions of pantomime do not appear to have survived into the Middle Ages, but descriptions of pantomime by authors such as Lucian have had an important influence. When formal theatrical performances began again in the fifteenth century in Italy, many plays included extensive narrative dances, an attempt to imitate pantomime. In the eighteenth century similar dances became an important part of opera, and the founders of modern ballet such as John Weaver in Britain (1673–1760) and Jean-Georges Noverre in France (1727–1810) looked to pantomime for their inspiration.

> The first permanent theatres of modern Europe, constructed in Italy in the sixteenth century, were modelled on ancient Roman theatres, as is evident in the *Teatro Olimpico* (9.1) designed by the great architect Andrea Palladio (1508–80) and built in Vicenza, Italy. Note the large arch with a scene painted in perspective behind it at the middle of what looks like a Roman *scaenae frons*. Arches such as this one would lead eventually to the proscenium arch, the frame that separates the performance space from the audience in many modern theatres.

9.1

Teatro Olimpico

> 1 What features of modern comic performances do you find similar to what we know of Roman mime performance? Do you think those similarities are more likely to derive from continuities in performance traditions, or from similarities in how farcical performance works in different societies?
> 2 What dance traditions are you familiar with? How do they compare with what we know of ancient pantomime?
> 3 What features of the *Teatro Olimpico* are similar to Roman theatres? In what ways does it differ from those theatres?

Seneca

The Renaissance brought both a new interest in ancient Greece and Rome and a rebirth of tragic theatre. The new tragic playwrights turned to Seneca as their model. Much Renaissance tragedy, therefore, included the following Senecan features:

1 Plots centred on revenge.
2 An acute sense of the power of evil, often with a focus on political tyranny.
3 Emphasis on connections between human actions and natural events (the pathetic fallacy).
4 Extensive use of declamatory rhetoric.

5 Characters whose obsessions with their goals override common standards of morality.

6 A large amount of grotesque and violent action.

7 Much attention to madness and its effects.

Neo-Senecan tragedy appeared in Italy, France and elsewhere, but it was especially important in England. Several of the plays of Christopher Marlowe (1564–93) are tragedies in the Senecan style, and the *Spanish Tragedy* (1592) of Thomas Kyd (1558–94) is a classic neo-Senecan tragedy of revenge. The influence of Seneca on William Shakespeare (1564–1616) is profound.

> By far Shakespeare's most Senecan tragedy is *Titus Andronicus* (c. 1590). After defeating the Goths, a barbarian people, the Roman general Titus Andronicus suffers horrendous indignities at the hands of the Gothic queen Tamora, her sons Chiron and Demetrius, her lover Aaron and the emperor Saturninus, whom Tamora marries. Because of them Titus loses his hand, two of his sons and his son-in-law; and Chiron and Demetrius rape his daughter Lavinia and cut off her hands and tongue. When Titus learns who is responsible for these crimes, he kills Chiron and Demetrius and feeds them to their mother. The play's final scene begins when Titus' surviving son Lucius, who has led an army of Goths against Saturninus, has agreed to meet with Saturninus, Tamora and Gothic and Roman leaders for a banquet at Titus' house (*Titus Andronicus* 5.3.26–65).

9.2 *Servants bring forth a table. Trumpets sounding, enter Titus, like [i.e., dressed as] a cook, placing the dishes, and Lavinia with a veil over her face … and others.*

TITUS	Welcome, my lord; welcome, dread queen;
	Welcome, ye warlike Goths; welcome, Lucius;
	And welcome all. Although the cheer be poor,
	'Twill fill your stomachs; please you eat of it.
SATURNINUS	Why art thou thus attired, Andronicus? 30
TITUS	Because I would be sure to have all well
	To entertain your highness and your empress.
TAMORA	We are beholding to you, good Andronicus.
TITUS	And if your highness knew my heart, you were.
	My lord the emperor, resolve me this: 35
	Was it well done of rash **Virginius**
	To slay his daughter with his own right hand
	Because she was enforced, stained, and deflowered?

Virginius according to a story from the early history of Rome, Virginius killed his daughter Virginia so that she would not be raped. Titus gets the story wrong, suggesting that she was raped before the murder.

SATURNINUS	It was, Andronicus.	
TITUS	Your reason, mighty lord?	
SATURNINUS	Because the girl should not survive her shame,	40
	And by her presence still renew his sorrows.	
TITUS	A reason mighty, strong, and effectual;	
	A pattern, precedent, and lively warrant	
	For me, most wretched, to perform the like.	
	Die, die, Lavinia, and thy shame with thee,	45
	And with thy shame thy father's sorrow die. (*He kills her.*)	
SATURNINUS	What hast thou done, unnatural and unkind?	
TITUS	Killed her for whom my tears have made me blind.	
	I am as woeful as Virginius was,	
	And have a thousand times more cause than he	50
	To do this outrage; and it now is done.	
SATURNINUS	What, was she ravished? Tell who did the deed.	
TITUS	Will't please you eat? Will't please your highness feed?	
TAMORA	Why hast thou slain thine only daughter thus?	
TITUS	Not I, 'twas Chiron and Demetrius;	55
	They ravished her and cut away her tongue,	
	And they, 'twas they that did her all this wrong.	
SATURNINUS	Go fetch them hither to us presently.	
TITUS	Why there they are, both bakèd in this pie,	
	Whereof their mother daintily hath fed,	60
	Eating the flesh that she herself hath bred.	
	'Tis true, 'tis true, witness my knife's sharp point. (*He stabs the empress.*)	
SATURNINUS	Die, frantic wretch, for this accursèd deed. (*He kills Titus.*)	
LUCIUS	Can the son's eye behold his father bleed?	
	There's **meed** for meed, death for a deadly deed.	65
	(*He kills Saturninus.*)	

Lucius and Titus' brother Marcus explain the crimes of Tamora and her relatives, and the Roman people proclaim Lucius emperor. Tamora's lover Aaron, who has been captured, is then brought before them (5.3.175–199).

9.3 [A ROMAN] You sad Andronici, have done with woes. 175
Give sentence on this execrable wretch
That hath been breeder of these dire events.

---

meed   what one deserves.

LUCIUS	Set him breast-deep in earth and famish him;
	There let him stand and rave and cry for food.
	If anyone relieves or pities him,
	For the offence he dies; this is our doom.
	Some stay to see him fastened in the earth.
AARON	Ah, why should wrath be mute and fury dumb?
	I am no baby, I, that with base prayers
	I should repent the evils I have done;
	Ten thousand worse than ever yet I did
	Would I perform, if I might have my will.
	If one good deed in all my life I did,
	I do repent it from my very soul.
LUCIUS	Some loving friends convey the emperor hence
	And give him burial in his fathers' grave.
	My father and Lavinia shall forthwith
	Be closèd in our household's monument.
	As for that ravenous tiger, Tamora,
	No funeral rite, nor man in mourning weed,
	No mournful bell shall ring her burial;
	But throw her forth to beasts and birds to prey.
	Her life was beastly and devoid of pity,
	And being dead, let birds on her take pity. (*Exeunt.*)

Although *Titus Andronicus* is Shakespeare's most conspicuously neo-Senecan play, the influence of Seneca is evident in all Shakespeare's tragedies, including his greatest. Macbeth shows an immoral wilfulness reminiscent of characters like Atreus. *King Lear* combines a chilling presentation of the power of evil with grotesque violence, elaborate declamation and natural events that seem to respond to human wrongdoing. *Hamlet*, a tragedy of revenge, owes much to its Senecan predecessors. Indeed Polonius, when he boasts of the players hired to perform for Hamlet's uncle, claims, 'Seneca cannot be too heavy, nor Plautus too light' (*Hamlet* 2.2.419–20).

Seneca's influence on drama faded after the seventeenth century. More modern audiences and critics have tended to find the Senecan style of declamation, grotesque violence and elaborate imagery from nature excessive. Characters whose obsessions transcend the norms of society, however, have remained a standard feature of drama, film, and novels. Figures such as the monster of Mary Shelley's *Frankenstein* (1818), Stephen Sondheim's *Sweeney Todd* (1979), and Clint Eastwood's Dirty Harry (1971, sequels through to 1988) owe much, if indirectly, to their Senecan ancestors.

> 1 Compare the final scene of Shakespeare's *Titus Andronicus* with the end of Seneca's *Thyestes* (8.6). What do the two scenes have in common?
>
> 2 What aspects of *Titus Andronicus*' final scene differ from the end of *Thyestes*? What might those differences suggest about how Shakespeare's world view differs from Seneca's?
>
> 3 What Shakespearean tragedies have you read or seen? What Senecan features do you find in those tragedies? In what ways do they differ from tragedy as Seneca wrote it?
>
> 4 What Senecan features do you notice in contemporary plays, films and literature?

Plautus and Terence

The Roman playwrights who have had the greatest influence on modern theatre and literature are Plautus and Terence. During the Middle Ages the plays of Plautus were largely ignored, but Terence became a core part of the educational curriculum and a model for Latin style. Hrotsvit (*c.* AD 935–*c.* 1002; her name is also sometimes spelled Rotswitha, Hrotsvitha or Hrotswitha), a canoness in a convent in Gandersheim, Germany, wrote six plays with Christian themes inspired in part by the plays of Terence. Whether these plays were performed in the convent or were intended only for reading is uncertain.

> Hrotsvit discusses her relationship to Terence in her preface to the plays (1–3).

9.4 There are many Christians who prefer the frivolity of pagan books, with their more eloquent and cultured language, to the usefulness of the sacred scriptures. I find that completely unforgivable. There are also others who remain loyal to the sacred texts and who spurn other pagan authors, but nevertheless continue to read the creations of Terence too often: Terence's sinful plots pollute them, even as his pleasing language delights them. That's why I, the Mighty Voice of Gandersheim, have decided to imitate in writing the author others cultivate in reading. Using the same style with which Terence describes the foul and unchaste deeds of lustful women, I will celebrate, as far as my modest talent allows, the praiseworthy chastity of holy maidens.

> Hrotsvit's plays are thus modelled on Terence's but are in many ways anti-Terentian. Whereas Terence's plays celebrate the romantic union of men and women, the heroes and heroines of Hrotsvit's plays reject earthly love in favour of chastity. Several plays even include martyrdom, which for Hrotsvit was a 'happy ending' far greater than an earthly marriage, for it led to union with Christ in heaven.

In the Renaissance both Plautus and Terence became very popular. We have noted the possible influence of mime on *commedia dell'arte*. The influence of Plautus and Terence on that genre is more certain: *commedia dell'arte*'s creators drew many of their plot motifs and stock characters from the Roman playwrights. Meanwhile, actors and playwrights in Italy also began to produce what was called **commedia erudita**: plays with written texts. These consisted primarily of productions of Plautus and Terence in Latin and in Italian translation, and of plays written in both Latin and Italian inspired by Roman comedy. *Commedia erudita* led to comedies inspired by Plautus and Terence throughout Europe.

The character who gives his name to Nicholas Udall's *Ralph Roister Doister* (c. 1552), probably the first comedy written in English, is a boastful fool modelled on the braggart soldiers of Plautus' and Terence's plays. For his *The Comedy of Errors* (composed before 1594), Shakespeare borrowed from Plautus' *The Menaechmus Brothers* a pair of identical twins separated as very young boys. One twin, searching for his long-lost brother, arrives in the town where that brother lives but only finds him after a great deal of comic confusion caused by the twins' identical appearance. Inspired by Plautus' *Amphitryo*, in which Jupiter disguises himself as Amphitryo and Mercury as Amphitryo's slave Sosia, Shakespeare added a second pair of twins, servants to the first pair. He also expanded considerably the role of the resident twin's wife, added a love story between the visiting twin and the resident twin's sister-in-law, and framed his play with a tale of separation, danger and reunification involving the twins' father and mother.

> Both *The Menaechmus Brothers* and *The Comedy of Errors* include scenes in which the resident twin mocks a quack healer. In Plautus' play the visiting twin has feigned insanity to escape from his brother's father-in-law (called simply *Senex*, or 'the old man'). The father-in-law goes to fetch a doctor, but when they return the visiting twin has left and his brother, the old man's actual son-in-law, is on stage (*The Menaechmus Brothers* (*Menaechmi*) 910–34).

9.5

	DOCTOR	Greetings, Menaechmus. Tell me, please, why do you open your arm like that? Don't you know how much you are exacerbating that illness you have?	910
	MENAECHMUS	Why don't you go hang yourself?	
	SENEX	Can you feel anything?	
	MENAECHMUS	Of course I can!	
	DOCTOR	Oh, this is bad, I don't think even an acre's worth of **hellebore** could cure it. But listen, Menaechmus.	
	MENAECHMUS	What do you want?	

hellebore   a herb used to treat insanity.

	DOCTOR	Answer my questions. Do you drink your wine white or black?	915
	MENAECHMUS	Why don't you go get crucified?	
	DOCTOR	By god, he's starting to show the first signs of madness.	
	MENAECHMUS	Why don't you ask me whether I eat bread that's scarlet, purple or pink? Or whether I eat scaly birds or feathered fish?	
	SENEX	Oh dear! Do you hear what ravings he spouts? Why are you hesitating? Give him some medicine before his madness takes possession of him!	920
	DOCTOR	Just wait. I need to do more diagnosis.	
	SENEX	You're killing me with your chatter.	
	DOCTOR	Tell me this: do your eyes ever become hard?	
	MENAECHMUS	What? Do you think I'm a lobster, you bastard?	
	DOCTOR	Tell me: do you ever feel your insides rumbling?	925
	MENAECHMUS	When I'm full, they don't rumble. When I'm hungry, they do.	
	DOCTOR	This doesn't seem like the answer of a madman to me. Do you sleep through until dawn? Do you sleep restfully?	
	MENAECHMUS	I sleep through, if I've paid my debts. Jupiter and all the gods destroy you and your questions!	930
	DOCTOR	Now the man is starting to rave. Watch out when he talks like that.	

In *The Comedy of Errors* both twins are named Antipholus, and their twin slaves are each named Dromio. Because of the confusion caused by the visiting twins, the resident Antipholus is believed to be mad by his wife (Adriana), his sister-in-law (Luciana) and his girlfriend (called simply the 'Courtesan'). The women bring on an allegedly learned man named Pinch, who claims he can exorcize evil spirits (Shakespeare, *The Comedy of Errors* 4.4.35–75).

9.6	ANTIPHOLUS	Come, go along; my wife is coming yonder.	35
	DROMIO	Mistress, *respice finem* – 'respect your end', or rather, to prophesy like the parrot, '**Beware the rope's end**.'	
	ANTIPHOLUS	Wilt thou still talk? (*He beats Dromio.*)	
	COURTESAN	How say you now? Is not your husband mad?	
	ADRIANA	His incivility confirms no less.	40
		Good Doctor Pinch, you are a conjurer.	
		Establish him in his true sense again,	
		And I will please you what you will demand.	
	LUCIANA	Alas, how fiery and how sharp he looks!	
	COURTESAN	Mark how he trembles in his ecstasy.	45

Beware the rope's end earlier in the play Antipholus had threatened to beat his wife with a rope because she refused to allow him in her home (she was with the other Antipholus, thinking he was her husband).

PINCH	Give me your hand, and let me feel your pulse.	
ANTIPHOLUS	There is my hand, and let it feel your ear. (*He strikes Pinch.*)	
PINCH	I charge thee, Satan, housed within this man,	
	To yield possession to my holy prayers.	
	And to thy state of darkness hie thee straight.	50
	I conjure thee by all the saints in heaven.	
ANTIPHOLUS	Peace, doting wizard, peace. I am not mad.	
ADRIANA	O that thou wert not, poor distressèd soul!	
ANTIPHOLUS	You, minion, you, are these your customers?	
	Did this companion with the saffron face	55
	Revel and feast it at my house today,	
	Whilst upon me the guilty doors were shut,	
	And I denied to enter in my house?	
ADRIANA	O, husband, God doth know you dined at home,	
	Where would you had remained until this time,	60
	Free from these slanders and this open shame.	
ANTIPHOLUS	Dined at home? (*to Dromio*) Thou, villain, what sayst thou?	
DROMIO	Sir, sooth to say, you did not dine at home.	
ANTIPHOLUS	Were not my doors locked up, and I shut out?	
DROMIO	Perdie, your doors were locked, and you shut out.	65
ANTIPHOLUS	And did not she herself revile me there?	
DROMIO	Sans fable, she herself reviled you there.	
ANTIPHOLUS	Did not her kitchen-maid rail, taunt, and scorn me?	
DROMIO	Certes she did. The kitchen vestal scorned you.	
ANTIPHOLUS	And did not I in rage depart from thence?	70
DROMIO	In verity you did. My bones bears witness,	
	That since have felt the vigour of his rage.	
ADRIANA	Is't good to soothe him in these contraries?	
PINCH	It is no shame. The fellow finds his vein,	
	And yielding to him humours well his frenzy.	75

> 1 How does Plautus' Doctor compare with Shakespeare's Pinch?
> 2 What has Shakespeare borrowed from Plautus in this scene?
> 3 How does Shakespeare's scene differ from Plautus'? How would those differences have changed the effects of the scene?
> 4 What Shakespearean comedies have you read or seen? What features of those comedies are similar to Roman comedies? In what ways are they different from the plays of Plautus and Terence?

No other Shakespearean play has as great a debt to Roman comedy as *The Comedy of Errors*, but borrowings from Terence and, especially, Plautus pervade Shakespeare's comedies. *The Taming of the Shrew*, for example, features a servant named Tranio, who, like his namesake in Plautus' *The Haunted House*, carries out an elaborate deception to help out his younger master.

France's greatest comic playwright is Jean-Baptiste Poquelin, known by his stage name Molière (1622–73). Besides borrowing characters and motifs from Plautus and Terence throughout his career, Molière based the plots of four of his plays on Roman comedies: *The School for Husbands* (1661) is an adaptation of Terence's *The Brothers*, *Amphitryo* (1668) derives from Plautus' play of the same name, *The Miser* (1668) draws heavily on Plautus' *The Pot of Gold*, and *The Deceptions of Scapin* (1670) relies for much of its plot on Terence's *Phormio*. In each of these plays Molière made changes – sometimes extensive ones – to his Roman models; but on occasion he followed the Roman plays very closely.

Compare, for example, the following scenes from Plautus' *The Pot of Gold* (9.7) and Molière's *The Miser* (9.8). In each play a miser (Euclio in Plautus' play, Harpagon in Molière's) enters in a panic after he has discovered that the treasure he has been hiding has been stolen.

9.7 EUCLIO I'm finished! Dead! Ruined! Where should I run? Where should I not run? Grab him! Grab him! Grab who? Who is it? I don't know! I can't see anything! I'm blind, and I can't even tell for sure where I'm going or where I am or who I am! Please, you folks, I beg you, I beseech you, help me, and show me the guy who stole it. What is it? What are you all laughing at? I know the whole lot of you! I know there are plenty of thieves here, hiding in their **nice white clothing** and sitting there as if they were decent people. (*He addresses a member of the audience.*) What do you say? I've decided to trust you, for I can tell from your face that you're good. Hey! Doesn't one of these guys have it? You've killed me! Tell me, then, who has it? You don't know? Oh, poor me! I've died a terrible death, I'm completely ruined, utterly destroyed: this day has brought me so much misery and evil and sadness, hunger and poverty. I'm the most miserable person in the whole world. What's the point of living, when I've lost all that gold, which I guarded so carefully? I've cheated myself of everything I might desire or enjoy, and now other people rejoice in this, in my suffering and loss. I can't bear it. 715

720

725

Plautus, *The Pot of Gold* (*Aulularia*) 713–26

9.8 HARPAGON Thief! Thief! Assassin! Murder! Justice, by God! I'm finished! I'm murdered! My throat's been cut! My money's been stolen! Who can it be? What's become of him? Where is he? Where's he hiding? What should I do to find him? Where to run? Where not to run? Isn't he there? Isn't he here? Who's this? Stop! Give me my money back, you scoundrel! (*He grabs his own arm.*) Oh, that's me. I'm in such

---

nice white clothing Euclio probably points to leading citizens, sitting in the front rows wearing white togas.

distress, I don't know where I am, who I am, or what I'm doing. Oh, my poor money, my poor money! My dear friend, they've taken you from me, and with you I've lost my support, my consolation, my joy. Everything is finished for me, and I have no more purpose in life. Without you I can't go on living. It's over. I can't bear it. I'm dying. I'm dead. I'm buried. Isn't there somebody who wants to bring me back to life, by giving me back my dear money, or telling me who stole it? Well? What do you say? Nobody.

Whoever did it must have watched carefully for his chance: he picked exactly the time I was talking with that **villainous son** of mine. All right, then, let's go. I'm going to demand justice and question the entire household under torture: maids, valets, son, daughter, even myself.

Look at all these people here! Everybody I look at rouses my suspicions: they all look like the thief to me. Hey! What are they talking about over there? About the guy who robbed me? What's that noise up there? Is my thief there? Please, if somebody has news about my thief, I beg you, tell me. Is he hidden there among you? They're all looking at me and laughing at me! You'll see that they're all accomplices in the theft of my property: I'm sure of it. Quick! Captains, police, marshals, judges, racks, gallows, executioners! I want everybody hanged! And then if I don't find my money, I'll hang myself!

Molière, *The Miser* Act 4, Scene 7

> 1 What has Molière borrowed from Plautus in this scene?
> 2 In what ways does Molière's scene differ from Plautus'? What would be the effects of these differences?
> 3 Why might talented playwrights like Molière draw on ancient drama?

Creators of comic drama have continued to make direct use of Plautus' and Terence's plots up to the present day. The French playwright Jean Giraudoux (1882–1944) gave his 1929 adaptation of Plautus' *Amphitryo* the title *Amphitryo 38*, alluding to how many versions of that play have been produced. In fact Giraudoux underestimated: *Amphitryo* has inspired far more than 38 plays through the centuries. One of the most recent adaptations of a Roman comedy is British playwright Peter Oswald's *The Storm*, a modernization of Plautus' *The Rope* (2005).

Roman comedies have been an especially rich source of inspiration for the

---

villainous son   Harpagon has disowned his son for opposing Harpagon's marriage to a young woman with whom the son himself is in love.

American musical. Musicals drawn from Plautus have included *The Boys From Syracuse* (1938), an adaptation of *The Comedy of Errors* by Richard Rodgers (music), Lorenz Hart (lyrics) and George Abbott (book); and Cole Porter's *Out of This World* (1950, book by Dwight Taylor and Reginald Lawrence), yet another adaptation of *Amphitryo*. The most successful Broadway version of Plautus has been *A Funny Thing Happened on the Way to the Forum* (1962, filmed 1966). Its authors Stephen Sondheim (music and lyrics), Burt Shevelove (book) and Larry Gelbart (book) drew characters and plot motifs from numerous plays of Plautus to create a rollicking farce about how a clever slave – named Pseudolus after the title character of Plautus' *Pseudolus* – manages to unite his young master with his beloved by tricking his old master, his neighbour, a pimp and a braggart soldier.

> In the scenes leading up to the passage below, Pseudolus has ensconced in his home his young master's slave-prostitute girlfriend and has concocted a sleeping potion with mare's sweat which he plans to give her so that she will fall asleep and the young master can carry her away. Pseudolus' old master, Senex, returns home unexpectedly and meets the girlfriend. When Pseudolus, improvising an explanation for the girlfriend's presence in the house, says she is Senex's new maid, Senex plans his own tryst with her. Pseudolus and his fellow slave Hysterium must keep Senex out of the house and away from the girl (*A Funny Thing Happened on the Way to the Forum*, Act 1).

9.9 SENEX   I know how busy both of you are. Therefore, it is for *me* to instruct her in the niceties of housework. (*starting for his house*) We shall start in my room.

HYSTERIUM   Sir!

PSEUDOLUS   Sir, your son is in there!

SENEX   Oh! (*thinks a moment, then:*) Before my friend and neighbour, **Erronius**, went abroad in search of his children stolen in infancy by pirates, he asked me to look into his house from time to time. (*goes to Erronius' house, takes key from ledge and opens door*) This seems as good a time as any. I shall have a chat with the girl in here. Send her to me.

PSEUDOLUS   Sir.

SENEX   Yes?

PSEUDOLUS   Only my great devotion to you allows me to speak so frankly. (*Unseen by Senex, Pseudolus sprinkles [the mare's sweat] on him.*) You trudged along the road quite some way, and I fear that the great physical exertion … (*sniffs*)

Senex, Hysterium, Erronius note that Sondheim, Shevelove and Gelbart have continued Plautus' practice of giving characters foreign-sounding names that reflect their personalities and their roles.

SENEX	(*sniffing*) Is that me?!
PSEUDOLUS	Yes, sir.
SENEX	My heavens, I smell like an overheated horse! I shall have to bathe.
PSEUDOLUS	At least!

Senex exits into Erronius' house.

Erronius also returns home unexpectedly while Senex is bathing in his house.

9.10

ERRONIUS	How good it is to see this street once more. These tired old eyes fill with tears at the sight of the little they see … (*going to his house*) Well, at least I have the comfort of my lonely house.

Hysterium rushes to door of Erronius' house.

HYSTERIUM	Sir!
ERRONIUS	And who are you?
HYSTERIUM	Hysterium, sir, servant to Senex.
ERRONIUS	(*to pillar*) Yes, of course. I should have known you anywhere. (*Senex is heard singing from inside house …*) What was that?
HYSTERIUM	I didn't hear anything. (*Senex sings a bit more.*) I didn't hear that either.
ERRONIUS	You did not hear that eerie sound?
HYSTERIUM	Eerie?
ERRONIUS	Eerie, as if haunted.
HYSTERIUM	(*to himself*) Eerie, as if haunted? (*to Erronius*) Sir, what I am about to tell you is eerie … Your house is … is haunted.
ERRONIUS	Haunted?
HYSTERIUM	As haunted as the day is long!

Pseudolus enters … listens.

ERRONIUS	Impossible! My house haunted, you say? Strange.
HYSTERIUM	But true. Perhaps you ought to stay with relatives … distant relatives.
ERRONIUS	Yes! No! Fetch me a soothsayer.
HYSTERIUM	A soothsayer?
ERRONIUS	Yes, I must have him search my house immediately.

Pseudolus puts cloth over his head, runs to Erronius, chants ghoulishly.

PSEUDOLUS	You are in need of a soothsayer?
ERRONIUS	How did you know?
PSEUDOLUS	I'd be a fine soothsayer if I didn't.
ERRONIUS	There is a spirit in my …
PSEUDOLUS	Silence! I am about to say the sooth! Wait! (*chants incoherently*) I see it. I see everything. (*Hysterium steps behind Erronius, pantomimes distance*) You have been abroad.

ERRONIUS	Yes, yes.
PSEUDOLUS	For ... (*looks at Hysterium, who flashes his ten fingers twice*) ... twenty years! (*Erronius nods vigorously. Hysterium shades his eyes with one hand.*) You have been searching ... for ... (*Hysterium cradles his arms, rocks them.*) A child! (*Hysterium holds up two fingers.*) Two children!
ERRONIUS	Yes, yes! (*Hysterium flexes his muscles.*)
PSEUDOLUS	A fine, big boy.
ERRONIUS	Yes.
PSEUDOLUS	And ... (*Hysterium places hand on his hip, pantomimes a girl*) A strange, little boy. (*Hysterium shakes his head no.*) A girl! A girl! A boy and a girl!
ERRONIUS	Yes! Can you find them for me?
PSEUDOLUS	Certainly. I can find them for you.
ERRONIUS	(*takes ring from his finger, gives it to Pseudolus*) Each wears a ring on which is engraven a gaggle of geese.
PSEUDOLUS	A gaggle of what?
ERRONIUS	A gaggle of geese. Look! (*points to ring*) There are only two others like it in the world. And my children wear them.
PSEUDOLUS	How many geese in a gaggle?
ERRONIUS	At least seven.
PSEUDOLUS	Seven? Then before I say the sooth again you must walk seven times around the seven hills of Rome.
ERRONIUS	Seven times?
HYSTERIUM	Slowly.
ERRONIUS	Seven times around the seven hills? (*Sailors enter with more baggage.*) Take it all back to the harbour! (*proudly*) *My* house is haunted. (*Sailors exit with baggage. Senex is heard singing again. Pseudolus joins in, eerily.*) And the spirit?
PSEUDOLUS	It shall be gone by the time you have done my bidding.
ERRONIUS	Thank you.
PSEUDOLUS	To the hills!
ERRONIUS	To the hills!

> 1 Compare Pseudolus' deception of his master and neighbour with Tranio's deceptions in Plautus' *The Haunted House* (**3.5–6**). What have the creators of *A Funny Thing Happened on the Way to the Forum* borrowed from Plautus?
> 2 How does Pseudolus' deception differ from Tranio's?
> 3 Tranio and Pseudolus belong to a long line of clever slaves and servants found in drama and literature from Plautus' day to our own. Can you think of some other examples of the type?

Plays and films that borrow directly from the plays of Plautus and Terence are only the tip of the iceberg. Roman comedy is in fact the foundation of most European and American comic drama since the Renaissance. As was noted in chapter 2, Plautus and Terence based their plays on now-lost plays of Greek New Comedy. The authors of New Comedy invented the basic plot of love overcoming obstacles that has become the mainstay of western comedy, and they employed numerous stock characters and plot elements such as opposition between fathers and sons, deception, and surprise recognition of family members. Plautus and Terence adapted and expanded these elements of plot and character and handed them on to all writers of comedy thereafter. Hence Plautus and Terence lie behind countless plays and films that are not explicitly adaptations of their works. To cite just a few examples: in Oscar Wilde's *The Importance of Being Earnest* (1895) union of two sets of lovers becomes possible when one lover proves to be a long-lost relative; Bertolt Brecht and Kurt Weill's *The Threepenny Opera* (1928) offers a cynical view of the comic conventions of love overcoming obstacles and the surprise happy ending; and Mike Nichols's *The Graduate* (1967), for all its hip satire of American life, is ultimately a time-honoured story of a man winning a woman in spite of obstacles. Television situation comedies, with their 20-minute storylines and characters that reappear for weeks, usually do not use the standard love plot found in so many comic plays and films; but many of their character types, plot devices and modes of humour go back ultimately to Plautus and Terence.

Nor has the influence of Plautus and Terence been restricted to comic drama. Roman comedy's opposition of young love to various obstacles has also been central to much tragedy and melodrama: witness, for example, Shakespeare's *Romeo and Juliet* and James Cameron's *Titanic* (1997). Most novels since the eighteenth century have followed New Comedy's love plots at least to a degree; and some, like those of Charles Dickens (1812–70), feature stock characters and repeated plot elements reminiscent of those of Roman comedy.

> 1 In what elements of contemporary entertainment and literature do you detect the influence of Plautus and Terence?
>
> 2 In what ways do you think modern forms of entertainment and literature have diverged from what Plautus and Terence offered? What do you think those differences might suggest about developments in society since the second century BC?

Recommended reading

General discussions

Richard C. Beacham, *The Roman Theatre and Its Audience* (Cambridge, Mass., 1992). General introduction.

Margarete Bieber, *The History of the Greek and Roman Theater* (2nd edn., Princeton, 1961).
Review of archaeological evidence for theatrical practice in Greece and Rome.

Eric Csapo and William J. Slater, *The Context of Ancient Drama* (Ann Arbor, 1995).
Collection of ancient sources for Greek and Roman theatre.

Gesine Manuwald, *Roman Drama: A Reader* (London, 2010).
An introduction to Roman dramatic texts, including passages from various authors in Latin and in English translation.

Gesine Manuwald, *Roman Republican Theatre* (Cambridge, 2011).
History of Roman theatre until the end of the Republic.

Roman comedy

Translations

Deena Berg and Douglass Parker, *Plautus and Terence: Five Comedies* (Indianapolis, 1999).

Lively, sometimes freewheeling translations of Plautus' *The Bacchis Sisters*, *The Menaechmus Brothers* and *The Braggart Soldier*, and of Terence's *The Brothers* and *The Mother-in-Law*.

Secondary works

W. Geoffrey Arnott, *Menander, Plautus, Terence* (Oxford, 1975).
Excellent short introduction to the three playwrights.

George E. Duckworth, *The Nature of Roman Comedy: A Study in Popular Entertainment* (Princeton, 1952).
Remains the standard work in English on Roman comedy.

Sander M. Goldberg, 'Plautus on the Palatine', *Journal of Roman Studies* 88 (1998), pp. 1–20.
Discusses the performance of Roman plays in front of temple steps.

David Konstan, *Roman Comedy* (Ithaca, NY, 1983).
Provocative essays on the social significance of Plautus' and Terence's plays.

Matthew Leigh, *Comedy and the Rise of Rome* (Oxford, 2004).
Argues that many features of Plautus' and Terence's plays reflect political concerns of their time.

C. W. Marshall, *The Stagecraft and Performance of Roman Comedy* (Cambridge, 2006).
The best guide to the performance of Plautus and (to a lesser extent) Terence.

Timothy J. Moore, *Music in Roman Comedy* (Cambridge, 2012).
The most thorough study of music in Plautus' and Terence's plays.

Erich Segal (ed.), *Oxford Readings in Menander, Plautus, and Terence* (Oxford, 2001).
Essays by various authors reprinted.

T. B. L. Webster, *Monuments Illustrating New Comedy* (3rd edition, revised by J. R. Green and A. Seeberg, 2 vols., London, 1995).
Catalogue of artwork from Greece and Rome showing plays, characters and motifs of New Comedy, along with essays on such matters as the different types of masks.

John Wright, *Dancing in Chains: The Stylistic Unity of the* Comoedia Palliata (Rome, 1974).
Argues that all writers of *palliatae* except Terence followed very similar rules of style, characterization and plot.

Plautus

Translations

Wolfgang de Melo, *Plautus: Works*, vols. 1–2 (Cambridge, Mass., 2011).
Replaces Nixon (below) for many of Plautus' plays. The rest of the plays will follow.

Paul Nixon, *Plautus* (5 vols., London, 1916–38).
Latin texts of all Plautus' plays with facing English translation.

Amy Richlin, *Rome and the Mysterious Orient: Three Plays by Plautus* (Berkeley, 2005).
Translations of Plautus' *Curculio*, *The Persian* and *The Little Carthaginian* in the style of hip hop.

Erich Segal, *Plautus: Four Comedies* (London, 1996).
Engaging translations of *The Braggart Soldier*, *The Pot of Gold*, *The Menaechmus Brothers* and *The Haunted House*.

David R. Slavitt and Palmer Bovie (eds.), *Plautus: The Comedies* (4 vols., Baltimore, 1995).
Translations by various authors of each of Plautus' plays.

Secondary works

William S. Anderson, *Barbarian Play: Plautus' Roman Comedy* (Toronto, 1993).
Demonstrates how Plautus deconstructs his Greek originals to make a new kind of comic theatre.

Eduard Fraenkel, *Plautine Elements in Plautus*, trans. T. Drevikovsky and F. Muecke (Oxford, 2007).
Translation of Fraenkel's 1922 *Plautinisches im Plautus*, the most important work on how Plautus added comic elements when he adapted Greek plays.

Kathleen McCarthy, *Slaves, Masters, and the Art of Authority in Plautine Comedy* (Princeton, 2000).
Argues that Plautus' plays reinforce the ideology of Roman slaveholders.

Timothy J. Moore, *The Theater of Plautus: Playing to the Audience* (Austin, Tex., 1998).
Demonstrates how the close relationship Plautus encouraged between his actors and their audience contributes to the meaning of his plays.

Erich Segal, *Roman Laughter: The Comedy of Plautus* (2nd edn., London, 1987).
An overstated but nevertheless important argument using the Freudian 'pleasure principle' to explain Plautus' 'Saturnalian' comedy.

Niall W. Slater, *Plautus in Performance: The Theatre of the Mind* (2nd edn., Amsterdam, 2000).
Argues that what makes Plautine theatre work is its awareness of its own theatricality.

Terence

Translations

John Barsby, *Terence* (2 vols., Cambridge, Mass., 2001).
Latin text with facing English translations of all Terence's plays.

Peter Brown, *Terence: The Comedies* (Oxford, 2006).
Highly readable translations of all Terence's plays.

Secondary works

Walter E. Forehand, *Terence* (Boston, 1985).
A good introduction to Terence's plays.

Sander M. Goldberg, *Understanding Terence* (Princeton, 1986).
Remains the best book in English on Terence.

L. W. Jones and C. R. Morey, *The Miniatures of the Manuscripts of Terence Prior to the Thirteenth Century* (2 vols., Princeton, 1930–1).
Descriptions of the manuscripts that contain illustrations, and plates of the drawings.

Republican tragedy

Translations

E. H. Warmington, *Remains of Old Latin* (4 vols., Cambridge, Mass., 1935–40).
Latin texts with facing English translations of fragments of Livius Andronicus, Naevius, Ennius, Pacuvius and Accius, as well as of the comic playwright Caecilius.

Secondary works

A. J. Boyle, *Roman Tragedy* (London, 2006).
Useful chapters both on Republican tragedy and on Seneca.

Robert A. Brooks, *Ennius and Roman Tragedy* (New York, 1981).
Examination of how Ennius Romanized Greek plays.

H. D. Jocelyn, *The Tragedies of Ennius* (Cambridge, 1967).
Latin text with commentary. Includes a very good introduction to Ennius and his plays.

Mime

Mario Bonaria, *Romani mimi* (Rome, 1965).
Includes fragments and references to mime and pantomime in Roman literature and inscriptions.

Costas Panayotakis, *Decimus Laberius: The Fragments* (Cambridge, 2010).
Latin text and translation of the fragments of Laberius with extensive commentary. Includes an excellent introduction to the genre of mime.

Imperial theatres and pantomime

Edith Hall and Rosie Wyles (eds.), *New Directions in Ancient Pantomime* (Oxford, 2008).
Essays on various aspects of pantomime and its reception.

E. J. Jory, 'Continuity and Change in the Roman Theatre', in *Studies in Honour of T. B. L. Webster* (Bristol, 1986), pp. 143–52.
Demonstrates that 'the heyday of the Roman theatre was not in the Republic but in the Empire'.

Ismene Lada-Richards, *Silent Eloquence: Lucian and Pantomime Dancing* (London, 2007).
Thoughtful assessment of what Lucian's 'On The Dance' tells us about pantomime and about Graeco-Roman society.

Ruth Webb, *Demons and Dancers: Performance in Late Antiquity* (Cambridge, Mass., 2008).
Includes useful chapters on both pantomime and mime.

Seneca

Translations

David R. Slavitt (ed.), *Seneca, The Tragedies* (2 vols., Baltimore, 1992–5).
Translations by Slavitt and others of each of the plays attributed to Seneca.

Emily Wilson, *Seneca: Six Tragedies* (Oxford, 2010).
Translations of *Phaedra, Oedipus, Medea, The Trojan Women, Hercules Furens* and *Thyestes*.

Secondary works

A. J. Boyle, *Tragic Seneca: An Essay in the Theatrical Tradition* (London, 1997).
Detailed analysis of Seneca's plays and a discussion of their influence in the Renaissance.

P. J. Davis, *Seneca: Thyestes* (Duckworth Companions to Greek and Roman Tragedy, London, 2003).
Introduction to the play, its context and its themes.

John G. Fitch (ed.), *Seneca* (London, 2008).
Collection of reprinted essays by various authors.

George W. M. Harrison (ed.), *Seneca in Performance* (London, 2000).
Essays from various perspectives on how Seneca's tragedies may have been performed.

Roland Mayer, *Seneca: Phaedra* (Duckworth Companions to Greek and Roman Tragedy, London, 2002).
Introduction to the play, its context and its themes.

Anna Lydia Motto, *Seneca* (New York, 1973).
Good brief introduction to Seneca and his works.

Gregory A. Staley, *Seneca and the Idea of Tragedy* (Oxford, 2010).
Argues that Seneca's plays reflect a Stoic conception of tragedy.

The legacy of Roman theatre

Fiona Macintosh (ed.), *The Ancient Dancer in the Modern World: Responses to Greek and Roman Dance* (Oxford, 2010).
Includes essays on the influence of pantomime.

Robert S. Miola, *Shakespeare and Classical Comedy: The Influence of Plautus and Terence* (Oxford, 1994).
Thorough review of Shakespeare's use of Plautus and Terence.

Robert S. Miola, *Shakespeare and Classical Tragedy: The Influence of Seneca* (Oxford, 1992).
Argues that Seneca was important in determining how Shakespeare responded to the problem of evil.

Erich Segal, *The Death of Comedy* (Cambridge, Mass., 2001).
Reviews how the idea of comedy, formed in Greece and solidified by Plautus and Terence, continued and changed through the twentieth century.

Glossary

aediles Roman magistrates who were responsible for, among other things, the organization of *ludi*. Curule aediles were in charge of the *Ludi Romani* and the *Ludi Megalenses*, plebeian aediles the *Ludi Florales*.

alliteration use of the same consonant to start words in close proximity to one another (e.g. 'pick a peck of pickled peppers').

archimimus, ***archimima*** the leading actor or actress in a troupe of mime performers.

assonance repetition of vowel sounds (e.g. 'messages sent frenetically').

Atellan play a type of farcical skit including much improvisation, brought to Rome from the town of Atella south of Rome.

augur an official who interpreted signs sent by the gods through natural phenomena such as the flight-patterns of birds.

aulaeum a curtain lowered into a slot in front of the stage to reveal the stage and raised to conceal it.

canticum a portion of a Roman play sung to the accompaniment of the *tibia* (contrast *deverbium*).

cavea the area in a Roman theatre where the spectators stood or sat.

censors two magistrates chosen from among Rome's elder statesmen every five years to take the census and oversee public works.

chlamys a kind of cloak worn over the tunic of some characters in Roman comedy, especially soldiers.

choragus a businessman who provided costumes for Roman theatrical productions.

cithara a large lyre (lyres are instruments in which strings of equal length, attached to a sound box, are plucked or strummed to produce notes).

commedia dell'arte a type of improvisational comedy first recorded in Italy in the sixteenth century AD.

commedia erudita plays of the Italian Renaissance with written texts (contrast *commedia dell'arte*).

consul Rome's chief magistrate during the Republic. Two consuls were elected for a one-year term each year.

crotala wooden or metal hand-clappers similar to castanets.

declamation (*declamatio*) an important part of Roman education in which students honed their speaking skills by making speeches about historical events or imaginary law cases.

deverbium a portion of a Roman play spoken without accompaniment (contrast *canticum*).

didascaliae production notices preserved with the manuscripts of several plays of Plautus and Terence.

drachma a unit of money, one hundredth of a mina.

Empire Rome's third period of government, from 27 BC to AD 476.

epilogue the final verses of a comedy, in which actors ask for the spectators' applause.

equites (singular *eques*) the second highest social class in Rome. *Equites* were rich (each had an estate of at least 500,000 *sestertii*), but they usually were not involved in politics.

Etruscans a people of unknown origin who lived in a region of central Italy known as Etruria. Between 800 and 300 BC they had a powerful empire and controlled Rome for part of that period.

exodium (plural *exodia*) a short piece of dramatic entertainment put on after a longer performance.

fabula palliata a comedy performed in Greek dress. Plautus' and Terence's plays are *fabulae palliatae*.

fabula praetexta a play with a plot drawn from Roman history; the name comes from the *praetexta*, a toga with a purple border worn by Roman magistrates.

fabula togata a play set in Italy, where characters wore togas, in contrast to *fabulae palliatae*, which were set in Greece and featured characters wearing *pallia*.

false maiden a freeborn woman, lost at a young age, usually enslaved and about to enter a career as a prostitute, whose status is revealed before the end of the play.

Fescennine verses insults, often obscene, which were directed at the bride and groom at wedding ceremonies and were also delivered on other occasions.

forum Rome's central square, centre of the city's political, economic and religious life. Plays were sometimes performed there.

fragment a passage of a lost work of ancient literature quoted by a later author. These quotations are all that remain of many Roman plays.

fresco a type of wall painting painted on wet plaster so that the colours penetrate the plaster and become fixed. Roman frescoes, especially those buried by the eruption of Mount Vesuvius in AD 79, are valuable sources for many aspects of Roman theatre.

grammarian a scholar who wrote works on language and literature. The works of grammarians are important sources of both information on Roman theatre and fragments of lost works.

iambic senarius the second most common metre in Roman comedy, spoken without accompaniment.

infamia a removal of rights normally granted to citizens. Actors, prostitutes, gladiators and criminals were subject to *infamia*.

ludi public games sponsored by the state in honour of one or more divinities or by aristocrats as part of funerals of their deceased relatives. *Ludi* could include theatrical performances, chariot-races, gladiatorial combats and other types of entertainment.

Ludi Apollinares games held in the spring in honour of the god Apollo.

Ludi Florales games held in the spring in honour of Flora, a vegetation goddess.

Ludi Megalenses games held every April in honour of the goddess Cybele, also called *Magna Mater* (The Great Mother). During this festival plays were performed in front of Cybele's temple.

Ludi Romani games held every September in honour of Jupiter.

mime (*mimus*) a type of farcical theatre involving much improvisation.

mina a unit of money, just under a pound of silver, or one-sixtieth of a talent.

mode a type of melody. Different modes were used in ancient music to distinguish different characters and moods. Exactly how the modes differed from one another is not clear.

Monarchy the first period of Roman government, traditionally from 753 to 509 BC.

neo-Senecan tragedy a type of tragedy inspired by Seneca that developed in the Renaissance.

New Comedy a type of domestic comedy first produced in Athens in the fourth century BC. Its greatest practitioner was Menander.

Oscans an Italic people, ethnically related to the Romans, who inhabited a region of Italy south of Rome.

pallium a Greek type of cloak worn by most characters in *fabulae palliatae*.

pantomime presentation of myths or other stories through gestures and dance, usually by one performer accompanied by a chorus and instrumentalists.

papyrus a kind of paper made out of reeds.

parasite a stock character of Roman comedy who gets his livelihood by getting free meals off others.

parasites of Apollo an organization of actors.

plebeian the lower of Rome's two most basic social divisions, plebeians and patricians.

polymetric changing verse forms frequently (contrast stichic).

portico a covered walkway.

praetor one of several elected magistrates second to consuls in authority. Praetors had various duties, including the maintenance of order in the city of Rome. One praetor, the urban praetor, was responsible for the *Ludi Apollinares*.

proscaenium the area of a Roman stage in front of the *scaenae frons*.

Republic the second period of Roman government, from 509 to 27 BC.

saffron a sweet-smelling, orange-yellow spice.

Saturnalia a Roman festival in late December which included extreme social inversion. Roman comedy is sometimes described as 'Saturnalian' because of the overturning of social hierarchy and everyday morality that often occurs in the plays.

scabillum a pair of wooden, or sometimes metal clappers worn as a shoe by a *tibia* player, used to reinforce rhythm in the musical accompaniment of mime, pantomime and other Roman performances.

scaena stage.

scaenae frons the large wall behind the stage that, together with the semicircular *cavea*, enclosed Roman theatres in their fully developed state.

Senate an assembly of Roman aristocrats who had the most power in the Roman Republic.

sententiae clever phrases, often expressing moral ideas, a common stylistic feature of both oratory and drama in Rome.

sestertius a Roman coin, the value of which varied over time.

siparia onstage curtains used as backdrops or to conceal parts of the stage.

socci slipper-like footwear worn by most characters in *fabulae palliatae*.

stichic continuing in the same metre for many verses (contrast polymetric).

stock character a type of character whose basic characteristics remain the same from play to play.

Stoic, Stoicism a philosophical school popular in Rome that held that the highest good was virtue, obtained by subjecting emotions to reason.

talent a very large unit of money, equivalent to over 25 kilograms (55 pounds) of silver.

Theatre of Balbus a stone theatre in the city of Rome, dedicated by Lucius Cornelius Balbus in 13 BC.

Theatre of Marcellus a stone theatre in the city of Rome, built by the emperor Augustus in memory of his nephew Marcellus and dedicated in 13 or 11 BC. A large part of this theatre still stands.

Theatre of Pompey the first permanent stone theatre in the city of Rome, built in 55 BC.

tibia a woodwind instrument made up of two pipes, each with a double reed. The *tibia* was played during almost all theatrical performances in Rome.

tibicen, *tibicina* a male or female player, respectively, of the *tibia*.

tragoediam cantare (tragic singing) a musical performance of excerpts from tragedies by a soloist, who was called a *tragoedos*.

trochaic septenarius the most common metre in Roman comedy, sung to the accompaniment of the *tibia*.

tunica a type of cloak usually worn underneath a *pallium* or other outer garment. Slaves sometimes wore just a *tunica* with no outer garment.

tympanum a shallow, round drum similar to a tambourine but without jingling metal discs.

velarium an awning used to cover Roman theatres during performances.